Literary Education and Digital Learning:
Methods and Technologies for Humanities Studies

Willie van Peer, University of Munich, Germany

Sonia Zyngier, Federal University of Rio de Janeiro, Brazil

Vander Viana, Queen's University Belfast, UK

Information Science REFERENCE

INFORMATION SCIENCE REFERENCE

Hershey · New York

Director of Editorial Content:	Kristin Klinger
Director of Book Publications:	Julia Mosemann
Acquisitions Editor:	Lindsay Johnston
Development Editor:	Julia Mosemann
Publishing Assistant:	Travis Gundrum
Typesetter:	Deanna Jo Zombro
Quality control:	Jamie Snavely
Cover Design:	Lisa Tosheff
Printed at:	Yurchak Printing Inc.

Published in the United States of America by
Information Science Reference (an imprint of IGI Global)
701 E. Chocolate Avenue,
Hershey PA 17033
Tel: 717-533-8845
Fax: 717-533-8661
E-mail: cust@igi-global.com
Web site: http://www.igi-global.com

Library of Congress Cataloging-in-Publication Data

Literary education and digital learning : methods and technologies for humanities studies / Willie van Peer, Sonia Zyngier, and Vander Viana, editors.
p. cm.
Includes bibliographical references and index.
Summary: "This book provides insight into the most relevant issues in literary education and digital learning, covering literary aspects both from educational and research perspectives"--Provided by publisher.
ISBN 978-1-60566-932-8 -- ISBN 978-1-60566-933-5 (ebook)
1. Literature and the Internet. 2. Literature--Research--Data processing. 3. Literature--Study and teaching--Technological innovations. 4. Literature--Computer network resources. 5. Web-based instruction. I. Peer, Willie van. II. Zyngier, Sonia. III. Viana, Vander.
PN56.I64L57 2010
802.85--dc22

2010016305

British Cataloguing in Publication Data
A Cataloguing in Publication record for this book is available from the British Library.

Editorial Advisory Board

Table of Contents

Detailed Table of Contents

Although authorship attribution is simply the determination of who wrote a document by analysis of its content, it is a long-standing problem both in the humanities and in computational text analysis. While traditional methods involve identifying key aspects of style through close reading, new developments in computational science permit a more objective approach through the statistical analysis of superficial characteristics such as vocabulary and word choice. If a writer can be shown (statistically) to have a particular stylistic quirk ('stylome') that appears broadly across his or her writing, then other writings also displaying that quirk are good candidates to also be by that author. The present chapter describes some of the statistical techniques used to make such judgments, and describes one particular computer program (JGAAP) that is freely available for this purpose. This type of analysis is capable of determining authorship with relatively high accuracy. The potential creates some significant implications for authorship questions across the humanities curriculum, as well as broader impacts in the world outside the academy. In light of these implications, I argue for the inclusion of more mathematics into the humanities curriculum.

This study investigates the expression of stance in Samuel Beckett's prose work. Following Biber and Finegan (1989), a wide variety of stance markers are identified and calculated in the texts. A multivariate statistical methodology is then used to analyze the way in which these markers of stance interact in the texts. The results are plotted two-dimensionally to enable visualizing the similarities and differences between the texts. These are also illustrated using examples from the texts. Some of the findings are a little surprising and, therefore, a new tool is used to plot the results three-dimensionally, enabling a better understanding of how stance is reflected and how the texts resemble and deviate from one another. Finally, the usefulness of this analysis is discussed.

In this chapter, we describe the development and application of language technology for intelligent information access to the content of digitized cultural heritage collections in the form of Swedish classical literary works. This technology offers sophisticated and flexible support functions to literary scholars and researchers. We focus on one kind of text processing technology (named entity recognition) and one research field (literary onomastics), but we try to argue that the techniques involved are quite general and can be further developed in a number of directions. This way, we aim at supporting the users of digitized literature collections with tools that enable semantic search, browsing and indexing of texts. In this sense, we offer new ways for exploring the large volumes of literary texts being made available through national cultural heritage digitization projects.

Until fairly recently, linguistics has been classified as a 'science' by definition, averral, and ideology rather than because of the uniformity of its practices across its many

Foreword

LOST AND FOUND IN THE READING MACHINE

It is a pleasure to write this foreword for the volume that follows, which contains fascinating explorations of some of the literary new-found land opened up by computing and digitization. As costs reduce, the new technologies are yielding to more and more of us, new ways of encountering literature and engaging with it, with hugely facilitated possibilities of searching, browsing, referencing, and linking. The single page at a time of codex reading is being displaced by multiple windows, multiple files, an indefinitely-extending array of images (static or moving), sounds (including music), and textual glosses and explanations. Anyone who starts out reading on the computer screen something brief like a Seamus Heaney sonnet can soon find themselves supplementing the bare fourteen lines of text with a variety of multi-modal resources unimaginable when illuminated medieval texts were in their heyday. With computers we can search and sort unprecedentedly large texts and corpora, and computerized text analysis is a burgeoning field. And with ever-increasing computing power, rapid access to huge stores of visual imagery (including moving images) and sounds and music promise an enriching of the immediate (that is, both spatially and temporally) contextualization of on-screen reading – at the click of a link. This in part is why champions of technologized literary reading, reception and interpretation emphasize the enhanced possibilities of visualization that digital resources create.

Still, and notwithstanding all these exciting kinds of cultural and experiential change, I want to enter some *caveats*. Here the reader will find some reminders of the limits to the new affordances, and of the enduring value in some of the old ways of doing things. I offer these not as a Luddite or a technophobe, but as someone wanting to relate the older practices of reading, analysis and interpretation to the new. I will begin with some comments on the extent to which, as one current view suggests, the reading of literature affords us a kind of mimetic simulation of the cognitive and emotional challenges (especially of interpersonal relationships) of everyday life. Critique of this view is important, I think, since it sometimes underwrites proponents' enthusiasm for a technology-dependent literary reading: the latter is argued to be an *enriched* version of the simulation that all literary reading is assumed to be.

1. Literature as Training for Real Life?

In a recent plenary talk at the Poetics and Linguistics Association (PALA) annual conference in Middelburg, The Netherlands, Keith Oatley (2009) used the following analogy in support of his thesis that literature offers readers a 'simulation' of everyday situations and experiences; "reading or watching fiction involves creating and entering a simulated social world" (Oatley 2009). He argued that this makes it possible for readers to experience emotions in themselves, in the imagined contexts that the author depicts the characters occupying. By means of reader-character empathy, readers take on various goals and plans in the fiction (usually the goals and plans of one or another character); and "with the goals and plans we have taken on, we experience our own emotions in the circumstances of the outcomes of the character's actions" (Oatley 2009). Much of this I agree with—intuitively or empathetically! But some of this I also find difficult, or inexplicit: for example, what exactly does 'taking on' entail, and what is it that readers 'get' from and in their engagement with the text that causes them to experience certain emotions in themselves, but in the characters' contexts (which, they know, fictional)?

Are there difficulties, in particular, with the metaphor of simulation? Oatley has written:

Just as we expect someone who learns to pilot a plane to benefit from time spent in a flight simulator, so we expect people who read a lot of fiction to develop better theory of mind and empathy. Recent studies by our research group (Maja Djikic, Raymond Mar, & Keith Oatley, see www.onfiction.ca) have shown such effects. (abstract, Oatley 2009; see also Oatley 2008)

The argument is that literary reading simulates real-life experience, so that the empathy developed in reading improves empathy 'performance' in real life. A crucial first step is that literary reading does simulate life experience, where by simulation is meant something virtually identical to the target activity while remaining fictional, pretence, without real-world consequences beyond the activity into a contiguous context, in the same ontological world. Thus doing really badly on a flight simulator – crashing the plane – may have consequences in the embedding ontological world where your performance is used to assess your suitability by the air force for further pilot training, for example; but there is no extending and expanding context in the world of the simulation itself, no strewn wreckage, no bodies to inter, no grief-stricken families.

With these considerations in view, there is a difficulty with the simulation analogy as invoked. Consider the flight simulator. These days, it includes a cockpit with a daunting array of instrument panels and screens supplying visual information, and the possibility of applying to those present the kinds of gravitational forces, thrust and banking sensations experienced in a real aeroplane cockpit. The best simulators today, to all intents and purposes, pass a kind of Turing test: if a pilot woke up in the middle of one, they might not be able to distinguish it from the real thing. In a flight simulator, a pilot *rehearses* any and all the manoeuvres they might have to perform in a real cockpit (including, presumably, spilling hot coffee, dealing with drunk and obstreperous passengers, coping with a hallucinating co-pilot who starts telling everyone that the cockpit they are in *is* only a simulation...).

The reading of literary fiction does not I believe relate to those things which the fiction represents in a way that is truly comparable. This is most immediately clear if one imagines reading a narrative about a character who is learning to fly: reading such a narrative is poor preparation, cognitively or emotionally, for flying a real plane. By contrast, spending time on a flight simulator would be quite good training. The other main difficulty with the analogy is the idea of improvement, the clocking of hours on the way to attainment of proficiency; it is doubtful that the steady growth in competence gained on flight simulators is paralleled by a steady growth in empathy with the increase in the number of novels we have read.

Let me emphasize that I recognize the centrality, in much art including verbal art, of the emotional engagement of the reader (my recognition of this is reflected in Toolan 2009 and Toolan in preparation). Art must be crucially, but not exclusively, emotionally engaging. It may be, too, that heightened sensitivity effects, or enhanced empathy, short-term or longer term, can be empirically confirmed among readers exposed to literature by comparison with those who are not: the work of Oatley and his associates in this regard is extremely interesting. What I question is whether emotional engagement derives from a process of simulation, and whether simulation misrepresents the practices of literary reading, even while it contains some truth. In a sense, I continue to see art as more *real* than the simulation figure (echoic of the Platonic idea of art as imitation, doubly removed from the ideal) assumes: a dramatization or articulation rather than a simulation. And, crucially, art depends on the addressee's imagination, whereas simulations require almost none (it is as real as the real thing!).

2. Contexts of Reading, Again

Another sign of the times comes in the abstract of a recent lecture given by Svenja Adolphs (2009), entitled "Corpus, Context and Ubiquitous Computing". Adolphs suggests that "everyday communication has evolved rapidly over the past decade with an increase in the use of digital devices" (although quite how one measures communicational evolution, as distinct from change, is unclear). She goes on to suggest that one of the most important challenges today is that of "being able to respond to the context of use" in our corpus and computational linguistics. As the abstract states: "The ability to understand how different aspects of context, such as location, influence language use is important for future context-aware computing applications." Besides position, she mentions movement, time and physiological state as contextual factors that may potentially cause variations in people's use of language. These are, to my mind, the tip of the contextual iceberg, but they are a useful reminder of how complexly contextually embedded is the actuality of language use, including that language use known as the reading of literature. On the other hand, are there specificities of context which the analyst of literary texts and literary reading is entitled to exclude from consideration? Even though they may affect particular readers and even whole groups of readers, are there contextual factors that are *not* integral to the designed and intended literary activity?

Consider three contexts of communication: one is the surreptitious sending of brief messages, scribbled on scraps of paper, between two adjacently-seated members of a panel, interviewing an expert witness in the course of a tribunal. The two members do not want the witness, or other panel members, to see these scraps of paper, let alone the messages they contain: they do not want the larger group to be aware that there is this covert dyadic deliberation going on. These contextual factors, I would say, directly and relevantly bear on the production and processing of the messages; on the production side, they may lead to rushed, less legible, more abbreviated and unintentionally ambiguous messages; on the reception side, rushed and covert reading might cause misunderstanding. But the rushed and covert qualities are integral to the nature of this two-party written communication.

A second scenario might be that of someone who begins reading Edgar Allan Poe's "The Tell-Tale Heart" as they step into a lift that is to take them 30 floors up in an office building; almost immediately the lift breaks down, the lights dim, and the emergency telephone advises the passenger that they will have to wait forty minutes to be rescued. During those forty minutes, with nothing else to do or read, the trapped person settles down and reads the whole Poe story. Under the contextual conditions, they find the story exceptionally disturbing: they begin to hyperventilate, feel that their own heart is about to burst, and by the time that the lift moves up to the nearest floor where they can alight, they are raving hysterically. That context of reading, however real for the person involved, is so atypical as to be no integral part of the normal or intended reading situation for that story. It is not a context of reading of "The Tell-Tale Heart" to which our computational analyses need be sensitive.

More difficult than the previous case, and really borderline, might be that of reading when ill enough to be hospitalized. This may not be the typical condition in which literary reading takes place, but it is hardly abnormal; literature is not often written expressly to be read by the unwell, but it is also clear that many people, even when so sick that their concentration is impaired, spend more time reading when ill than when not. It is very likely, and varying with the nature of the condition, that the reader's health condition will be a contextual effect on their attention to and evaluation of the literary text (as of their other communicational engagements). Nevertheless, when that person reads a new Alice Munro story in the *New Yorker* or a Kathleen Jamie poem in *The Guardian*, I would not want to include these contextual factors – the reader's illness – in the analysis or assessment of the literary text, or treat it as at the core of the reading experience. Again, this is not to deny the value and importance of what has come to be known as bibliotherapy, or to deny that someone with cancer may respond to a poem about chemotherapy rather differently from the other readers. But those are variations in readership; the poem itself stays the same, and is unchanged by those variations. And a poem about chemotherapy that is only striking to people who have undergone that treatment is a bit of a failure: a better one would be emotionally and cognitively engaging of a wider range of readers, regardless of health or other variable.

What do the three scenarios of reading reception suggest? In the first, I argued that the rushed and surreptitious conditions of production and reception are a permanently relevant part of the context of reading: someone coming across those texts years later should, in a sense, take that context into consideration when interpreting and evaluating the messages. In the Poe-story-in-lift example, I suggested that powerful as the particular context was for the trapped reader, this was not a contextualization that one should automatically incorporate into an interpreting of the text. And even in the third scenario, involving a whole category of readers (one could apply this to other categories of course: all white readers, all women readers, all deaf readers), I wanted to resist the idea that the Munro story or the Jamie poem should be somehow tagged or calibrated, at the outset and so as suitably contextualize subsequent analysis, along the lines that Adolphs (2009) persuasively argues is appropriate and necessary in computational study of other kinds of language event. The short explanation is that the Munro story or Jamie poem is designed to be read by anyone reasonably fluent, regardless of their personal or situational particularities. Adolphs (2009) mentions physical movement as sometimes contextually relevant, and one can easily imagine someone saying "I was reading Jamie's 'Mr and Mrs Scotland' on my way to work this morning, but I couldn't get into it because the bus was lurching around too much". Fair enough: the reading experience has been compromized here. But also totally unfair: the unsatisfactory reading is no fault of the poem or Kathleen Jamie. That person should do better by that poem, and read it under different and more suitable contextual conditions.

3. New Possibilities in the Dissemination of Literature (I): Audiofiction

The distinctions among the kinds of relevant and irrelevant context offered in the previous section are rudimentary and only preliminary, but may help me to focus on the more integrally relevant types of variation and development that emerge, in text-reader relations in the digital, hypertextual age, where decisions about what is within or outside 'the literary' will be newly tested. Let me begin with audiofiction, and in particular the listened-to *short story* (a much more interesting case than the audio*book*, I believe). There seems to be little objection to saying that an Alice Munro story, satisfactorily orally performed by a competent radio actor, would be just as much the whole literary experience as, say, a print version of the story in a hard copy of the *New Yorker*. In some ways the oral/aural version is less contaminated: in the *New Yorker*, the printed story may be flanked by advertisements for malt whisky and reproduction Shaker furniture, accompanied by a half-page pen-and-ink depiction of one of the story's settings, plus 'user damage' such as creased pages and greasy fingerprints.

What ideational and emotional *differences* might there be, between the experience of *reading* an Alice Munro, Tobias Wolff, or David Foster Wallace story and *listening* to it? We are only beginning to explore these issues thoroughly. We know that listening (like speech) is inescapably 'timed' or 'in' time, and that by contrast reading permits us to stretch time, and even (to a degree) to impose our own pacing on this linear activity. We know also that imposing a pause during listening is different from the one that can take place in reading. The former is normally for purposes of 'repair' (halting the flow recorded speech because of some external interruption, or in order to catch a phrase or development that one has missed). The latter, by contrast, has the potential to be a moment of 'reflection' (where, e.g., we lift our eyes from the text, or dwell on the words just read, in order to think again, or further, about the relevance and the implications of what has just been expressed).

There is little evidence of equivalent 'reflection' time in the typical consumption of audiofiction, although there could be one.

Understanding of the effects and consequences of auditory rather than visual processing of literary fiction is still quite speculative (and in need of empirical study). Since in audio stories the consumer has 'less time', it may be that some of the things in stories which arguably need more time – reconsideration, intertextual evoking and analogizing, the 'liberty' of the consumer to 'take' the given words in different ways--will tend to be curtailed. Alternatively, or additionally, the textual style of audio stories might change to better suit audio consumption. For example, if one way of delaying the flow time (giving the listener the kind of time that a reader can take to process a message) would be to use more repetition, then possibly certain kinds of reiteration and recapitulation, over and above the kinds of disambiguating uses we find quite normally in written stories, might come to be more often used in audiofiction. It is possible that forms of such reiteration are already developed in formats like the radio story and radio play. Time for listener-reflection can also be secured by the use of a sonic or musical interlude, but these are not usually part of the writer's conception of the piece and are therefore a kind of intrusion; even where graphic images accompany written stories they do not usually *interrupt* the flow of the text on the page. Some of the differences in the reading vs. listening experience have been probed in Bailly (2007); see also Toolan (2008). Bailly (2007) noted that the iPod-delivered short story differs from the printed version at least in the way the pace and flow of the discourse is essentially under the performer's (or performers') control, and by virtue of the presence (intrusion?) of the performer's voice(s). Bailly (2007) set out to see, by means of informant questionnaires, whether such factors render the audio story easier to consume but less cognitively and emotionally rich than the same story encountered in written form. His very provisional findings were not always as predicted: printed stories seemed to be somewhat more enjoyable than those in audio format – possibly either because the processing was under reader 'control', or because of subjects' greater familiarity with written story consumption. Stories in audio format were judged to be less demanding, possibly because in listening you do not have to create the narrative voice. And while the audio stories engendered more emotional responses, these were mainly 'fresh' ones, relating directly to the scenes/episodes described; by contrast the read stories seemed to elicit far more emotional memories, relating story situations to more removed and richer past experiences of the individual readers.

4. New Possibilities in the Dissemination of Literature (II): Poetry as Audiovisual Performance

But audiofiction, via the computer or, allowing much greater mobility, via one's MP3 player or iPod, is still a relatively traditional literary digitization. Why not bring our poets more directly to us, in future? As an alternative to the 'slim volume', printed and bound, why shouldn't Kathleen Jamie's next selection of poetry come to us on videodisc: *performed* by the poet herself, speaking directly to the screen (of one's computer or iPod), with accompanying images and background music as deemed appropriate? Or we could have Alice Oswald's poetry about the Dart river, spoken by the poet herself, intermittently in shot, accompanied by video of the tidal Dart under the different phases of the moon. Oswald's oral performance of the poetry need not preclude the presence of other sounds as background accompaniment (birdsong, river sounds), and a readable version of the lines spoken could be provided in a panel above, below or to one side of the main screen. How could this be less than, or not fully, the 'text' of Oswald's Dart poems? Might we not alternatively say that this is the way we have always wanted to experience poems – the next best thing to having the living poet reading in front of us – but have hitherto lacked the means? If the latter is, increasingly, accepted as an entirely usual way to 'read' contemporary poetry, then a different general conception of the modern poetic canon will gradually emerge, partially displacing more traditional outlets such as the slim volumes published by Faber and others. Poetry performances are already available on YouTube and other free and fee-charging websites (van Peer 2009), but the audiovisual download is not yet a prominent way of acquiring the latest Rita Dove or Seamus Heaney collection: this mode is not yet fully institutionalized and professionalized. And if the audiovisual download becomes a prominent and financially attractive means of poetry publishing, then those poems that do not lend themselves to visual depiction or are difficult to perform orally may lose ground in the struggle for readership and attention; the genre or genres will change, with something gained and something lost.

5. Reiterating Some Literary Fundamentals

By way of restraining a too-enthusiastic embrace of the digitization of all things literary, let me close with a reiteration of a few things that remain true even in the computerized era of Web 2.0, second life, twittering, texting and live cams.

5.1. We cannot actually *read* any quicker with computers than we did before they arrived; we can only cross-refer quicker, or with less effort (Planet Google and all its works has displaced our hard copy bound and printed version of *Encyclopedia Britannica*, the *OED*, *Gray's Anatomy*, the *Dictionary of National Biography*, etc.). Before long, any reader anywhere may enjoy direct on-the-screen access to every page in every book in the US Library of Congress. But you cannot *read* any of that material any faster than before. The affordances of digital technology of course nurture 'multi-tasking', browsing and scanning, but these 'advances' can be easily overstated; and recent psychological research on the "switch costs" of multitasking suggests that it is often counterproductive (Rubinstein, Meyer & Evans 2001). I have never seen a poet write two poems at the same time, and I know of no-one who can read two poems at the same time. Digital technology runs up against the Saussurean buffers known as the linearity of the linguistic sign. Access is neither consumption, nor understanding. There is an analogy here with the students of ten years ago, say, who photocopied the key readings for a course and thereby persuaded themselves that they had 'taken possession' of the material contained therein; today they – and we – download the ftp files to a hard disk and similarly risk conflating access with knowledge/understanding. So with digitization some aspects of written culture are greatly changed (speed of access), but other aspects are *not* changed in the slightest (speed of reading, speed of understanding).

5.2. We can certainly hope that the reading machine will enrich our understanding of the particular literature we are presently reading (by enabling us to link at once to a cornucopia of relevant contexts, glosses, analogous materials, in at least the aural and visual media and in many modes). But alongside the enrichment of hypertextual and paratextual supplements there is a risk of impoverishment, distraction, contamination. This is a new version of an old debate in literary circles over the desirability of reading the bare text or of reading the text heavily annotated and supplemented by critical exegesis and commentary, intratextual and intertextual reference, and a record of all variant textual forms. Of course we can say we need both, or that different editions can be argued to suit different purposes, but in actuality choices will and must be made (linearity and time again). You – whoever you are – cannot read at time *t* in room *r* one and the same text in a bare and in an annotated edition. Which will you read first? And if you read the abundantly hypertextually annotated version first, *can* you, subsequently, truly read the same work in its bare and unadorned form? In short, we should see that more (more glosses, more exegesis, more links to images) does not invariably mean better, and that less on occasion will be better. To prefer the glossed version to the unglossed text is akin to preferring that every joke come with an explanation added (to help cultural outsiders, for example); an inescapable side-effect is that the joke cannot then be properly experienced as contextualized joke.

There is a general point here that is too often neglected: that with *every* change (of technology, or theory, or practice, for example) some conditions or qualities will be lost or will deteriorate even as others clearly improve. Optimists and modernists do not always accept this, to me, thermodynamic truism, since they evaluate change from within a system of cultural values. Thus they think of the new digital music technology which can re-master old Toscanini or Beecham recordings, and suggest much is improved and *nothing* is lost. On the contrary, the old recording, with its crackles and hisses and audience coughs and fluffed horn entry, and much more of what was part of the original *valeur*, has gone. Like a facelift, the result is better in some respects, but some qualities (whether they are good or bad is secondary) have been removed.

5.3. If to read literarily is to be immersed in the text to the point of being undistractable, unaware of the page margins and gutters or even of the page, the print, all the footnotes and *hors-textes*, then all such textual dietary supplements are unhelpful at best, deleterious at worst (they tend to cause the attention to be divided). I think of how, as a student, I read Shakespeare plays in those cheap Signet classic editions, my eyes repeatedly pulled away from the characters' speeches to the explanatory notes at the foot of almost every page (sometimes explaining the blindingly obvious, sometimes asserting an interpretation of the sense of a phrase that would strike me as a complete surprise). How does such an experiencing of Shakespeare compare with the 'immersive' attendance at a performance of the same scene in a theatre (or even on film)? In the latter, of course, one is not reading at all, so I may be criticized for not comparing like with like. My point, though, is that in literary reading we may ideally (or sometimes, or mostly) want the experience to be more like the totally focused response that is – in my view – theatre at its best.

5.4. Humanities scholars – perhaps more than other researchers – are prone to take a metaphor and run with it as if it were real. We are so keen on metaphors that if the marketing team tells us that this machine or package can 'read' texts, identify main themes and patterns, sort this, make that connection, we are a bit quick to believe them. But computers cannot think, feel, interpret, understand, misrepresent… only people can. My computer has not told me a single story; not one. It has not created a single thing. It is a mechanical device of enormous complexity in a few respects, but of glaringly narrow repertoire and adaptability by comparison with, say, a bird or a fish – let alone a human being. And it is so *dependent* upon me, unlike a tree, for example: if I do not turn it on, it cannot do a darned thing.

5.5. Computer programs for text analysis do the sorts of 'analysis' of, for example, Russian, that someone who can see Cyrillic marks or hear Russian sounds but not actually speak it, read it, or write it, could do. Our computers do not know that what they are looking at is Russian, with all the multi-aspectual and boundaryless hinterland that (as language-makers and users) we know that a text in Russian entails. In fact, *not* having or knowing any of that hinterland, grasp of some of which is critical to knowing that a text or speech *is* Russian, is crucial to the creation of the computerized analysis software. Via digitization, the software 'looks' at Russian standardized writing not as Russian or as language but as recurring and non-recurring shapes along a line; nothing more.

5.6. A familiar theme of commentaries and guides to literary studies and literary appreciation in the digital age is that *now*, as never before, reading and responding can be collaborative, interactive, and shared. All shall enjoy equal posting rights on the Wiki or LAN, the Blackboard or WebCT discussion forum. The 'private pain' of solitary reading, where the student or amateur struggles alone to make sense of what they are reading without benefit of buddies, is banished. Again, I think we should beware of overstating the isolation of pre-digital reading, or the communalism of reading in the digital age. In the latter, it is true, a number of remotely-distributed readers can, even simultaneously, share their reactions to a poem in speech and writing; but that is when technology and practical provisions are optimal, and things are often less than optimal. More importantly, what underpins this 'intimate collaboration' is an acceptance of non-intimacy: a consenting to communicate via screen and digitized audio, rather than with physical, face-to-face interaction, and what I would call haptic proximity (*haptic*: the sense of touch). Call me a hopeless romantic, but for me an electronic computer-mediated two- or three-way discussion of, say, Yeats's "When you are old and grey and full of sleep" cannot fully compensate for the loss of those aspects of *embodied* interaction experienced in a *viva voce* conversation about this poem by people enjoying John Lyons's canonical situation of utterance: "one-one, or one-many, signalling in the phonic medium along the vocal-auditory channel, with all the participants present in the same actual situation able to see one another and to perceive the associated non-vocal paralinguistic features of their utterances, and each assuming the role of sender and receiver in turn" (Lyons, 1977: 637). My point then is that the old, face-to-face across-the-seminar-table way of reading and discussing Yeats was both a less private and a more embodied interaction than the new technologized fora. Less private and more embodied does not necessarily amount to 'better', or more supportive of the shy reader or the sensitive one (the loudest and most voluble seminar student is not always the most insightful!). But since such (old style) poetry discussions involve living, co-present, certain contact via two of the key senses (sound, sight) and potential contact via at least two more (touch, smell), the experience is more authentically embodied and collaborative than any virtual tutorial.

5.7. Living voice and human touch are important I believe, although I lack the space here to develop the argument fully. Let me instead refer to a moment of art-mediated intimacy in a celebrated film, by way of exemplification. Consider the episode in *Babette's Feast* (dir Gabriel Axel, 1987) where the opera-singer Achille Papin is giving a singing lesson to the pastor's sweet-throated daughter Philippa, eliciting from her a fully achieved performance of the famous love song in Mozart's *Don Giovanni* that begins (in the original Italian) *Là ci darem la mano, lá mi dirai di sí* ("There we will join hands, there you'll say yes to me."). The episode can be found on YouTube. Achille and Philippa become immersed in the situation they are creating or recreating. The music is partly outside its performers in some respects. Their voices project, and are audible, elsewhere in the house, and particularly audible to the possessive and puritanical pastor: the film cuts away twice during the song to shots of him seated with his other daughter at a table in an adjoining room, *their* hands joined in grief-stricken witness of the sinful seduction attempted by Papin or Mozart's black art. Also 'external' is the musical accompaniment that comes from the piano in the room, but significantly Papin abandons that mechanical aid quite early in the duet, opting instead to hum the orchestral line where it seems to be needed. But the music is also inside the couple, brought forth from within their bodies (and we hardly need to speculate about their mental representations at this point). Papin, as Giovanni, clutches Philippa/Zerlina's arm, her shoulders, and at the song's conclusion kisses her forehead. The duettists do not quite kiss, then, and the scene is not interpreted as one where Papin takes advantage of his pupil. But no viewer would deny that the imminent *possibility* of their hands and lips touching is central to their and our experiencing of the music, of the situation, and of themselves. No viewer doubts that Achille is really smitten with Philippa and her voice (unlike the love-making of Giovanni to Zerlina, ironically, there is no simulation here), and the 'canonical situation' of his singing with and to Philippa is critical. Their singing and communicating does not merely role-play or simulate love; it crosses a line (a line which the logic of simulation theory implies is absolutely uncrossable) to become an embodied experiencing of love. What started out as pretending and role-playing (playing the roles of Giovanni and Zerlina) becomes *on the strength of that pretending or imaginative immersion* no pretending at all, but Achille truly (and innocently, as the song puts it?) in love with Philippa, and her half in anxious love with him. That Philippa shortly terminates the singing lessons (at her father's implicit behest and to what we interpret to be his idea of intense pleasure) only makes the now-abandoned connection the more palpable. The whole episode (like the film in which it arises) shows rather than tells the power of art, and then the curbs on that power. But what my description has failed to mention so far is the *quality* of Philippa's singing: Achille, the 'resting' professional, sings well enough; but Philippa's singing is transcendent, so pure, committed, and beautiful. It is a performing of the art-love-beauty nexus that (I believe) Axel and Blixen intended. Mozart's beautiful love song is here as compelling a demonstration of the power of art and the artist as one can imagine (and we viewer-listeners, like the protagonists, are persuaded by the demonstration); in a parallel way, later in the film, Babette's feast will achieve the same goal.

5.8. If there was one most noteworthy area of development that I would want to pick out for attention, among the multiple practices of literary reading that have emerged over the past twenty years, it would not be literary weblogs, or net-based slash fiction, or hyper-fiction, or the growth of reading of the great authors via online critical editions. It would not be a high-tech development at all, but reading groups. Agreed, some of these rely on mass-media communication – the Oprah Winfrey book selections, the one city one book programmes in Seattle, Chicago, and now worldwide (these are civic initiatives that try to get everyone in a city to read and discuss the same book) – but even these are using relatively old technologies (on reading groups see the work of Swann, Allington and O'Halloran 2008 and Fuller 2008). And the larger growth in reading groups, at least in North America and the UK, has mostly occurred with a minimum of technological facilitation. For reasons not easily fathomed (decline in institutional religious belief and church-going? increased affluence and leisure time? a hunger for kinds of fluid or intermittent community outside the traditional bases in family, class, ethnicity, profession?), small groups of like-minded people are taking the trouble to meet in person on a fairly regular basis, to share their thoughts about whatever literary work they have agreed to read. The reading group standardly conforms to Lyons's (1977) conditions for "the canonical situation of utterance" (where *utterance* could easily be replaced by the richer term *communication*). I believe they do so precisely because in that way more of their senses, more of their bodies (not just hearing and sight but touch also and even smell (e.g., of each other, or of the books or paper in hand) are engaged in the act of literary reading, broadly understood (and the sense of taste too, where refreshments accompany the book discussion).

5.9. Alongside the growth in the communal but low-tech shared literary reading that is the reading group, another distinct and enduring affordance of literary reading should not be neglected: that of private and undivided attention. The writer Colm Tóibín has recently re-asserted that literature is special by virtue of being art which can have a private impact, on one person at a time: "The business of reading and writing are done alone… There is a lovely privacy and power about that… You are affecting someone when they are alone, probably the most powerful time to affect people." (Tóibín 2008). Tóibín (2008) contrasts this (potentially) private relation, of fiction and poetry, with the typically more public relation of films and plays; and he perhaps overstates his case, neglecting the possibilities of a powerful shared literary experience – not only in the theatre but at a poetry reading or, as implied earlier, in a reading group.

Still, as hinted at in 5.3 above, undivided attention remains a specially important element to take into consideration because in the modern world there are, to an unparalleled extent, endless ambushes upon semiological immersion, whether that comes under the aegis of hyperliterature, multi-tasking, split-screens or other multi-source multi-modal communication. I am not saying that multiple modes of communication cannot be synchronized and integrated. On the contrary, the thrust of integrational linguistic theory is that they routinely are (cf. the integrational principle of cotemporality – Harris 1981: 157-164). But I do want to suggest that a different kind of reading, and arguably sometimes a qualitatively inferior one, takes place when the eye must repeatedly move not steadily and syntagmatically along the line of text, but from one text to a para-text, from body text to margin or footnote, or from one window to another (and then back again, or on to yet another). As others have noted, *desultory* reading (in one of the earlier senses of *desultory*:

moving or jumping from one thing to another; disconnected) may militate against deeply engaged reading, one where there is both cognitive and emotional immersion in the narrative or situation literarily depicted (Ben Shaul 2009; Bauerlein 2008).

ACKNOWLEDGMENT

I am most grateful to the following for their helpful comments on drafts of this essay: Beatrix Busse, Dan McIntyre, Nina Nørgaard, Keith Oatley, Willie van Peer, Vander Viana, and Sonia Zyngier.

Michael Toolan
University of Birmingham, UK

REFERENCES

Adolphs, S. (2009, July). *Corpus, Context and Ubiquitous Computing*. Plenary talk at the Corpus Linguistics Conference, University of Liverpool.

Bailly, J. (2007). *Emotional responses to printed format and audio format stories*. Unpublished MA dissertation, University of Birmingham, UK.

Ben Shaul, N. (2009). *Hyper-Narrative Interactive Cinema*. Rodopi: Amsterdam.

Bauerlein, M. (2008). *The Dumbest Generation: How the Digital Age Stupefies Young Americans and Jeopardizes Our Future (Or, Don't Trust Anyone Under 30)*. Jeremy P. Tarcher/Penguin: New York.

Fuller, Danielle. (2008. Reading as Social Practice: The Beyond the Book research project. *Journal of Popular Narrative Media, 1*(2), 211-217.

Harris, R. (1981). *The Language Myth*. Duckworth: London.

Lyons, J. (1977). *Semantics* (Vol. 2). Cambridge University Press: Cambridge.

Oatley, K. (2009). *Such stuff as dreams: The psychology of fiction*. Plenary lecture to the Poetics and Linguistics Association, Wednesday 29 July, Middelburg, The Netherlands.

Oatley, K. (2008). The mind's flight simulator. *The Psychologist, 21*, 1030-1032.

van Peer, W. (2009). The Multidimensionality of Art. *Empirical Studies of the Arts, 27*(2), 217-222.

Rubinstein, J. S., Meyer, D. E. & Evans, J. E. (2001). Executive control of cognitive processes in task switching. *Journal of Experimental Psychology: Human Perception and Performance, 27*, 763-797.

Swann, J., Allington, D., & O'Halloran, K. (2008). *Contemporary reading groups and the reception of literature: an empirical approach.* Paper presented at the Poetics and Linguistics Association Conference, Sheffield: 23-26 July. 2008.

Tóibín, C. (2008). Radio interview with Michael Silverblatt. *KCRW's Bookworm.* First aired April 17, 2008. Archived at http://www.kcrw.com/etc/programs/bw/bw080417colm_toibin (last retrieved: August 3, 2009)

Toolan, M. (2008). Audiofiction: no time for deep thoughts and feelings? Online Proceedings of the Annual Conference of the Poetics and Linguistics Association (PALA). Retrieved from http://www.pala.ac.uk/resources/proceedings/2008/toolan2008.pdf

Toolan, M. (2009). *Narrative Progression in the Short Story: A Corpus Stylistic Approach.* New York and Amsterdam: John Benjamins.

Toolan, M. (in press). *Immersion and emotion: how textual patternings shape our experiencing of literary narrative.*

Preface

Progress (in education) is not in the succession of studies but in the development of new attitudes towards, and new interests in, experience. -- John Dewey (1897)

How many times do we come across quotes from centuries ago which, not having become anachronistic, still have not had the fortune to be heard by many? Dewey's (1897) statement in the epigraph is one such case. We live at a time of enormous readjustments, especially in the use and dissemination of media. We have gone past the era of storing and processing information into one of knowing how to access and manage it. In the area of literature, ever more information on literary production is being distributed and retrieved in electronic form (for instance, audiobooks and e-books; also see Toolan, this volume). New ways of reading emerge with consequences for learning and research environments at educational institutions. It is high time we open ourselves to these new possibilities and learn how to deal with them.

Today's popularization of modern technologies has allowed scholars in the Humanities, including literature specialists, to access an array of novel opportunities in the digital medium, which have also brought about an equal number of challenges and questions. However, very little has been provided for the advance of literary education. With a few exceptions here and there, the Humanities still resist turning to digital forms. This is vividly brought up by Davidson and Goldberg (2009: 8), who describe the present state in many schools around the world as one where "how we teach, where we teach, who we teach, who teaches, who administers, and who services – have changed mostly around the edges. The fundamental aspects of learning institutions remain remarkably familiar and have done so for something like two hundred years or more".

In fact, when faced with innovations in technology, the typical attitude of teachers of literature who resist change is to go from an initial rejection to a gruntled acceptance. They gradually adapt to new technology until it becomes naturalized (cf. Bax, 2003) and they cannot really do without it any more. Ironically enough, when they think they have mastered the technology, another new scenario will have appeared and the cycle repeats itself. One would expect, therefore, that learning processes would take place as a rule, so that new technological introductions would be embraced somewhat faster. Unfortunately, that does not generally tend to be the case.

Compared to the reaction of those working in the natural sciences, the vigorous rejection of any novel development in literary studies is in some ways worrying. For one, it is energy wasted because, as the cycle repeats itself again and again, it requires cognitive and emotional energy that could have been better spent on more useful ideas or projects. Adding to that, as the cycle eventually leads to full acceptance of the new technology anyway, it makes the initial refusal useless.

Aware of this situation, the contributors of *Literary Education and Digital Learning: Methods and Technologies for Humanities Studies* offer a deep probe into relevant issues in literary education and digital learning from both a research and an educational perspective. Admittedly, there is nothing wrong with not knowing everything about new gadgets. Today's youngsters have developed their own styles of communication regardless of our attitudes as adults and, indeed, there may even be some attraction in learning from them from time to time. We hope that once our readers evaluate the experiences collected here, they will be able to make a cost/benefit analysis of the current situation in literary studies with regard to information technology and decide for themselves the path to be taken.

Both the foreword and the afterword to this volume intend to bring provocative topics to light. These are meant to help readers position themselves in relation to the issues involved in digital literary learning. In the opening of the present volume, Michael Toolan (University of Birmingham) sets the tone by developing a number of possibilities which have been brought about to the literature field by new techonologies. At the same time, consious of its limitations, the foreword also expands on what computers have not done so far.

The book is then divided into two main parts: research and education. The first one, which comprises four chapters, collects studies that clearly indicate how technologies may be employed in literary research. In other words, its aim is to understand how computers and programs may help scholars and students investigate literary works in novel ways, thus bringing new perspectives to the area. In the first chapter, Patrick Juola (Duquesne University) discusses how feasible it is to uncover the author of a given text. In clear prose, he describes some of the possibilities of this evolving field and considers its application to literary studies. Also acknowledging the importance of authorship, Lisa Lena Opas-Hänninen (University of Oulu) addresses, from a statistical viewpoint, the topic of change in one's literary writing. In this case, she looks into eleven texts in prose written by Samuel Beckett in order to check their comparability in terms of stance. Moving on to Swedish literature, Lars Borin and Dimitrios Kokkinakis (University of Gothenburg) report on their work in literary onomastics – namely, the development of a system which allows users to gather several important background information as regards names mentioned in literary works. The authors also discuss the research possibilities which are opened up with the application of language tecnology to the literary field. Finally, Bill Louw (University of Zimbabwe) shifts the perspective to a more lexical/semantical one by analyzing word patterning as, for instance, that of 'day' in Philip Larkin's poetry. In his chapter, he points out how collocations may be used to enhance one's understanding of literature.

The second part of the book is dedicated to the education of literature students or, from a more general standpoint, readers. It consists of three chapters, ranging from a product-based approach to a process-based one. Opening this part, Stefan Hofer, René Bauer and Imre Hofmann (University of Zurich) explain how they have devised tEXtMACHINA, an e-learning environment which has been developed to account for the particularities of the literary field. The chapter also reports on the experience of using this web-based environment to enhance the possibilities of German literature teaching in the Switzerland context. In the following chapter, Jon Saklofske (Acadia University) also deals with the teaching of literature at universities. However, in this case, the author goes on to propose that games should be integrated in pedagogical practice. To this end, the chapter provides an overview of the technological tool the author designed as well as a detailed account of how it has been used in the Canadian setting. The educational part closes with William L. Heller (Teaching Matters) extending the discussion of literature teaching to the regular school background. Drawing on the concepts of the zone of proximal development and multiple intelligences, the author makes a case for teaching Shakespearean texts as early as possible. To illustrate his proposal, the chaper comments on and analyzes a real three-phase experience of teaching Shakespeare's to fifth-graders at a school in New York City.

Closing the present volume, David Miall (University of Alberta) invites readers to embark on his dream of a literary machine. This innovation, which is unfortunately unavailable to date, aims at encompassing several features to help enhance one's experience of literature reading. Miall's proposal is clearly illustrated by means of Coleridge's poetry, and its application to rearch and teaching are highlighted in the afterword.

All in all, the volume offers a survey of the potentials of inviting techonological innovation to the realm of literary research/education. This survey is inherently brief, as the area still lacks more solid production into the confluence of technology and literature. Ultimately, we hope the present book contributes to a change of attitude and a new way of using technology in education.

REFERENCES

Bax, S. (2003). CALL: Past, present and future. *System, 31*, 13-28.

Davidson, C. N., & Goldberg, D. T. (2009). *The future of learning institutions in a digital age* (The John D. and Catherine T. MacArthur Foundation reports on digital media and learning). Cambridge, Massachusetts: The MIT Press. Retrieved February 12, 2010, from http://www.uchri.org/images/Future_of_Learning.pdf

Dewey, J. (1897). My pedagogic creed. *School Journal, 54*, 77-80. Retrieved February 12, 2010, from http://dewey.pragmatism.org/creed.htm

Willie van Peer, University of Munich, Germany
Sonia Zyngier, Federal University of Rio de Janeiro, Brazil
Vander Viana, Queen's University Belfast, UK

Section 1
Research

Chapter 1
Authorship Attribution and the Digital Humanities Curriculum

Patrick Juola
Duquesne University, USA

ABSTRACT

Although authorship attribution is simply the determination of who wrote a document by analysis of its content, it is a long-standing problem both in the humanities and in computational text analysis. While traditional methods involve identifying key aspects of style through close reading, new developments in computational science permit a more objective approach through the statistical analysis of superficial characteristics such as vocabulary and word choice. If a writer can be shown (statistically) to have a particular stylistic quirk ('stylome') that appears broadly across his or her writing, then other writings also displaying that quirk are good candidates to also be by that author. The present chapter describes some of the statistical techniques used to make such judgments, and describes one particular computer program (JGAAP) that is freely available for this purpose. This type of analysis is capable of determining authorship with relatively high accuracy The potential creates some significant implications for authorship questions across the humanities curriculum, as well as broader impacts in the world outside the academy. In light of these implications, I argue for the inclusion of more mathematics into the humanities curriculum.

DOI: 10.4018/978-1-60566-932-8.ch001

INTRODUCTION

In 1983, the German magazine *Stern* published excerpts from what were believed to be the diaries of Adolph Hitler. A number of experts, including the leading historian Hugh Trevor-Roper, had examined them and pronounced them genuine. Within two weeks, however, analysis of the paper and ink used proved them conclusively to be false. What will happen in 2043, when someone publishes excerpts from the (electronic) diary of another world leader? Without paper and ink, will there be any way to examine them and determine if they are forgeries?

Authorship attribution is the science and art of examining documents and trying to determine who wrote them by analysis of the document content. While traditionally done by close expert reading, there has been an explosion in recent years of scholarship in search of ways to get computers to make the judgment based on statistical properties of the document such as word frequencies. This task will be shown both to be interesting in its own right (and highly solvable), but also a good illustration of the large question of how computers should interact with (and serve) traditional humanities disciplines such as literature.

TOUCHSTONES AND ERRORS

Assessing documents to determine who wrote them is a classic problem for scholars; you find a manuscript in an archive and look for quirks of handwriting and phrasing that may give a hint to who wrote it and when. Indeed, the problem of identifying groups of people by their language goes back, literally, at least to the Old Testament:

And the Gileadites took the passages of Jordan before the Ephraimites: and it was so, that when those Ephraimites which were escaped said, Let me go over; that the men of Gilead said unto him, Art thou an Ephraimite? If he said, Nay;

6 Then said they until him, Say now Shibboleth; and he said Sibboleth: for he could not frame to pronounce it right. Then they took him, and slew him at the passages of Jordan: and there fell at that time of the Ephraimites forty and two thousand (Judges 12:5-6).

This illustrates one of the simplest methods of determining the author of a text; if you can find a straightforward, all-or-nothing touchstone that only the person of interest would use (or would avoid using), find that in the relevant document and you have your answer. Wellman (1936) describes a similar event in a legal case: he had in his possession documents that would win the case if the jury could be persuaded that a specific witness had written them. These documents were notable for their repeated misspelling of **toutch*. By persuading the witness under some pretence to take dictation in court, he was able to show that she misspelled *touch* in exactly that same way (and thus presumably was the author he was looking for).

Another example comes from the famous Beale Manuscript (Singh, 2000). Ostensibly a letter written by Beale in 1822 but not published until 1860, it accompanies a famous set of coded directions to find a fortune in buried treasure. To this day, the directions have only been partly decoded and the treasure has never been found – if it ever existed at all. Scholars are justifiably suspicious on this point, in part because the letter uses words and phrases (such as *stampede* or *improvised tools*) that were not employed in 1822, but were in use by 1860 (Kruh, 1982, 1988).

Less formally, every teacher knows to look for damning similarities in answers, especially in wrong answers. If two students both write identical gibberish in response to a homework problem, something is up. Similarly, many teachers have adopted a standard practice of running a search engine like Google on suspicious phrases from essays in the hopes of finding the original source from which students have copied nearly word-for-word. All these examples have in common the idea that there is a single piece of information, a smoking gun, as it were, to prove or more commonly disprove the purported author.

There are two major problems with this approach. The first is that proving plagiarism via Google requires that the original source be available (and searchable); a student who copied from an unpublished essay in a fraternity file cabinet is more or less untouchable. The second is that many of the necessary touchstones are not very common. The Gileadites (and Wellman, with the power of the court system) were able to invoke *force majeure* to make sure the other party said or wrote what they needed, but in typical writing, the word *touch* is rather rare, and *stampede* rarer still. Can scholars rely on finding the right word in the right place in the right document?

STATISTICAL FINGERPRINTS

If individual words are too rare to be relied upon, it may be possible to use more common and far-reaching broad aspects of language to determine authorship. An early (and often-reinvented) idea can be first found in De Morgan (1851) and Mendenhall (1887), who observed that some people seem to use larger words than others. Yule (1938) suggested that the average number of words per sentence seemed to vary reliably between people. Superficially, it seems plausible that people with larger vocabularies will of necessity use longer words. Unfortunately, it has not proven possible to apply this observation usefully; average word length varies dramatically from document to document (even when written by the same person);

and documents of radically different style will have the same average word length. In the damningly understated words of Smith (1983 as cited by Holmes, 1994), "Mendenhall's method now appears to be so unreliable that any serious student of authorship should discard it" (p. 89).

On the other hand, there may be features of language that are both common and reliable enough to be useful. One candidate for such a feature is the set of near synonym pairs: the words *large* and *big* are close enough in meaning as to be nearly interchangeable, and which one you use is largely a matter of personal preference. Another candidate is the set of so-called function words, small, common words like prepositions, conjunctions, and pronouns that are not so much about the meaning of the sentence as about the relationship between the meaningful (or content) words. Consider, for a moment, trying to define what the meaning of *of* is, or the meaning of *an*. Does your neighbor live in the house *next to* yours, the one *near* yours, or the one *by* yours? Because these words are both common and topic-independent, they are strong candidates to use as features.

Mosteller and Wallace (1964) were among the first to apply this technique, but it has since become relatively standard. The researchers analyzed a group of political texts called *The Federalist Papers*, a collection of 85 anonymously published newspaper editorials published between 1788 and 1789. Historians now agree that John Jay wrote three of these essays, James Madison wrote 16, and Alexander Hamilton wrote 51, with three more written jointly by Madison and Hamilton. Both Hamilton and Madison, however, claimed to have written the remaining 12, which have become known to history as the disputed essays (although historians are confident that they were written by Madison on the basis of other evidence).

Mosteller and Wallace (1964) analyzed these works in terms of simple frequency statistics (e.g., in this document, the word *of* appeared 8 times per thousand words) and inferred probabilities (how likely it is that the word *of* will appear more than ten times per million words in the next document), a technique (to be discussed in more detail later) that would be known as the Naïve Bayes classifier (Lewis, 1998) and found that the probability that the disputed essays had been written by Hamilton was vanishingly small, while the corresponding probability that they had been written by Madison was much larger. This finding has been replicated by many others since (see Juola, 2006 for some examples).

Another example is the case of the fifteenth book of the *Oz* series, as studied by Binongo (2003). As before, there are two contending candidates for *The Royal Book of Oz* – L. Frank Baum, the creator of the original series, and Ruth Plumly Thompson, the person who took over the series after Baum's death. Again studying the distribution of function words, he was able to show both that Baum and Thompson had strongly different stylistic preferences in these words, and that the *Royal Book* much more closely matched Thompson's style.

Function words do appear, then, to be sufficiently idiosyncratic as to be useful features for this job. Similarly, if one imagines the difficulties involved in eschewing prepositions, articles, and conjunctions completely, they should also be common enough that we can expect to find them. Van Halteren et al. (2005) suggested that fundamental features like this should be termed a 'stylome', in a deliberate imitation of the genome that underlies individual biological differences.

WORKING WITH STYLOMES

An Example Algorithm

Function words, then, are a strong candidate for the possible elements that may make up a detectable stylome. From a practical standpoint, it is an obvious question to ask whether or not there are any other candidates. Another evident inquiry is how to best detect differences in style within the candidates. As an example, we present a brief description of one method of detection, the Naïve Bayes analysis method. This method has been chosen because the statistics are easier to explain than many other competitors (for a more detailed background, see Juola, 2006).

At its most fundamental, the Naïve Bayes method formalizes our intuitions that some things are less likely than others, and if we have a choice between causes, we pick the most likely explanation for what we observed. Suppose we have a large body of writing by two or three separate people, and we find that that one person uses (for example) color adjectives a lot, while noticing that a second uses them hardly at all, and the third uses them at about an average rate. If we find a new document with lots of color adjectives, we would incline to believe that the first person was more likely than the third, but both of them were more likely than the second, based on color adjectives alone. If we also found that the third and only the third wrote with an extensive use of metaphor (and the document itself used metaphor extensively), this would be yet more evidence against the second potential candidate – and might even shift our view of the relative likelihood of the first and third. Bayes' theorem, in turn, provides a formal and quantitative measurement of how our view should shift, given the relative frequencies of evidence for and against our hypothesis.

We thus have at least one intuitively plausible method of inferring the authors of a given document. The procedure is to identify a set of likely candidates, and for each one, collect enough authentic examples of their work (the usual term for these examples is the training set) that you can identify the characteristic quirks that distinguish their work from the other candidates in the set. When done informally, this is simply close reading and paying attention to style. If those same quirks appear in the unknown document as in one candidate's training set, then the same person probably wrote the unknown document. In a more formal setting, we can quantify the relevant characteristics of both the training set and the candidate document and apply Bayes' theorem. As with most statistical studies, the amount of data we need (for example, the size of the training set) will determine the strength of evidence we can obtain and therefore our confidence in the results. In the hypothetical example above, we have two hypothetical quirks that can be quantified and applied to infer that the second author probably did not write it, but that the third probably did.

These informal inferences can be coded into a computer and converted to exact numerical values based on just how extensive the use of metaphor is and how much each person varies in his/her use of metaphor. For Naïve Bayes, the statistics are relatively simple; each numerical trait is treated as a random variable and the distribution calculated. For each candidate, an average level of the trait and the distribution around the average is calculated. Using Bayes' theorem, we can therefore calculate the probability that any particular document was written by any particular author, and the one with the highest (numerical) probability is considered to be the most likely creator of the document. The exact algorithms are beyond the scope of this chapter, but are well-known and easy to code up. The chief difficulty in applying this method is to produce numerical measures of authorial quirks. While some traits (such as word length) can be quantified easily, other attributes (such as use of metaphor) may be difficult or impossible for a computer to measure. Even here, human judgment can be used (for example, by asking experts to quantify metaphor on a Likert scale) and the resulting numbers fed into the Naïve Bayes system. The mathematics, as stated before, are not difficult for the statistically trained.

Programmatic Frameworks

For the statistically untrained, as an alternative to doing the math yourself, existing software can be used. In another paper (Juola et al., 2006), we have described a framework for analyzing authorship automatically using a variety of different techniques. The Java Graphical Authorship Attribution Program (JGAAP) is a freely-downloadable Java program (see www.jgaap.com for details) implementing this framework that provides over 2,500 different methods for analyzing texts.

Underlying the program is a three-phase theoretical framework describing a process for authorship attribution in terms of a simple pipeline of modular building blocks. The first phase, called canonicization, simply converts documents to a standard or canonical form. For example, line breaks and carriage returns can be an informative feature when studying poetry. In most normal prose, however, line breaks are more a function of the editor and publisher than of the writer– or perhaps even of the typesetting program used. The words, however, are selected by the author. An editor's reformatting will not typically change his or her choice of words. Therefore, a program should be able to ignore or neutralize format changes. The canonicization phase can therefore (at least in theory) effect any needed format changes. Similarly, the program can de-edit (Rudman, 2005) the text to eliminate any irrelevant changes made by the editor such as the intrusion of page numbers or the alteration of spelling (if the editors insist on changing the discussion above to *colour* adjectives, then that is not really my terminology – in fact, *colour* vs *color* is often seen as an important cue when the editor and publisher leave the author's choice alone). The canonicizer should therefore in theory eliminate as many distracting and uninformative sources of variation as possible (although some types of de-editing are not currently practical for computers, such as reversing human-editorial changes). However, many changes are computationally tractable such as variations in inter-word spacing introduced by line justification, or even numbers when the numbers themselves are not part of the individual style (as in sports reportage – what is important for analysis is not the score, but the words used to describe the score). At the end of this phase, the text to be analyzed should ideally be in as close to a unified format, as close to the originally intended manuscript, and stripped of as much irrelevant and distracting variation as possible.

Of course, this is not always possible. Converting Web pages to flat text is relatively easy since the necessary markup (HTML) is both well-defined and obvious. Stripping numbers is easy. Converting Word documents to plain text is harder because there is no well-known standard for MS Word, and Microsoft has hitherto guarded the specifications. Fixing typographic errors is harder yet. The JGAAP software package implements only a few of the many possible ways to canonicize documents.

The second phase of the JGAAP framework is the generation of an event set from the canonicized document, essentially identifying the relevant events to be analyzed later. If we are interested only in patterns in the comparative distribution of adjectives (without regard to their colligational environment), for instance, then the events would be words, and we would be well-served not only to pay attention to words, but to throw out all the words that were not adjectives. On the other hand, analyzing patterns in sentences would involve the identification of sentential events, while analyzing distributions of characters would of course lead to event sets comprised entirely of characters. Again, while this may seem an easy task, it may prove to be easy or hard depending upon the exact details; identifying characters is easy in typewritten documents, hard in handwritten ones. Identification of words is relatively easy in English (which has spaces between words) but hard in Chinese, and of course identification of metaphors is probably beyond the scope of current technology (although research continues on this very interesting topic).

The third and final phase is the application of inferential statistics to figure out which author is (most likely to be) responsible for the text. Again, there are several different methods that can be employed. The Naïve Bayes method has already been described. A simpler method is simply to group similar events into histograms (for example, making a histogram of the fifty-or-so most common words, which are very likely to be function words), then looking at the closest documents. This method goes by the rather off-putting name of 1-nearest neighbor, but is based on the very intuitive idea that if this document has a similar distribution of words as a document by Sinclair Lewis (where similarity is measured via the abstract notion of a distance), there is a good chance it is his.

The 1-nearest neighbor method can be improved in a number of ways. First, as there is always the possibility that any one document might be unusual or unrepresentative, you can take the five closest documents and let them vote on who the author is – if four of the five agree, you have your answer. This method is called 5-nearest neighbor. You can apply statistical transformations to your data set such as Principle Component Analysis (PCA), which reduces the fifty or so variables to two, and displays them in clusters that (one hopes) reflect authorship. An example of such an analysis is given in Figure 1.

In this analysis of five authors, we see clear visual groupings based on the frequency of the most common words in the document. And, of course, if an unknown document were to be placed in, say, the upper right corner of the diagram, we could infer that it was more likely to be written by Sinclair Lewis than by James or Wharton.

Figure 1. Principle Component Analysis (courtesy of David Hoover)

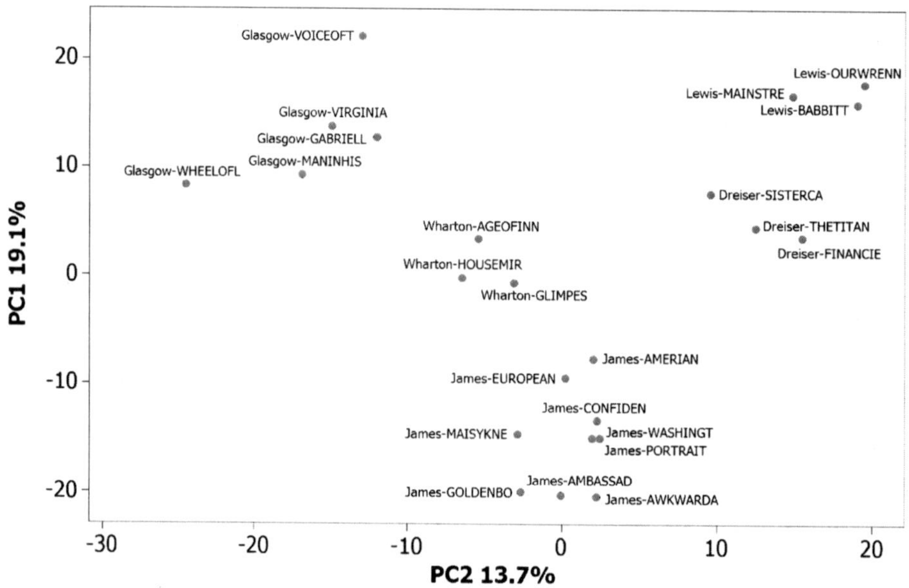

As with prior stages, the number of possible analytic methods far exceeds the number that have actually been incorporated into JGAAP at this writing, or will ever been incorporated. Rudman (1998) has estimated that over 1,000 different event sets alone have been proposed over the century-long history of this task. But even with the 2,500 or so that JGAAP currently encompasses, we have material enough to ask which, if any, are effective and accurate.

Authorship Testing

The most obvious way to determine which methods work is to test them empirically. To this end, one needs to obtain a set of validated documents of known authorship, apply the methods in question, and grade them on the accuracy of their outputs. Unfortunately, this has not always been practical. Many techniques have been proposed in the context of a specific question of interest to the proposer and only to the proposer – a scholar interested in Marlowe might develop an *ad hoc* method to study a document he or she found in an archive, apply the method, then move on to a different document from a different archive. Large-scale testing requires the cooperation of many different researchers and research groups, the collection of a large group of texts for testing, and in many cases, shows more about how incompatible the different software can be. There are, nevertheless, a few examples of large-scale testing and no doubt more are forthcoming.

To more fully understand some of the issues involved in testing, consider the test corpus compiled by Baayen et al. (2002) and Juola and Baayen (2005). Baayen et al. (2002) collected – really, had written-to-order – nine tightly topic-controlled essays each by eight undergraduate students at the University of Nijmegen. These essays, three fiction, including a retelling of the Dutch version of *Little Red Riding Hood*, three descriptive, and three argumentative) averaged about 900 words each and provide a very difficult test corpus, precisely because the essays are so similar. The writers are very close in age, education, socio-economic status, and so forth, and the essays are relatively short (at least in comparison to the hundreds of thousands of words of Shakespeare available). Despite this, several researchers have tried to infer the authorship of these documents, with mixed success. Simple function word PCA (Principle Component Analysis performed on function words) as described above fails to extract any useful information (the results obtained were no more accurate than chance), but an extension of PCA called Linear Discriminant Analysis (LDA – a method of inferring separating hyperplanes in an abstract high-dimensional feature space) is moderately accurate, as is a variation on 1-nearest neighbor using an unusual distance measure called cross-entropy (Juola, 1997; Juola and Baayen, 2005). Cross-entropy is an information-theoretic measure of how unpredictable a given set of test data is in comparison with our expectations from a set of training data.

One might wonder about what these results really say. If we suppose, for a moment, that these findings on the Dutch corpus cannot be further improved simply by tweaking the software such as making minor changes to parameters, does this mean that LDA is a better technique for authorship attribution than PCA? Or does it mean that LDA when applied to function words is better than PCA? Or maybe that LDA is better than PCA when applied to documents of fewer than 1,500 words, or perhaps documents in Dutch, or documents written by university students, or a pleasant combination of any or all of these factors. A university instructor in the United States could legitimately question whether the structure of Dutch is similar enough to English to make this finding applicable to his/her work. Obviously, larger-scale testing is needed to determine whether or not LDA and cross entropy are, in general, better inference methods than PCA.

One larger example of such testing (although barely large-scale in absolute terms) is the Ad-hoc Authorship Attribution Competition (AAAC) organized in 2004 in Gothenburg, Sweden although carried out over the Internet (Juola, 2004). The contest included thirteen problems in a variety of languages, genres, and lengths. Problem A, for example, asked participants to analyze a group of English-language essays collected from a Duquesne University freshman composition class, while Problem D asked participants to analyze Elizabethan and Jacobean plays by classic playwrights like Marlowe, Shakespeare, and Jonson. Problem F presented excerpts from the *Paston Letters*, a classic of Middle English, while problem K presented excerpts from a 13th-century Serbian-Slavonic text *The Lives of Kings and Archbishops.* Problem M was the Dutch corpus described above. In theory, this should permit us to compare performance across many genres and languages. Thirteen sets of solutions were submitted by eleven research groups across the world.

These results (presented in detail in Juola, 2008) illustrated both the strengths and the weaknesses of authorship attribution. The results were strong and heartening in that almost every participant scored well, often beating chance by substantial percentages. The results were also heartening in that the participants that scored well on the large documents (such as the plays and novels) also tended to score well on the smaller documents (the letters and essays) – and the participants that scored well on the English documents tended to score well on the non-English documents. This suggests that a good method is likely to stay a good method when moved to a different language or genre – that LDA is likely to outperform PCA on English school essays as well as Dutch ones, or even on English personal letters or financial reports. On the other hand, none of the methods, even the high-performing ones, were accurate enough overall to justify relying highly on, especially if the stakes were high (for example, in an accusation of plagiarism or in a court case). This is a point to which we shall return.

Perhaps least heartening of all is the unfortunate fact that the highest scoring participant cheated. Instead of analyzing the documents computationally, he resorted to the age-old trick of close reading and Google searching. Many of the problems involved classic documents with which any English professor would be familiar as a matter of course, but the Library of Google will catch even the obscure works. But even the works that were not available online could sometimes be identified by searching, for example, for characteristic spelling mistakes or personal information. Has Google made it possible to extend **touch* into a practical large-scale authorship attribution technique?

Other Types of Attribution

Besides the simplest type of attribution described in the previous section, there are many other related problems that can be approached via similar technology. In fact, the problem described above is arguably the simplest type of problem, where we have a well-established set of candidate authors (such as Hamilton and Madison) and are interested only in which one wrote the document. A more realistic, but much more difficult scenario would involve the possibility of a none-of-the-above response, just on the offhand chance that Jefferson decided to try his hand at writing a political pamphlet. Technology has not yet come up with a complete solution to this version of the problem.

Even within the 'closed-class' version of the problem, there are a number of interesting extensions to the problem, depending upon how one defines the concept of 'author'. Charles Dickens, for example, wrote professionally for thirty years (and Henry James for forty); did the young Dickens have the same style as the old Dickens? Or, to phrase the problem another way, could we use the methods of the previous section to date documents, or to analyze the development of style?

Perhaps unsurprisingly, the answer is *yes*; experiments of this sort have been done. David Hoover (2006) again provides an example. He analyzed 19 novels by Henry James for evidence of a large-scale shift in writing style over time. Using PCA on the 900 most common words these novels show clear evidence of such a shift. In the diagram, presented here as Figure 2, we see clear indications of a left-to-right progression in this abstract space over the course of Henry James' writing career, and would allow us to guess at the date of a newly discovered James manuscript found in a desk drawer somewhere (Hoover, 2006).

Similarly, by adjusting our concept of creator, one can apply authorship attribution techniques to inferring group characteristics; simply take a large collection of female authors as Author A, a large collection of male ones as Author B, and see what, if

Figure 2. 19 Novels by Henry James analyzed via PCA (Hoover, 2006, p. 79)

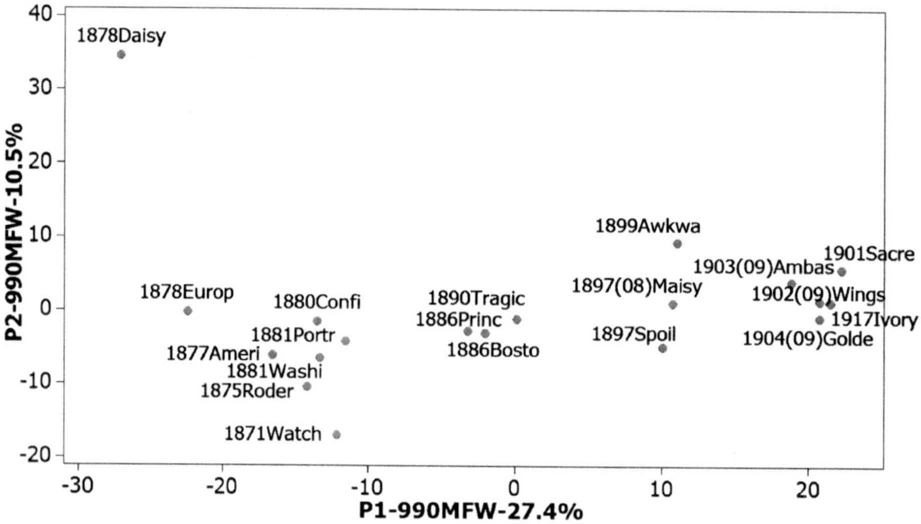

any, characteristic quirks are both shared among the A group and distinct from those of the B group. Studies like this could in theory examine the sociolinguistics of any category of interest, whether gender, race, nationality, socioeconomic status, national origin, region, education, and so forth. Many such studies have been performed; a good example is Koppel et al. (2002) and their study of gender and authorship.

Another interesting area is the classification of texts by personality. Pennebaker has done extensive work in this area, for example, by matching traits to their writing styles (Pennebaker and King, 1999; Pennebaker et al., 2003). It is probably safe to say that any method by which people can be grouped could be studied via authorship techniques. While I have no reason to believe that left-handed redheaded flute players write any differently than right-handed bald guitarists, there is nothing except common sense preventing someone from running a study to check it.

This, however, raises another question, and one for which research has not yet provided a satisfactory answer. Once we have learned that a particular marker is useful for distinguishing between bald guitarists and redheaded flute players, what does that tell us about hair or musicians? Especially with the type of low-level, easily machine-computable features that are generally studied, the idea that guitarists use the word *of* more often than flute players does not seem particularly insightful no matter how well-validated it is. Ultimately, the interpretation of authorship judgments, especially in trying to understand more about the authors in question, is something that computers cannot and may never be able to do for us. So while investigating differences between musicians is easy; one simply gathers a collection of writings sorted by instrument preference and analyzes it using a program like JGAAP, interpreting the results of such a study still requires creativity and scholarly insight.

APPLICATIONS OF AUTHORSHIP ATTRIBUTION

The empirical findings from computer programmers appear to be good, then. The technology we have now has the long-term promise of being able to determine authorship in a wide variety of contexts with usefully high accuracy. But what are the actual implications for a typical literature or language scholar?

Why We Care

We will start with the basics: authorship attribution may become a powerful technology in the ongoing fight against plagiarism. Teachers have traditionally been limited by their personal ability to judge authorship of submitted papers, and have often found themselves hampered by an inability to present a convincing case for sanctions in the event that they cannot find the original source, it being buried inaccessibly in a library or a fraternity filing cabinet, for instance. While technology has made plagiarism much easier (I can access web sites that will write a paper to order for me), it can also make detection much easier, especially when the teacher is in a position to point to the results of the computer analysis and say "these two term papers you submitted were written by two different people; were either of them you?"

More generally, computational authorship attribution can be a useful tool for analyzing the body of work associated with any particular person, whether by supporting claims for anonymous works (as with the *Federalist* example) or by disproving accepted ones. It can also be used to analyze the unsigned documents of anonymous or corporate authorship – for example, which law clerk(s) really wrote most of the text of an important legal decision, and did those clerks go on to influence other aspects of legal or government policy? Who is the person in the Ministry of Finance who is actually responsible for the most recent policy statement? Indeed, questions about which anonymous bureaucrat is responsible for what decision are standard bread-and-butter research topics for historians. This applies, of course, equally well to literature scholars interested in extending or narrowing the canon of documents attested to a particular person; for example, unsigned legal opinions may be associated with a scholar of recognized literary merit such as Sir Thomas More.

Authorship attribution can also be of crucial importance in the legal system, especially as more and more documents are created and published online. In an ordinary criminal investigation, the identity of the writer of a document such as a ransom note or a suicide note could be critical. In the case of a traditional handwritten document, the standard techniques of handwriting analysis, known to every manuscript historian and armies of forensic document examiners can give authorities the answers they need. Even for typewritten documents, the individual typewriters usually have some sort of quirk such as a worn *q* key or an off-line *m*. However, a purely electronic document has no such quirks; one flat-ASCII A is identical in all respects to any other. Again, this is not confined to the legal; literature scholars have been using manuscript evidence for centuries, but what can be done with modern writers for whom the manuscripts are electronic?

A cautionary tale can be extracted from the writings of conservative columnist Jack Cashill (www.cashill.com). In his Sept. 18, 2008 column, he suggested that presidential candidate Barack Obama had not, in fact, written the 1995 memoir *Dreams From My Father*. He states instead that Bill Ayers had been brought in to ghostwrite the book, on the basis of perceived stylistic similarity. Of course, if true, this could prove to be the basis of a major attack on the honesty and character of a major political candidate. If plagiarism and misrepresentation of one's own work is a problem for a college freshman, it should be a problem for a freshman senator as well. But if false, these allegations could still be the basis of a major attack, a classic October smear campaign of the sort that US history is littered with. This is one instance where classic approaches to literary scholarship could in theory have substantial political implications.

This, of course, is the major problem with authorship attribution. How confident are we that our attributions are correct? This is a problem with traditional methods as the anti-Stratfordian camp in Shakespeare studies illustrates (people who believe that Shakespeare did not write the plays attributed to him, typically preferring candidates like Bacon or the Earl of Oxford), but it is equally a problem with the non-traditional methods of statistical analysis described in this chapter. Indeed, it may even be a more serious problem with computer-based analysis, simply because the apparently scientific use of the computer and of statistics. This problem was alluded to in the discussion of the Naïve Bayes inference, but is more generally true – statistics can only provide evidence, but not certainty.

The problem comes in when you have a large number of somewhat reliable techniques. Every marketing expert is familiar with this; if you have a movie (or a new flavor of ice cream) you want to sell, get a hundred people to review it or to run surveys. Even if 95% of the polls come back saying that it is the worst thing in living memory, there will always be that 5% that liked it, and you can publicize their responses on national TV while quietly burying the other 95%. With well over 2,500 possible analysis techniques, it would be easy for an unscrupulous spin doctor to try every possible turn and twist in the JGAAP software until he gets the one result that he likes, whether it shows that Ayers wrote every line of *Dreams* or that Ayers had never even seen a copy until he bought his at the bookstore. Similarly, a convinced anti-Stratfordian could analyze and re-analyze every sonnet until a suitable result was found.

What We Need To Know

This problem – not just that of inaccuracy, but the one of interpreting results in light of potential inaccuracy – illustrates some things that still need to be done by literature specialists. For example, the research thus far has generally used a very naïve view of authorship as the basis for its judgments. A document has one writer, one time of writing, one genre, and so forth. That person is solely and singly responsible for everything about the document (although one will sometimes grudgingly admit the existence of an editor who puts page numbers at the bottom and such) from the spelling of the individual words to the formulation of grammatical sentences to the fundamental ideas. However, this is nonsense. Even if you can correctly identify direct quotations (Rudman, 2005) and eliminate them, there is still the problem of indirect quotation, paraphrase, and simple sloppy scholarship where the scribe or typist leaves out the quotation marks.

Put simply, what is actually authorship? Does the authorial process include selecting quotations? Does it involve responding to critical suggestions, or adjusting the format to fit publishers' norms? And if not, how can we distinguish between aspects of the document that are authorial from those that are not?

Abandoning the assumption of single authorship is no less problematic. Of course, since some documents officially have several authors, we must accept that multiple authorship is possible. But how many different forms can it take? In some cases, a senior colleague will simply sign the manuscript and thereby lend political support to it. In others, different participants will write different sections of the document and the final manuscript is assembled with a stapler. In other cases, an author or authors will produce a relatively completely preliminary draft which is lightly edited – or completely rewritten – by another person, hopefully one with a better grasp of the mechanics of composition. It could even be the case where one has an idea and shares it with a colleague who writes it down. Who should be credited with ownership of the words in these cases and others like them?

Similarly, documents are not plagiarized or stolen as a unit; students will usually pick up key phrases or passages, and in many cases will alter the wording of the passage in minor ways. Composition instructors are at pains to point out that this is still plagiarism, the misrepresentation of another author's work as their own. But the line between plagiarism and adaptation – the point at which an altered work becomes one's own – is neither clear nor easily describable.

These are problems even to a traditional literature scholar, comfortably sitting in an armchair and far away from a computer. But they become more serious when computers enter the mix, simply because computers deal so badly with vagueness and ambiguity. To analyze a document for authorship, for example, I need to be able to explain to the analyst exactly what the document includes. Does it include the page numbers? The section breaks? The document title? The formatting of the footnotes? While I might be able to tell the human analyst something vague such as to ignore the page numbers, I would need to define for the computer exactly what that is, how a collection of letters like *xi* could be a 'number', and how the location of page numbers can vary, even within a single work.

Defining for a computer exactly what is to be done is usually the most difficult and time-consuming part of software development. Unfortunately, the people most skilled in making such definitions (professional computer programmers) are often very unskilled in the domain expertise needed to solve the problem in the first place. Defining for the computer that *touch* is a five-letter word is fairly simple, especially in English where word boundaries are clearly marked by spaces. Defining for the computer that **toutch* is misspelled or that the word *stampede* was first used in the 1850s is a little harder and will often require giving the computer some sort of database. However, it can still be done with relative ease, and one can feel almost as confident of the computer's judgment as one can of the accuracy of a good dictionary. By contrast, it becomes almost impossible for a typical programmer to tell the computer what a metaphor is, what constitutes personification, or what a trope is. Even literature specialists may feel uncomfortable if pressed to give an exact definition of how to recognize irony.

Unfortunately, they are the only ones who will be able to do it. As the potential for computer-aided literature analysis (and the demand for it) increases, it will become increasingly apparent that this kind of analysis can only happen when humanists can communicate in terms that the computers, and their programmers, can understand. Fortunately, such a language is available.

MATHEMATICS, THE DIGITAL HUMANITIES, AND LITERATURE

Life and research are going digital. The days when only specialists needed computers and most practicing professors could survive with a set of index cards are gone, and even the most arcane academician in the history of ancient civilizations probably writes papers using a text processor, communicates with the journals via e-mail, and looks for references and recent scholarship using a search engine like Google. Indeed, Google may be one of the most powerful and revolutionary tools for teaching, learning, and research developed in the 20th century.

And, of course, Google relies upon computers as well as a sophisticated mathematical definition of how to figure out what a Web page is about in order to deliver the appropriate content to the user. As Google and similar projects expand, it is reasonable to expect the type and content of computational offerings for education to similarly expand and for the practice of researchers (generally) to adapt to the new offerings. As a simple example, Google is currently working on making the entire contents of several major libraries completely available over the Internet. It will soon be possible, if indeed it is not already possible, to access more books on a given subject than any practitioner could read in a lifetime.

But what are the new offerings likely to be, and who is likely to be creating them? The application of computer and digital technology to research in the humanities, a discipline called *digital humanities* or sometimes *humanities computing*, has seen an increase in attention in recent years, but unfortunately not much uptake (Juola, 2008). Instead, software changes seem to be driven by a combination of large companies and general purpose markets, without necessarily considering the needs of the relatively small academic community. This effect has been particularly pronounced in the humanities disciplines, where the necessary skills to do self-programming are often lacking, and the funding necessary to hire programming is not forthcoming.

The funding picture may be improving, for instance, with the establishment of the Office of Digital Humanities at the United States National Endowment for the Humanities and similar efforts in other countries. However, what is needed is improvement in the skill set, if not to the point of allowing self-programming, at least to the point of being able to describe the needed program and approaches.

This works out to be skill in mathematics. But it is so in a rather specialized sort of mathematics, and unfortunately a sort that is not often taught to literature specialists, the skill of abstract structural representation. For example, everyone knows that you can add the same thing to both sides of an equation – if x equals y, then x+x equals y+y. But what would this mean if x were, say, a color, or a shape, or an abstract concept? Does it even make sense to add two colors? That the answer is yes may or may not surprise the reader – after all, adding two colors together is routine when mixing paints – but what is more likely to be surprising is that the adding of colors, metaphorically, turns out to have an exact mathematical interpretation in terms of numbers. Indeed, the only way that computer graphic programs like Paint can operate is by representing colors as numbers, operating upon these numbers, and then reinterpreting the results of the (mathematical) operation as colors again. Google has made billions interpreting meaning into an abstract algebraic space in which two documents that are close in subject are also, literally, close in space.

Something similar is performed by the authorship transformations such as PCA, where documents that are close in style become (physically) close on the printed page that represents the transformed space. But PCA is itself a rather easy application of concepts from a second-year (but post-calculus) mathematics course. To a professional computer scientist, the calculations underlying PCA are not difficult, but understanding what needs to be represented in those calculations – Words? Concepts? Ideas? Tropes? – is difficult. To a literature professor, understanding the concepts to represent is easy, but actually representing them is difficult. For example, a digital library of a million books represents almost too large a knowledge base to be useful. At a rate of a book a day, a human reader would take 30,000 years to read one million books – or a computer could read all million in a few hours and report back with a list of the useful ones if you could tell the computer what type of books are useful, or what sort of information you want to extract, or even what sort of examples you were looking for.

To truly progress, practitioners in the digital humanities will need to re-embrace mathematics as a traditional humanities discipline (as indeed it once was). I have argued elsewhere (Juola, 2002; see also Juola & Ramsay, in press) that what humanists really need is exposure to the fundamentals of about six different math classes, no more, perhaps, than they would learn in the first month or so of class in a traditional setting. But these basic concepts are critical to being able to represent humanistic knowledge in a useful way.

CONCLUSION

Authorship attribution – determining who wrote a particular document by examining it – has been a traditional problem in the humanities, and the idea of automating the analysis process and using some sort of emergent statistics has been around for over a century. Modern technologies, using more sophisticated statistics and the power of a computer to do the calculations, have been shown to be very accurate, if somewhat spotty. Research continues into the best way to improve this technology – again, this research requires a strong mathematical background.

At the same time, understanding the techniques and findings of statistical authorship attribution methods requires a strong background in traditional humanities scholarship. Knowing a specific set of words that the computer has identified as being characteristic means little or nothing without a context, an environment, and an explanation about what those words show about the author and his/her style.

We see, therefore, that a proper analysis of authorship attribution requires strong humanist interaction with the computers and their programmers. The authorship models used in most studies are naïve at best and outright wrong at worst, the features used may not be especially interesting to literature scholars, and the conclusions are not always trustworthy. There is a strong need for humanists to be involved in this kind of research to provide domain expertise.

The link between these two groups is mathematics, both pure and applied. Mathematics is both a traditional liberal art, used for representing and quantifying abstraction, and also the language underlying all modern computer programs. However, most humanists are limited in their ability to provide this expertise by their limited understanding of abstract mathematics. While it may not be reasonable to expect humanists to be familiar with the arcane of computer programming languages (especially given the rapid changes in technology), it is also not reasonable to expect computer programmers to be familiar with literary theory or to be able to identify interesting abstractions without expert guidance. We therefore argue that the incorporation of mathematics into a traditional humanities curriculum will be more and more important as computational methods for authorship attribution or text analysis become more common, influential, and important.

REFERENCES

Baayen, R. H., van Halteren, H., Neijt, A., & Tweedie, F. (2002). An experiment in authorship attribution. In [St. Malo: Universite de Rennes.]. *Proceedings of JADT, 2002*, 29–37.

Binongo, J. N. G. (2003). Who wrote the 15th book of Oz? An application of multivariate analysis to authorship attribution. *Chance, 16*(2), 9–17.

de Morgan, A. (1851/1882). Letter to Rev Heald 18/08/1851. In de Morgan, S. E. (Ed.), *Memoirs of Augustus de Morgan by his wife Sophia Elizabeth de Morgan with selections from his letters*. New York: Adamant Media.

Holmes, D. I. (1994). Authorship attribution. *Computers and the Humanities, 28*(2), 87–106. doi:10.1007/BF01830689

Hoover, D. (2006). Stylometry, chronology, and the styles of Henry James. In [Paris: Sorbonne.]. *Proceedings of Digital Humanities, 2006*, 78–80.

Juola, P. (1997). What can we do with small corpora? Document categorization via cross-entropy. In *Proceedings of the Workshop on Similarity and Categorization (SimCat 97)*. Edinburgh: University of Edinburgh.

Juola, P. (2002). Humanities mathematics: when computing doesn't work. In (Ed.), *Proceedings of COSH/COCH 2002*. Toronto: University of Toronto.

Juola, P. (2004). Ad-hoc authorship attribution competition. In *Proc. 2004 Joint International Conference of the Association for Literary and Linguistic Computing and the Association for Computers and the Humanities (ALLC/ACH 2004)*. Gothenberg: Univerity of Gothenberg.

Juola, P. (2006). Authorship attribution. *Foundations and trends in information retrieval, 1*(3), 1-112.

Juola, P. (2008). Killer applications in digital humanities. *Literary and Linguistic Computing, 23*(3), 73–85.

Juola, P., & Baayen, H. (2005). A controlled-corpus experiment in authorship attribution by cross-entropy. *Literary and Linguistic Computing, 20*(1), 59–67. doi:10.1093/llc/fqi024

Juola, P., & Ramsay, S. (in press). *Mathematics for humanists*. Oxford: Oxford University Press.

Juola, P., Sofko, J., & Brennan, P. (2006). A prototype for authorship attribution studies. *Literary and Linguistic Computing, 21*(2), 169–178. doi:10.1093/llc/fql019

Koppel, M., Argamon, S., & Shimoni, A. R. (2002). Automatically categorizing written texts by author gender. *Literary and Linguistic Computing, 17*(4), 401–412. doi:10.1093/llc/17.4.401

Kruh, L. (1982). A basic probe of the Beale cipher as a bamboozlement: Part I. *Cryptologia, 6*(4), 378–382. doi:10.1080/0161-118291857190

Kruh, L. (1988). The Beale cipher as a bamboozlement: Part II. *Cryptoogila, 12*(4), 241–246. doi:10.1080/0161-118891863007

Lewis, D. D. (1998). Naïve Bayes at forty: The independence assumption in information retrieval. In *Proc ECML-98* (pp. 4-15).

Mendenhall, T. C. (1887). The characteristic curves of composition. *Science, 9*(241), 237–249. doi:10.1126/science.ns-9.214S.237

Mosteller, F., & Wallace, D. L. (1984). *Inference and disputed authorship: The Federalist*. Reading, MA: Addison-Wesley.

Pennebaker, J., Mehl, M., & Niederhoffer, K. (2003). Psychological aspects of natural language use: Our words, our selves. *Annual Review of Psychology, 54*, 547–577. doi:10.1146/annurev.psych.54.101601.145041

Pennebaker, J. W., & King, L. A. (1999). Linguistic styles: Linguistic use as an individual difference. *Journal of Personality and Social Psychology, 77*, 1293–1312. doi:10.1037/0022-3514.77.6.1296

Rudman, J. (1998). The state of authorship attribution studies: Some problems and solutions. *Computers and the Humanities, 31*, 351–365. doi:10.1023/A:1001018624850

Rudman, J. (2005). The non-traditional case for the authorship of the twelve disputed Federalist Papers: a monument built on sand. In *Proceedings of ACH/ALLC 2005*. Victoria, BC: University of Victoria.

Singh, S. (2000). *The code book: The science of secrecy from ancient Egypt to quantum cryptography*. London: Anchor.

Smith, M. W. A. (1983). Recent experience and new developments of methods for the determination of authorship. *Bulletin of the ALLC, 11*, 73–82.

van Halteren, H., Baayen, R. H., Tweedie, F., Haverkort, M., & Neijt, A. (2005). New machine learning methods demonstrate the existence of a human stylome. *Journal of Quantitative Linguistics, 12*(1), 65–77. doi:10.1080/09296170500055350

Wellman, F. L. (1936). *The art of cross-examination*. New York: MacMillan.

Yule, G. U. (1938). On sentence-length as a statistical characteristic of style in prose, with application to two cases of disputed authorship. *Biometrica, 30*, 363–390.

Chapter 2
Multivariate Analysis of Stance in Fiction: A Case Study

Lisa Lena Opas-Hänninen
University of Oulu, Finland

ABSTRACT

This study investigates the expression of stance in Samuel Beckett's prose work. Following Biber and Finegan (1989), a wide variety of stance markers are identified and calculated in the texts. A multivariate statistical methodology is then used to analyze the way in which these markers of stance interact in the texts. The results are plotted two-dimensionally to enable visualizing the similarities and differences between the texts. These are also illustrated using examples from the texts. Some of the findings are a little surprising and, therefore, a new tool is used to plot the results three-dimensionally, enabling a better understanding of how stance is reflected and how the texts resemble and deviate from one another. Finally, the usefulness of this analysis is discussed.

INTRODUCTION

This study investigates how Samuel Beckett's prose texts express attitude and assessment, in particular emotions, moods and degree of certainty of knowledge. Samuel Beckett's literary style developed over his career from a traditional, third-person

DOI: 10.4018/978-1-60566-932-8.ch002

narrative style to a highly innovative, minimalist one (Brienza 1987). It is widely acknowledged that in the third part of his trilogy, *The Unnamable*, he began to move towards the greater abstraction of his later works and in the 1960s Beckett made his first attempts towards the kind of minimalist style that he is so well known for in the prose and drama his later years (for a discussion on this see Knowlson and Pilling 1979). These later texts are often verbless, impressions of surroundings, told by no one in particular and addressed to no one either. Therefore, it could be assumed that his prose works are also likely to show differences in the way in which attitudes and assessments, or *stance*, is expressed.

The marking of attitude is related to the concept of reader involvement, in that by making him or her privy to the attitudes of the narrator or character(s), the reader is drawn into the texts. This is in accordance with reader response theory, which has taken many forms, including reader response criticism, reception theory and phenomenology (Ballaster 2007). Common to these is an emphasis on the role of the reader in creating meaning, and the relationship between the reader and the text. Some of the differences between the various approaches lie in the notion of textuality. Some claim that the text is self-contained and meaning is centered in the text; others claim that meaning is reader-centered and that the reader brings his or her knowledge and experience to the text, shaping it in the process (Bleich 1978; Davis 2002; Fish 1980; Hamilton & Schneider 2002; Harker 1992; Iser 1974; Jauss 1982; Riffaterre 1978; Selden, Widdowson & Brooker 1997). Its early forms include the work of semioticians such as Umberto Eco (1979), who argued that some texts, such as Joyce's *Finnegan's Wake*, positively invite the reader to participate in the making of meaning. In Beckett's case, this is of particular interest, since the later texts are written in such a minimalist style; they are like impressions in the mind of the narrator that are being related to some perceived listener. His prose works are almost telegraphic in style and are stripped of many of the markers of syntax. The reader has to bring much of the meaning into the text himself or herself in order to interpret it, thus also becoming involved in the manuscript. It is therefore particularly interesting to investigate how the narrator's attitudes and assessments are conveyed in Beckett's prose texts.

In recent years, linguists have become increasingly interested in how attitudes and assessments are expressed in speech and writing. Such studies have used a variety of different terms. Sometimes researchers talk about *evaluation* (Hunston 1994; Thompson and Hunston 2001), referring to how writers/speakers talk about their positive and negative opinions on a topic. Other concepts include *affect* (Ochs 1989), *evidentiality* (Chafe 1986), *hedging* (Holmes 1988, Hyland 1996), *appraisal* (Martin 2001), and *stance* (Barton 1993; Beach and Anson 1992; Biber and Finegan 1988, 1989; Kärkkäinen 2003). Broadly speaking, some of these focus more on the writer's attitudes, e.g. affect and appraisal, whereas others refer more to their judgement on the likelihood of events, e.g. evidentiality and hedging, and yet others, e.g. stance and evaluation, combine the two aspects, covering both attitude and judgement. What is common to all, though, is that they discuss the expression of opinions from the speaker's or writer's point of view, and not necessarily from what is embedded in the language items themselves. Leech (1974: 15-18) discusses this in making a distinction between *connotative meaning* (i.e., the meaning of an expression that is derived from the 'real-world experience' one has had, and *affective meaning*, that is, meaning derived from the 'personal feelings of the speaker'). People have *attitudes*, whereas linguistic items have *connotations* (Thompson and Hunston 2001: 2).[1]

Here I follow Biber and Finegan's (1989) methodology to investigate the expression of attitude in Beckett's texts because it is one of the few studies that uses quantitative statistical methods. For the same token, I use the term *stance*, which refers to the expression of attitude, in particular the way in which speakers express their attitudes towards the topic of discussion. One way of looking at stance is to say that there are two different types of expressions of attitude, namely evidentiality and affect. Evidentiality refers to the evidence that a speaker/writer may have for the claims he or she is making (Anderson 1986: 273; Thompson and Hunston 2001: 3). Traditionally, of course, we speak about modality, that is, the speaker's estimate of the likelihood of events (e.g. Halliday 1994). Evidentiality means that the reader becomes privy to the speaker's attitudes towards whatever knowledge the speaker has, the reliability of that knowledge and how the speaker came about that knowledge. Affect refers to the personal attitudes of the speaker, that is, his/her emotions, feelings, moods, etc. Another way to look at stance is to divide it into three categories, like Conrad and Biber (2001) did in their study on adverbial expression of stance. These three categories comprise epistemic, attitudinal and style stance. Epistemic stance in Conrad and Biber's (2001) terms covers the same ideas as evidentiality in Thompson and Hunston (2001). In other words, it refers to the speaker's/writer's knowledge of the truth value of the proposition. Attitudinal and style stance, on the other hand, together cover what Biber and Finegan (1989) named affect (i.e., the expression of personal attitudes). Epistemic stance has also been studied with regard to degree modifiers by Paradis (1997; 2000), Simon-Vandenbergen (2008) and Simon-Vandenbergen & Aijmer (2007) and more broadly by Kärkkäinen (2003). Levorato (2009) studied how personal stance and authoritativeness was conveyed by pamphlet writers in the time leading up to the 1800 Union between Great Britain and Ireland. Lempert (2008) investigated epistemic stance in poetic structure, specifically a form of argumentation, moving to the concept of interactional stance. Riddle Harding (2007), on the other hand, discussed speakers' attitudes towards counterfactual scenarios and specifically the effects these have in literature. Finally, Biber (2006) studied a wide range of lexico-grammatical markers of stance in spoken and written university registers, noting that there are differences in the way stance is expressed and whether it is expressed at all.

Whether it be called stance, evaluation, appraisal, evidentiality or affect, the concept of conveying attitudes and known or imagined reliability of propositions has been widely studied. Although many scholars have more recently begun to view stance as an interactional phenomenon, taking also into account non-verbal data, which has been afforded by the emergence of more multimodal data, for the purposes of this study, given that it deals only with textual data, it is better to turn to the more familiar sense of the word, that is, to look at the lexical and grammatical resources for expressing affect and evaluating propositional content.

MATERIAL AND METHODOLOGY

Biber and Finegan (1989) investigated adjectival, verbal and modal markers of stance. They grouped these markers into 12 different categories as follows: certainty adverbs (e.g. *definitely, undoubtedly*), doubt adverbs (e.g. *apparently, possibly*), certainty verbs (e.g. *know, prove*), doubt verbs (e.g. *doubt, seems*), certainty adjectives (*certain, irrefutable*), doubt adjectives (e.g. *alleged, improbable*), affective expressions (e.g. *love, fear, glad, upset, luckily, sadly*), hedges (e.g. *almost, maybe, sort of*), emphatics (e.g. *for sure, really, so*+ADV, *such a*), and necessity (*can, may, might, could*), possibility (*ought, should, must*) and predictive modals (*will, would, shall*) (Biber and Finegan 1989: 119-122). Using 500 texts from 24 genres and the cluster analysis technique, they showed that different text types are likely to express stance in different ways. For example, personal letters are likely to have frequent affect markers, certainty verbs, doubt verbs and emphatics, that is, they show 'emphatic expression of affect'. Conversations, on the other hand, are likely to show involved interaction, in which evidentiality is frequently marked, that is, interactional evidentiality. Finally, many written genres are likely not to express stance to any considerable degree (i.e. faceless stance) (Biber and Finegan 1989: 115-117).This means that many written texts are likely to be impersonal, not taking a stand or expressing attitude, but rather stating facts. Finding this kind of stance in a literary work would be interesting indeed, because it would mean that the text is rather factual and certainly does not draw the reader into the world of the novel through appealing to his/her emotions.

Opas and Tweedie (1999) used the same markers of stance with principal components analysis (PCA) to investigate romance fiction and showed that three different types, namely the Harlequin Presents series, the Regency Romance series and Danielle Steel's novels, can be broadly speaking separated by their expression of stance. The first two types can be called formulaic romance texts, since there are guidelines for writing such novels. The first of these represent contemporary plots with passionate characters expressing their emotions. The latter type consists of text set in the Regency period, where the hero and heroine wooed with words. Danielle Steel's novels represent women's fiction and are set in modern times. The results showed that her novels were characterized by more hedges and emphatics than the other novels and thus could be labelled portraying interactional evidentiality (cf. Biber and Finegan 1989). Some of the Regency Romance novels showed more prediction and necessity modals than the other texts and could thus be in Biber and Finegan's (1989) taxonomy labelled texts exhibiting predictive persuasion. The Harlequin Presents series and some of the Regency Romance series, however, showed no particular features that would be used more than in other texts. They were called texts with faceless stance according to Biber and Finegan's (1989) proposal.

These studies both used similar methodologies to investigate the expression of stance and demonstrated that different types of texts portray evidentiality and affect in different ways. The present study will use the same stance markers with principal components analysis to show that this can also be seen in the texts of one author who experimented with style during his career.

This study uses a corpus of Samuel Beckett's novels and short prose works, comprising eleven works and covering each decade from the 1930s to the 1980s. The first text is *Murphy* (1936)[2], his first full-length novel. The following one is *First Love*, which, although first published in 1970, was written in 1946 and is the only novella he wrote between *Murphy* and the well-known trilogy: *Molloy*, *Malone Dies* and *The Unnamable* (written 1947-1950). Having written this, Beckett turned to drama and did not write any prose until the late 1950s, when he produced most of the *Fizzles*, a collection of short prose texts[3]. Although the *Fizzles* have been published together as one book, they resemble each other and show repetition across texts. Here they were treated as one unit, since many of them are too short to be dealt with individually in an analysis of this nature. Of the half a dozen prose texts Beckett wrote in the 1960s, perhaps the most well-known are *All Strange Away*, *Enough* and *Imagination Dead Imagine* and thus they were chosen to represent this decade. In the 1970s he wrote *Company* and *Ill Seen Ill Said* was written in 1979-1980. For copyright reasons, all texts were random sampled, with the exception of the *Fizzles* and *Imagination Dead Imagine*, which were too short to sample and expect to get a reliable result. Each sample was approximately 1,000 words and a sufficient amount was taken from each text to make up at least 10% of the whole. This has been deemed sufficient to catch most features of style in a text (Biber 1990). The individual samples were chosen using a table of random numbers, such as can be found in any introductory statistics book or even on the web. The table will look something like Figure 1.

Figure 1. Random numbers

17459	63323	78063	54356	61705
59783	41068	30754	23117	80367
93023	25962	93683	27000	38256
55492	79540	46970	49708	25136
88467	55267	17621	63860	44852

Assuming that the text to be sampled has less than 300 pages, you would start on the first row of the table and take the first sample from page 174 onwards. Then you would go along the table until you find the next three digits that fall within your page range. In this case your second sample would begin on page 237 and the third one on page 63. This is repeated until you have the required amount of samples. The total corpus here is approximately 37,000 words (see Appendix).

The next step was to count all the features of stance within Biber and Finegan's (1989) model for each of the texts. To this end, WordSmith Tools (Scott 2004) was used, although any concordance program would have done equally well. WordSmith was chosen because it is readily available, runs on all Windows platforms, including those that do not have DOS capability, accepts many different formats of markup in texts and being a wysiwig (what you see is what you get) program, is suitable even for researchers who are not very familiar with concordance tools. For example, the doubt adjective *possible* was used as the search item. The WordSmith concordancer would then produce a list of all instances of that item with one line of text around each case, indicating, among other things, the number of the example and which text it came from. The number of instances of an individual item could thus be seen at a glance. Because some items are not necessarily consecutive in a sentence, they had to be searched for using the function of 'X with the context word Y within a certain amount of words to the left or right of the main item X' (e.g. *I/we* (ADV/MODAL/AUX) *expect that*, where one would be searching for *expect that* with the context word *I* within 3-5 words to the left of *expect* and the results would turn up all instances of *I/we expect that*, *I/we always expect that* and so on). Obviously, some items were such that one searched for the main item and then had to manually go through all the hits to see which ones to keep and which to discard (e.g. *so* + ADV). Due to the different amounts of words in the texts, these raw results were then standardized to 1,000 words. The results can be found in Figure 2.

Looking at Figure 2, we see that we have 12 groups of features and we are interested in how they interact with each other in 11 texts. Such interactions are far too complex to attempt to visualize. We are used to visualizing the interaction between two features, such as one can plot on x and y axes, and we can even visualize the

Figure 2. Results for all features counted

	I CERTAINTY ADVERBS	II DOUBT ADVERBS	III CERTAINTY VERBS	IV DOUBT VERBS	V CERTAINTY ADJECTIVES	VI DOUBT ADJECTIVES
Murphy	2.45017	0.16334	0.81672	0.98007	0.98007	0.49003
First Love	1.99600	0.99800	1.99600	0	1.99600	0.99800
Molloy	1.58382	5.23879	2.80214	1.82748	2.31481	0.97465
Malone Dies	1.58572	1.78394	1.98216	1.58572	2.57680	1.58572
The Unnamable	0.77833	5.29265	7.47198	3.11332	1.86799	0.46699
All Strange	0	2.02020	0	0	1.01010	1.01010
Imagination	0	0	2.72479	4.54132	0	2.72479
Fizzles	1.11892	2.23785	2.55754	1.27877	4.15601	1.75831
Enough	0	0.94607	2.83822	0	0.94607	0.94607
Company	0.99900	0	0.99900	5.99400	2.99700	2.99700
Ill Seen	0.95057	1.90114	0	5.70342	0.95057	0

	VII AFFECTIVE EXPRESSIONS	VIII HEDGES	IX EMPHATICS	X POSSIBILITY MODALS	XI NECESSITY MODALS	XII PREDICTIVE MODALS
Murphy	2.45018	1.14341	6.86050	7.84057	1.14341	5.55374
First Love	3.99201	0.99800	6.98602	9.98004	0.99800	2.99401
Molloy	2.55848	1.09649	9.86842	5.11695	2.43664	6.09161
Malone Dies	1.58572	1.18929	6.34291	4.36075	2.77502	5.15361
The Unnamable	3.42465	0.77833	5.29265	8.56164	4.82565	8.56164
All Strange	0	2.02020	14.14141	1.01010	0	0
Imagination	0.90826	3.63306	8.17438	4.54132	0	0.90826
Fizzles	0.95907	1.43861	11.50895	3.67647	1.75831	5.11509
Enough	0	0.94607	11.35289	5.67644	0.94607	6.62251
Company	0	0.99900	3.99600	3.99600	0.99900	0.99900
Ill Seen	3.80228	0	12.35741	6.65399	0.95057	3.80228

interactions between three features, e.g. inside a cube. But visualizing how more than three features or dimensions interact becomes difficult. This means that we would ideally like to see the important interactions between the features and ignore the less important ones, thus reducing the number of interactions we need to look at to an amount that we are able to visualize. In order to do this, we need to turn to statistical methods common in authorship studies and stylistic analysis (e.g. Burrows 1987, 1996; Hoover 2003, 2004, 2007; McKenna and Antonia 2001; Mosteller and Wallace 2007; Opas 1996; Tabata 1995, 2004). These methods can be carried out using any standard statistics package, such as SPSS (Statistical Package for the Social Sciences) or PAST (PAleontological STatistics). In this study, SPSS was used, simply because it is probably the most well-known among humanities scholars.

The statistical method used in this study is principal components analysis (PCA), one of a family of so-called dimension-reducing techniques. These calculate the axes through which we can see the most variation between our texts, thus being able to differentiate between them. PCA will return as many components as one has features in the data, so in this case it will calculate 12 components. If, on the other hand, one were using the 50 most common words (as is common in authorship attribution studies), PCA would return 50 components. It is likely that not all of these will distinguish between the texts to any significant degree. In fact, many of them will represent the minor variation that one precisely does not want to deal with.

One of the plots that SPSS will produce is called a scree plot, as seen in Figure 3.

The 12 components produced by SPSS are on the x-axis. The y-axis shows the eigenvalues for each component (i.e., how much of the variance in the data that component explains). Note how the curve drops initially and then begins to taper off. This means that each of the components at the tail end of the curve explains very little of the variation and can thus be ignored. Normally, we should look at the plot and find the first 'step' (like in a staircase) after the 'drops' and then 'cut' above it, in other words, consider only the components above it. In this case, however, the first 'step' is between components 2 and 3 and we cannot cut above it, since that would give only one component and we need at least two in order to see how they interact. Thus, we need to look at the first and the second components.

Figure 4, produced by SPSS, shows the eigenvalues of each of the components (i.e., what was plotted on the y-axis of Figure 3).

Note how for each component the table shows the percentage of the variance that the component explains and the cumulative variance (i.e., the variance explained by that component together with all others before it). We now see that the first and second components together explain 55.55% of the variation in the data, which in statistics is considered quite good, since it accounts for more than half of the variation in the data. While one might think that a few more components would mean that a lot more could be taken into account, in statistical terms all the components

Figure 3. Scree plot for the Beckett data

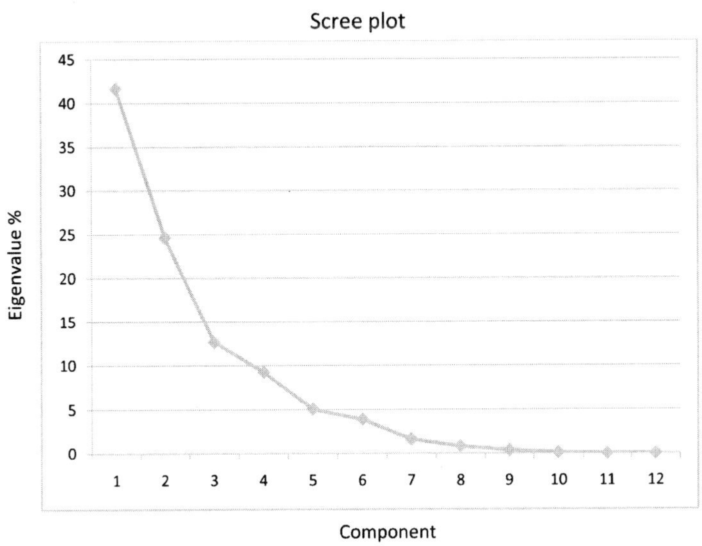

Figure 4. Total variance explained in Beckett data

Total Variance Explained

Component	Initial Eigenvalues			Extraction Sums of Squared Loadings		
	Total	% of Variance	Cumulative %	Total	% of Variance	Cumulative %
1	4,643	38,689	38,689	4,643	38,689	38,689
2	2,023	16,859	55,547	2,023	16,859	55,547
3	1,865	15,539	71,087	1,865	15,539	71,087
4	1,375	11,456	82,543	1,375	11,456	82,543
5	,999	8,327	90,870			
6	,539	4,493	95,363			
7	,276	2,302	97,664			
8	,191	1,593	99,258			
9	,067	,559	99,817			
10	,022	,183	100,000			
11	3,279E-16	2,732E-15	100,000			
12	-5,645E-17	-4,704E-16	100,000			

except the first one are not important, as the scree plot above showed, and they can be ignored. They simply muddy the waters, because they explain so little of the variation. Regardless of this we do need to take components two and three into account if we are to visualize any of the variation, either two-dimensionally or three-dimensionally.

Using the PCA function, SPSS has also calculated a score for each text on each principal component (see Figure 5). It is these scores that are then used to look at to what extent the texts are similar to or different from each other.

RESULTS

In Figure 5, we can see the results of the principal components analysis. The table shows the first three components because, although the scree plot in Figure 3 indicated that it is the first two components which should be looked at, we need to retain the third component to carry out a three-dimensional analysis at a later stage.[4] The table shows that although *Murphy* and *Malone Dies*, for example, are quite similar on the first component (i.e., their scores are similar; they are quite different on the second component, one having a negative score and the other a positive result, and somewhat different on the third component, since the scores are apart, though both negative).

The best way to understand the results of the principal components analysis presented in Figure 5, is to visualize how each of the components interacts with the

Figure 5. Scores for the first three components

TEXT	COMPONENT_1	COMPONENT_2	COMPONENT_3
Murphy	0.38167	-0.96972	-1.21965
First Love	0.56519	-0.75760	-1.31197
Molloy	0.75574	0.05115	0.71187
Malone Dies	0.26139	0.61935	-0.19867
The Unnamable	1.91914	1.10640	0.83425
All Strange	-1.43563	-0.93266	1.37029
Imagination	-1.50220	0.80684	-0.21709
Fizzles	-0.07366	0.58765	0.70922
Enough	-0.24073	-0.51390	1.07569
Company	-0.87772	1.54155	-1.33846
Ill Seen	0.24682	-1.53905	-0.41548

next one. To do this, we need to plot these scores on x and y axes. As was explained earlier, we should be looking at components 1 and 2 in the first instance. SPSS will draw a graph using those two components as input and label the cases using the abbreviated titles given (see Figure 5). The result can be seen in Figure 6.

This figure shows us that the texts *The Unnamable* (1950), *Company* (1979), *Imagination Dead Imagine* (1965) and *All Strange Away* (1964) are quite different from all the other texts, and also different from each other. On the other hand, it also shows us that the texts *Ill Seen Ill Said* (1980), *Murphy* (1936) and *First Love* (1946) are fairly similar to each other. The texts *Malone Dies* (1948) and *Fizzles* (1960-75) are also similar to each other. *Molloy* (1947) seems to be close to *Malone Dies* than it is to *The Unnamable*, which is as one would expect. Compared to the other texts of its period (i.e., *All Strange Away* and *Imagination Dead Imagine*, *Enough* (1965) seems to be somewhat on its own, but on the other hand, it is closer to centre of the graph and thus more like the other texts that lie around it). What the figure does not show is *how* similar or different they are in their expression of stance. For this, we need to look at the correlation coefficients of the 12 different types of markers of stance investigated for each of the components (Figure 7).

For each stance feature, SPSS calculated how important it is in each of the 12 components that the program returned. Figure 7 shows these figures for the first three components.

One might think of the coefficient as showing how much ‘pulling power’ the feature has and in which direction on the component axis. In other words, a feature like predictive modals (0.852) will ‘pull’ texts in one direction on component 1 and a feature like hedges (-0.650) will ‘take’ them in the opposite direction. On the other hand, a feature like doubt verbs (-0.117) is not very strong and thus does not make much difference on component 1. To see how these features are reflected in the texts, we need to plot component 1 against component 2 on the x and y axes. Since SPSS does not do this,[5] we need to use Excel to plot the two axes.

Figure 6. PC 1 plotted against PC 2 with text titles (A) and dates of production (B) as labels

A)

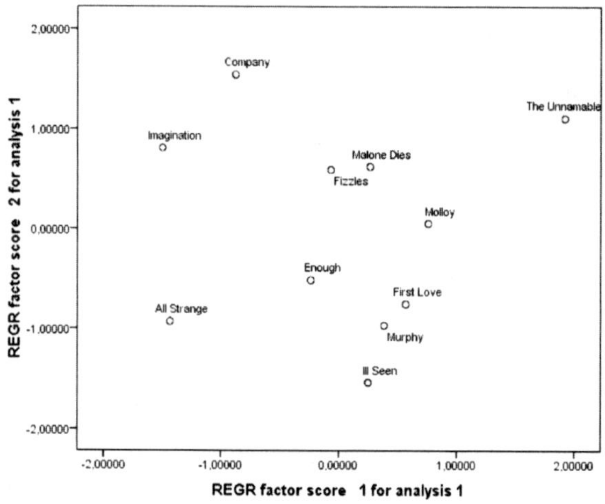

B)

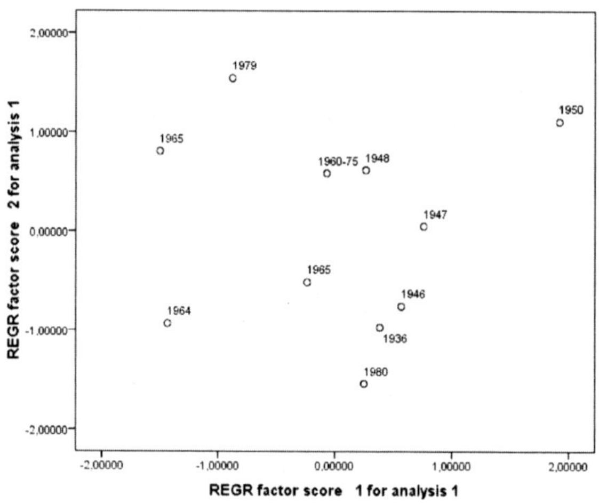

Figure 8 presents the correlation coefficients for each of features investigated for PC1 and PC2, plotted against each other. For each feature in the graph, we can see in which direction it is 'pulling' the texts. For example, doubt adjectives and hedges are pulling texts to the upper left-hand side of the graph while emphatics are pulling texts to the lower left-hand side. We then need to compare this with Figure 6, which plots the texts on PC1 and PC2. If we imagine the x- and y-axis in Figure

Figure 7. Correlation coefficients for all stance markers

Component matrix			
	Component		
	1	2	3
I Certainty adverbs	0,538	-0,149	-0,615
II Doubt adverbs	0,664	0,125	0,583
III Certainty verbs	0,613	0,542	0,349
IV Doubt verbs	-0,117	0,337	-0,360
V Certainty adjectives	0,266	0,466	-0,015
VI Doubt adjectives	-0,617	0,725	-0,225
VII Affective expressions	0,754	-0,328	-0,322
VIII Hedges	-0,650	0,300	0,128
IX Emphatics	-0,333	-0,623	0,621
X Possibility modals	0,721	-0,191	-0,463
XI Necessity modals	0,850	0,427	0,218
XII Predictive modals	0,852	0,050	0,275

Figure 8. Correlation coefficients for the features of stance on PC1 and PC2

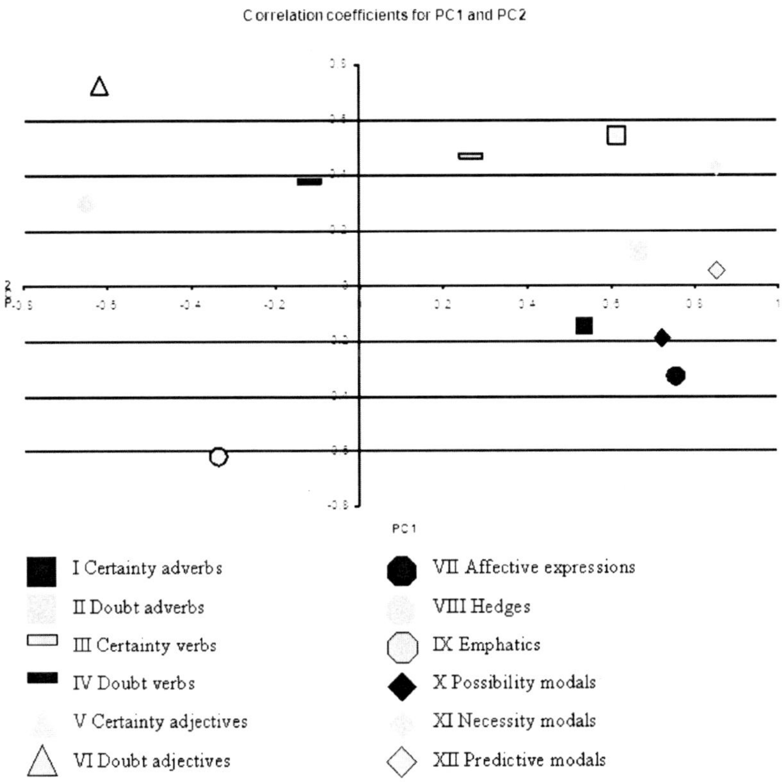

6A crossing at 0, it means that those texts which are in any of the four corners of Figure 6A are likely to contain more of the features that are in the same corner of Figure 8 than all the other texts.

Looking at Figures 2 and 3, we can see, for example, that texts like *Imagination Dead Imagine* and *Company*, both of which are in the upper left-hand corner of Figure 6, are likely to show more hedges and doubt adjectives (the two features in the upper left-hand side of Figure 8) than the other texts. In fact, we find that *Imagination Dead Imagine* has more than twice as many hedges (*more or less*) as all but one of the other texts (3.63 per 1,000 words, see Figure 2 for this and subsequent feature counts) and the second highest number of doubt adjectives (*possible*; 2.72 per 1,000 words). This can be seen in the text itself:

It is ***possible*** *too, experience shows, for rise and fall to stop short at any point and mark a pause,* ***more or less*** *long, before resuming, or reversing, the rise now fall, the fall rise, these in their turn to be completed, or to stop short and mark a pause,* ***more or less*** *long, before resuming, or again reversing, and so on, till finally one or the other extreme is reached.(Imagination Dead Imagine, p. 64; emphasis mine)*

Company, on the other hand is clearly marked by doubt adjectives (*imaginable*, *possible*), having more of them than any other text (2.997 per 1,000 words). It also has a fair amount of hedges (0.999 per 1,000 words), though clearly less than *Imagination Dead Imagine*. On the other hand, *Company* is being pulled upwards, to the positive side of PC2, by doubt verbs (*appears*, *seems*; 5.994 per 1,000 words), although these are a less strong force. Some of these features can be seen in the following extract.

Not in another as once seemed ***possible****. The same. As more companionable. And that his posture there remained to be devised. And to be decided whether fast or mobile. Which of all* ***imaginable*** *postures least liable to pall? Which of motion or of rest the more entertaining in the long run? (Company, p. 60; emphasis mine)*

These two texts, *Imagination Dead Imagine* and *Company*, also show us that when a text lies in a certain area of Figure 6, it does not mean that the text necessarily exhibits an abundance of all the features that ‘pull’ texts in that direction; in fact, it may only contain an abundance of one or two of the features, particularly if the features have strong enough ‘pulling power’. We must also bear in mind that the features that pull texts in one direction or the other only do so because the data that is being used is what it is; with another data set, these features might group themselves in a completely different way. This methodology is supposed to tease apart the data that is being analyzed, in other words to answer the question of which features tend to appear together in the data.

In the lower right-hand corner of Figure 6, we find *All Strange Away* standing somewhat apart from the other texts. Figure 8 indicates that it should be characterized by emphatics and possibly hedges, since they pull strongly to the negative side of PC1 but less strongly to the positive side of PC2 than doubt adjectives. In fact, looking at Figure 2, we find that the *All Strange Away* has more emphatics (*more, most, so*+ADJ) than any other text (14.14 per 1,000 words) and nearly twice as many as six of the others. It also seems to have nearly twice as many hedges (*more or less*) as most other texts, with only *Imagination Dead Imagine* having more.

***So** dark and cold any length, shivering **more or less**, feeble slaps want of room at all flesh within reach, little stamps of hampered feet, so on. Same system light and heat with sweat **more or less**, cringing away from walls, burning soles, now one, now the other. (All Strange Away, p. 13; emphasis mine)*

*Physique, too soon, perhaps never, vague bowed body bonewhite when light at full, nothing clear but ashen glare as imagined, no, attitudes too with play of joints **most** clear **more** various now. For nine and nine eighteen that is four feet and **more** across in which to kneel, arse on heels, hands on thighs, trunk best bowed and crown on ground.(All Strange Away, p. 14-15; emphasis mine)*

If we then turn to look at the opposite side of Figures 2 and 3 (i.e., the right-hand side, we find the text *The Unnamable* in the far right-hand top corner of Figure 6). Looking at the upper right-hand side of Figure 8 we note that the features that characterize texts in that area include a high amount of certainty verbs (*know*), necessity modals (*should, must*), predictive modals (*shall*) and doubt adverbs (*perhaps*).

*For to go on means going from here, means finding me, losing me, vanishing and beginning again, a stranger first, then little by little the same as always, in another place, where I **shall** say I have always been, of which I **shall know** nothing, being incapable of seeing, moving, thinking, speaking, but of which little by little, in spite of these handicaps, I **shall** begin to **know** something, just enough for it to turn out to be the same place as always, the same which seems made for me and does not want me, which I seem to want and do not want, take your choice, which spews me out or swallows me up, I'll never **know**, which is **perhaps** merely the inside of my distant skull where once I wandered, now am fixed, lost for tininess, or straining against the walls, with my head, my hands, my feet, my back, and ever murmuring my old stories, my old story, as if it were the first time.(The Unnamable, p. 277; emphasis mine)*

As can be seen from the example above (and Figure 2), the text does indeed have a high number of certainty verbs (7.47 per 1,000 words), in fact two to three times as many as the others. It also has far more predictive modals (8.56 per 1,000 words) than the other texts, more than twice as many necessity modals as most others (4.82 per 1,000 words) and more than twice as many doubt adverbs as the other texts (5.29 per 1,000 words), with the exception of *Molloy*, which has almost the same amount.

We now turn to look at those texts which are vaguely in the middle of the graph in Figure 6 (i.e., around the point where the x-axis and the y-axis cross each other). It is noticeable that many of these texts are quite near the 0 point on the x-axis (i.e., the first component, but are separated from each other by being spread along the y-axis, that is, the second component). This means there are no features which would be 'pulling' them strongly in any direction on the first component. Four of these are among the earliest works of Beckett (i.e. 1936-48). The first of these, *Murphy* (1936), has somewhat more certainty adverbs than many other texts, and is at the top end in the number of possibility and predictive modals, but otherwise seems to be fairly nondescript on all other features (see Figure 2). The next one, *First Love* (1946), also has somewhat more certainty adverbs than many others, and is at the top end in the number of affective expressions and possibility modals, but is very unremarkable on the other features. *Molloy* (1947), on the other hand, has as many doubt adverbs as *The Unnamable* (i.e., twice as many as the other texts, or more). It also has a fair amount of affective expressions, emphatics, possibility modals, necessity modals and predictive modals. *Malone Dies* (1948) has a fair amount of necessity and predictive modals, but is not remarkable on any of the other features. The *Fizzles* (1960-75) and *Malone Dies* are seemingly similar (Figure 6), yet the only feature that they both have a fair amount of is predictive modals, in addition to which the *Fizzles* have a large number of emphatics and more certainty adjectives than all other texts. *Enough* (1965), like the *Fizzles* has a large amount of emphatics and quite many predictive modals, in addition to which it has a fair amount of possibility modals, yet it is seemingly more different from the *Fizzles* than *Malone Dies* is. Finally, *Ill Seen Ill Said* (1980), like *Enough*, has a large number of emphatics and possibility modals, in addition to which it has a fair amount of doubt verbs and affective expressions, yet it is seemingly closer to *Murphy* than to *Enough* (cf. Figure 6). Overall, on the basis of the results, these texts are really only separated from each other on PC2, and even then sometimes group together in a way that does not correspond to the intuition of the reader.

From a reader's point of view, *Murphy*, *First Love*, *Molloy* and *Malone Dies* seem more like each other than like the later works, perhaps because they are seemingly written as more 'traditional' novels, with either a first person or a third person narrator, several characters and events. The later texts are more like the internal thoughts of a character, fleeting impressions on the mind. *The Unnamable* is perhaps the bridge between these types, since although being part of Beckett's trilogy, it has more stream-of-consciousness type narration than the other early works. To the reader, it is not surprising that *All Strange Away*, *Company* and *Imagination Dead Imagine* portray stance differently from all the other works, because they are seemingly thoughts in the mind of the speaker which the reader can still follow fairly easily. Nor does it surprise the reader that *The Unnamable* differs from the rest of the trilogy. What is surprising, however, is that *Malone Dies* and the *Fizzles* seem to express stance in a similar way and that *Ill Seen Ill Said* is fairly close to *Murphy* in this respect, since these texts are not at all like each other from a reader's point of view. Although the scree plot (Figure 3) showed that we need only look at the first and the second components, it seems worthwhile to take the third component into consideration and model all three components together 3-dimensionally to determine whether this will help us to see some aspect of those central texts that a 2-dimensional plot is not able to show.

In order to do this, a tool was built[6] which reads the data in Figure 5 from an Excel file and then produces the three-dimensional model, showing its most optional angle first (i.e., the one which best separates the texts). This is shown in Figure 9.

The first thing to note about this figure is how the 0 point cutting lines on all three components are visible, which makes it easier for us to see how the principal components divide the data. Beginning with PC 1, we note that in this figure only *Murphy*, *First Love* and *The Unnamable* are on the positive side, whereas all the other texts lie on the negative side. Looking back at Figure 7, we note that the two features which are strongly pulling texts to the negative side of PC 1 are hedges (-0.650) and doubt adjectives (-0.617). This means that the texts on the negative side seem to express some kind of uncertain doubt, whereas the other texts, most notably *The Unnamable*, express stance in other ways.

Principal component 2 seems to divide the texts again into two groups, the few on the negative side and the rest of the texts. Figure 7 indicates that the strong features pulling texts to the negative side of the component are emphatics (-0.623) and to some extent affective expressions (-0.328). Thus, the texts on the negative side are likely to express emphatic affect. Of the four texts on this side of PC2, *All Strange Away* stands out, because the only feature pulling it to this side is emphatics, it has no affective expressions and it has none or very few of the other two features that have a weaker negative pull, namely certainty adverbs and possibility modals. *Murphy* and *First Love*, while not scoring very high on the emphatics, have a combination of the other three negative features, scoring reasonably high on all of them, which explains why they are on the negative side of PC2. It should be noted, however, that none of the four texts are very far out on the negative side. There are several markers of evidentiality that are pulling texts towards the positive side of the component,

Figure 9. Components 1, 2 and 3 in three-dimensions

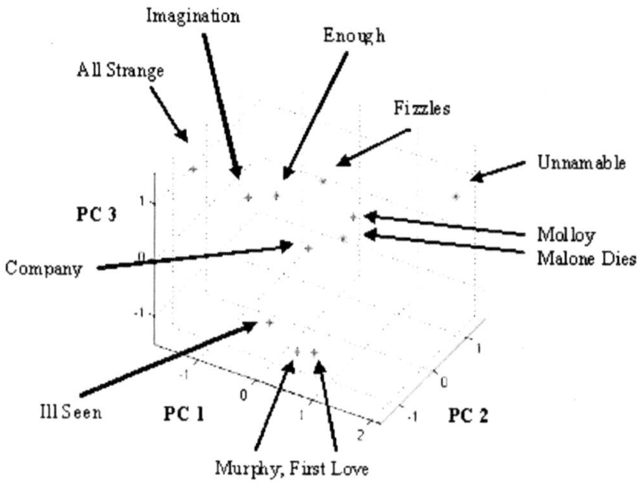

e.g. doubt adjectives (0.725), certainty verbs (0.542), certainty adjectives (0.466) and necessity modals (0.427).

Finally, PC 3 seems not to distinguish the texts quite so clearly from each other, at least visually. Looking at the figure, it seems like there are only two texts on the positive side of PC3. However, looking at Figure 5, we note that there are in fact five texts on this side. This is a problem with looking at the results three-dimensionally and for this reason, one should look at the results from different angles (i.e., 'turn the cube around', as has been done later). Those texts that are on the positive side of the component are being strongly pulled there by emphatics (0.621) and doubt adverbs (0.583). In other words, they seem to express emphatic doubt. On the other hand, the strong forces pulling texts to the negative side of the component are certainty adverbs (-0.615) and possibility modals (-0.463). It is almost as if these texts expressed more possible certainty.

Turning to look at the individual texts in this figure, we see some new aspects of them. Notice how *Murphy*, *First Love* and *Ill Seen Ill Said* are now grouped closer together and further away from the other texts that were in the middle of Figure 6. This is because we are now looking at them 3-dimensionally and taking into consideration PC3 simultaneously with PC1 and PC2. The features that they all seem to share are a fair amount of affective expressions, emphatics and many possibility modals. In fact, *Ill Seen Ill Said* is the only text that was written after 1950 which has a significant amount of affective expressions. These texts should then contain expressions such as *love*, *like*, *hate*, *so*, *really*, *can* and *may*. This can be confirmed by looking at some examples from the texts:

*"**Just** so," said Neary. "Now then. For whatever reason you **cannot love** in my way, and believe me there is no other, for that same reason, whatever it **may** be, your heart is as it is. And again for that same reason --"*

*"Whatever it **may** be," said Murphy.*

*"I **can** do nothing for you," said Neary.*

"God bless my soul," said Murphy.

*"**Just** so," said Neary. "I should say your conarium has shrunk to nothing." (Murphy, p. 6; emphasis mine)*

*I reminded her that the parsnip season was fast drawing to a close and that if, before it finally got there, she **could** feed me nothing but parsnips I'd be grateful. I **like** parsnips because they taste like violets and violets because they smell like parsnips. (First Love, p. 28; emphasis mine)*

*She **cannot** see it from her door. Blindfold she **could** find her way. With herself she has no **more** converse. (Ill Seen Ill Said, p. 12, emphasis mine)*

On the other hand, *Molloy* and *Malone Dies* seem to be more like each other than in Figure 6, as a reader would have expected. Interestingly, *Company* does not seem to be such an extreme text any longer, but has in fact moved closer to *Molloy* and *Malone Dies*. Figure 2 indicates that these three texts share a high number of certainty adjectives (i.e., 2.31, 2.58 and 3.00, respectively). *Molloy* and *Malone Dies* also have a fairly high amount of certainty adverbs (i.e., 1.58 and 1.58, whereas *Company* has much less, for example 1.00). Thus, it seems that they mark adjectival certainty and, to some extent adverbial certainty also. This can be seen in the following extracts:

*At a given moment, pre-established if you like, I don't much mind, the gentleman turned back, took the little creature in his arms, drew the cigar from his lips and buried his face in the orange fleece, for it was a gentleman, that was **obvious**. Yes, it was an orange pomeranian, the less I think of it the more **certain** I am. (Molloy, p. 13; emphasis mine)*

*"**To be sure**," he said, "**to be sure**, I am out of sorts." He added, after a pause, "Nice name, without its being quite **clear** whether this tribute was aimed at the nice name of Moll or at the nice name of Macmann."(Malone Dies, p. 235; emphasis mine)*

*Mainly blue in this position the natural pallor you so admire as **indeed** from it no doubt wholly blue your own.(Company, p.56; emphasis mine)*

Note also that *Imagination Dead Imagine* has now moved closer to *Enough* and the *Fizzles* than has been shown previously. This would indicate that it is more similar to those texts and somewhat less extreme than Figure 6 showed. This is again due to the fact that we are now looking at the components three-dimensionally and thus able to see other aspects of the variation. Both of these latter cases are a little surprising, since in each one there seem to be no features that all three texts would have a great deal of.

Finally, both *The Unnamable* and *All Strange Away* are also in this figure apart from the other texts and can thus be interpreted as being quite different from all other texts. *The Unnamable*, being far on the positive side of PC 1 should have very few hedges and doubt adjectives, which can be confirmed by looking at Figure 2. The text also exhibits an unusually high amount of possibility, necessity and predictive modals, all of which pull strongly onto the positive side of the component, as do the many affective expressions, doubt adverbs and certainty verbs that the text shows. It seems to be clearly on the positive side of PC 2 and should thus contain some of the evidentiality markers that were pulling texts in that direction. Indeed, it has far more certainty verbs (7.472) than any of the other texts. It also has twice as many necessity modals (4.826) as any other text. Although the text does not score very high on doubt and certainty adjectives, both of which are also strong positive forces on PC2, it does have these features and together with its high scores they are enough to put it firmly on the positive side. On PC 3, *The Unnamable* is on the positive side, and while it does not have an unusually high amount of emphatics, it does show a very high amount of doubt adverbs (5.293). Overall then, the text is characterized by modals, verbal certainty and adverbial doubt:

*...I **can't** stir, I'm there already, I **must** be there already, **perhaps** I'm not alone, **perhaps** a whole people is here, and the voice its voice, coming to me fitfully, we **would** have lived, been free a moment,...(The Unnamable, p. 377; emphasis mine)*

All Strange Away lies in the opposite corner, far away from *The Unnamable*. It is far on the negative side of PC 1, meaning it should contain hedges and doubt adjectives. It does score high on the hedges (2.020) but fairly average on the doubt adjectives (1.010). On PC 2 it also lies on the negative side and shows more emphatics (14.141) than any other text, and on PC 3 it is clearly on the positive side, where it is being pulled by emphatics and to some extent doubt adverbs (2.020):

Physique, too soon, ***perhaps*** *never, vague bowed body bonewhite when light at full, nothing clear but ashen glare as imagined, no, attitudes too with play of joints* ***most*** *clear* ***more*** *various now. (All Strange Away, p. 14-15; emphasis mine)*

Since Figure 9 is three-dimensional, it follows that it can be turned around, just like a cube, and we can look at the results from a slightly different angle, such as in Figure 10, in the hope that this would shed more light on the relationships between the texts.

This figure shows *All Strange Away*, *Imagination Dead Imagine* and *The Unnamable* as texts that are different from the others; this was also seen in Figures 2 and/or 4. We need to rotate the figure to see the different effects of looking at it from different angles.

It also shows that *Murphy* and *First Love* resemble each other, as would be expected, and that *Ill Seen Ill Said* is fairly close to them, as did both the other figures. Also in accordance with Figure 9, this figure shows that *Molloy* and *Malone Dies* resemble each other, as one would expect. In fact, we can see it more clearly here than in Figure 6. The difference between this and the other figures lies in the way it portrays *Company*, the *Fizzles* and *Enough*, where the first two now resemble each other closely and are different from the last one. Looking at Figure 2, we can see that the features which seem to make *Enough* different from the other two texts, are a lack of certainty adverbs and doubt verbs, a much lower number of certainty and

Figure 10. Rotated 3-dimensional image of components 1-3

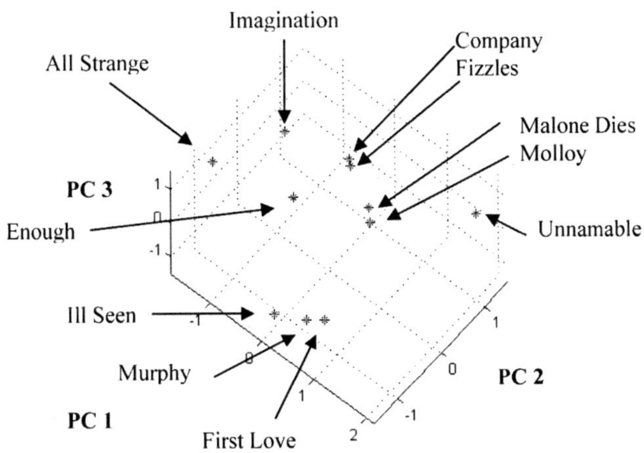

doubt adjectives and a greater amount of possibility modals. Here we are looking for the differences, not similarities and it is on PC2 where *Enough* is most different from the other two texts. On the other two components it groups itself closer to one text or the other. If we then look closely at the results in Figure 5, we notice that *Enough* should be on the negative side of PC 1, which it is in this Figure; it should be on the negative side of component 2 and the positive side of three, which is not visible in this figure. This is because the figure is three dimensional and we are looking at it from a particular angle. Nevertheless, this angle helped us see that two of three texts are seemingly more alike and also different from the third one, which we were not able to see in any of the other figures. As readers, however, we certainly feel that *Company* and the *Fizzles* feel similar:

The barest gist. Stilled when finally as always hitherto they do. You lie in the dark with closed eyes and see the scene. As you could not at the time. The dark cope of sky. The dazzling land. You at a standstill in the midst. The quarter boots sunk to the tops. The skirts of the greatcoat resting on the snow. In the old bowed head in the old block hat speechless misgiving.(Company, p. 52)

...it's impossible I should have a voice, impossible I should have thoughts, and I speak and think, I do the impossible, it is not possible otherwise, it was he who had a life, I didn't have a life, a life not worth having, because of me, he'll do himself to death, because of me, I'll tell the tale, the tale of his death, the end of his life and his death, his death alone would not be enough, not enough for me... (Fizzle 4)

Both of these texts seem like impressions on the mind (i.e., the first one paints a scene where the character finds himself and the second one is more like the character rattling on about his thoughts). *Enough*, on the other hand, feels more like the character reminiscing about days past and it is syntactically different from the other two in that it has complete sentences, that is, it is more like a traditional narrative:

In order from time to time to enjoy the sky he resorted to a little round mirror. Having misted it with his breath and polished it on his calf he looked in it for the constellations. I have it! he exclaimed referring to the Lyre or the Swan. And often he added that the sky seemed much the same. We were not in the mountains however. There were times I discerned on the horizon a sea whose level seemed higher than ours. Could it be the bed of some vast evaporated lake or drained of its waters from below? I never asked myself the question.(Enough, p. 57-58)

Thus, by rotating the figure, we were able to shed more light on how texts can be teased apart. It also enabled us to notice differences in texts that other angles do not show but that as readers we are at least unconsciously aware of.

DISCUSSION

The results shown in the previous section indicate that using statistical methods such as the one presented here can help to analyze in which ways texts resemble each other and in which ways they are different from one another. It does seem to make a difference whether one portrays the results two-dimensionally or three-dimensionally. In two-dimensional presentation, those texts which are seemingly most different from the other texts stand out clearly. On the other hand, the three-dimensional presentation seems to be able to shed more light on those texts that in the two-dimensional presentation do not differ from each other considerably. By rotating the three dimensional model, one can attempt to differentiate between some of the texts that the two-dimensional model does not separate, but that nevertheless seem intuitively to be clearly different.

In this particular case, it should be noted that the two earliest texts analyzed here, *Murphy* and *First Love*, seem to resemble each other, that the next two texts, *Molloy* and *Malone Dies*, while resembling each other closely, are also different from the first two texts (see Figures 4 and 5). The rest of the texts, however, are spread around the cube indifferent ways. As was mentioned earlier, the early texts *Murphy*, *First Love*, *Molloy* and *Malone Dies* seem similar to the reader, or at least more similar to each other than to the later texts, due to their first and third person narration, where series of events are clearly being recounted. This would also be in tune with the idea that they portray stance in a similar way, since they are more like 'traditional' narration, where the narrator also expresses opinions and feelings, and not the fleeting impressions on the mind of the speaker, if there even is one, seen in the later texts.

Although one can say that Samuel Beckett's texts have developed diachronically from the more traditional narrative forms to highly innovative forms of expression, this study shows that there does not seem to be any discernible diachronic pattern in the way stance is expressed in these texts. Critics have noted that Beckett is an experimental writer, who has stretched syntax to its limits and created a condensed, fragmented style which ignores the rules of grammar (Brienza 1987). From *The Unnamable* onwards, he experimented with ways of expressing himself, creating ever more condensed, fragmented, impressionistic styles that lead the reader into the mind of the character. It seems that this is also visible in his expression of stance in that many of the texts are unlike the others, seeming also to experiment with it, and

Ill Seen Ill Said, which is like *Murphy*, seems to have closed the circle. Beckett's range of styles is so extreme, from traditional narrative to very minimalist and bare ones, that generalizations about his style are very difficult to make (Opas 1990). Brienza (1987) pointed out that Beckett's texts are stylistically different because each one shows some innovation. This also seems to be confirmed by the present study. This combination of traditional literary criticism and quantitative analyses offers us a way into understanding and interpreting even the most innovative literature.

This methodology of using a standard statistical multivariate method of analysis and then plotting it in a new, non-standard, 3-dimensional manner is well worth exploring with other data. Normally, the results of a principal components analysis with large amounts of features will turn up an analysis in which one needs to take at least three components into account when interpreting the data. In such cases, it seems likely that three-dimensional modeling will greatly enhance how one can visualize the interactions of the various features on the texts and the differences between the texts. A number of previous analyses have used multivariate statistics in the analyses of literary texts (Burrows 1987, 1996; Hoover 2003, 2004, 2007; McKenna and Antonia 2001; Opas and Tweedie 1999; Tabata 1995, 2004). They have all presented their results two-dimensionally, but it would be interesting to see what the results would look like if they were plotted three-dimensionally and, in particular, whether it would change the results in any way. In some cases, visualizing the results three-dimensionally enables us to see more of the variation, to tease out the differences and similarities of texts and even to explain results that look surprising when seen in a two-dimensional space. In other cases, it might muddy the waters further, but more studies such as this one are needed to begin to fully understand the usefulness of the method. As the tools for three-dimensional plotting become more readily available, they will offer new ways of analyzing the results produced by standard statistical methods. The past few decades have seen a rise in application of computing in literary studies, and although it still is not considered mainstream it has become more widely accepted. Two main aspects have emerged: first, there is the electronic text, and second, the computer-assisted analysis of text. One embodiment of the former is the digital scholarly edition, others might include the hypertext and the computer game. The latter is equally broad, in that it might include the analysis of individual texts from a thematic or stylistic point of view, the analysis and comparison of various versions of a text, the investigation of the literary theoretical principles embodied in hypertexts, the rhetorical nature of computer games and other aspects of narrative studies in the electronic medium. The present study falls clearly into the ever-growing category of computer-assisted analyses of individual texts, which aim to demonstrate how these methodologies can help to shed light on the internal workings of individual texts and ultimately on their possible interpretations.

REFERENCES

Anderson, L. B. (1986). Evidentials, Paths of Change and Mental Maps: Typologically Regular Symmetries. In Chafe, W. L., & Nichols, J. (Eds.), *Evidentiality: The Linguistic Coding of Epistemology*. Norwood, NJ: Ablex.

Ballaster, R. (2007). What is reading? Ros Ballaster asks us to think about what we do when we read. *The English Review*, *17*(3), 6–9.

Barton, E. (1993). Evidentials, argumentation, and epistemological stance. *College English*, *55*, 745–769. doi:10.2307/378428

Beach, R., & Anson, C. M. (1992). Stance and Intertextuality in Written Discourse. *Linguistics and Education*, *4*, 335–357. doi:10.1016/0898-5898(92)90007-J

Biber, D. (1990). Methodological Issues Regarding Corpus-based Analyses of Linguistic Variation. *Literary and Linguistic Computing*, *5*(4), 257–269. doi:10.1093/llc/5.4.257

Biber, D. (2006). Stance in spoken and written university registers. *Journal of English for Academic Purposes*, *5*, 97–116. doi:10.1016/j.jeap.2006.05.001

Biber, D., & Finegan, E. (1988). Adverbial Stance Types in English. *Discourse Processes*, *11*, 1–34. doi:10.1080/01638538809544689

Biber, D., & Finegan, E. (1989). Styles of stance in English: lexical and grammatical marking of evidentiality and affect. *Text*, *9*, 93–124. doi:10.1515/text.1.1989.9.1.93

Bleich, D. (1978). *Subjective Criticism*. Baltimore, London: Johns Hopkins University Press.

Brienza, S. D. (1987). *Samuel Beckett's New Worlds. Style in Metafiction*. Norman, Oklahoma: Univ. of Oklahoma Press.

Burrows, J. F. (1987). *Computation into Criticism: A Study of Jane Austen's Novels and an Experiment in Method*. Oxford: Clarendon Press.

Burrows, J. F. (1996). Tiptoeing into the Infinite: Testing for Evidence of National Differences in the Language of English Narrative. In S. Hockey & N. Ide (Eds.), Research in Humanities Computing '92 (pp.1-33). No. 4 in the series Research in Humanities Computing. Oxford: Clarendon Press.

Chafe, W. L. (1986). Evidentiality in English Conversation and Academic Writing. In Chafe, W. L., & Nichols, J. (Eds.), *Evidentiality: The Linguistic Coding of Epistemology*. Norwood, NJ: Ablex.

Conrad, S., & Biber, D. (2001). Adverbial Marking of Stance in Speech and Writing. In Hunston, S., & Thompson, G. (Eds.), *Evaluation in Text. Authorial Stance and the Construction of Discourse*. Oxford: Oxford University Press.

Davis, T. F. (2002). *Formalist Criticism and Reader-Response Theory*. Gordonsville, VA: Palgrave Macmillan.

Eco, U. (1979). *The Role of the Reader: Explorations in the Semiotics of Texts*. Bloomington: Indiana University Press.

Fish, S. (1980). *Is There a Text in This Class? The Authority of Interpretive Communities*. Cambridge, MA: Harvard University Press.

Halliday, M. A. K. (1994). *An Introduction to Functional Grammar* (2nd ed.). London: Edward Arnold.

Hamilton, C. A., & Schneider, R. (2002). From Iser to Turner and Beyond: Reception Theory Meets Cognitive Criticism. *Style (DeKalb, IL)*, *36*(4), 640–658.

Harker, W. J. (1992). Reader Response and Cognition: Is There a Mind in This Class? *Journal of Aesthetic Education*, *26*(3), 27–39. doi:10.2307/3333011

Holmes, J. (1988). Doubt and Certainty in ESL Textbooks. *Applied Linguistics*, *9*, 20–44. doi:10.1093/applin/9.1.21

Hoover, D. L. (2003). Multivariate Analysis and the Study of Style Variation. *Literary and Linguistic Computing*, *18*(4), 341–360. doi:10.1093/llc/18.4.341

Hoover, D. L. (2004). Altered Texts, Altered Worlds, Altered Styles. *Language and Literature*, *13*(2), 99–118. doi:10.1177/0963947004041970

Hoover, D. L. (2007). Corpus Stylistics, Stylometry, and the Styles of Henry James. *Style (DeKalb, IL)*, *41*(2), 174–203.

Hunston, S. (1994). Evaluation and organization in a sample of written academic discourse. In Coulthard, M. (Ed.), *Advances in Written Text Analysis* (pp. 191–218). London: Routledge.

Hyland, K. (1996). Talking to the Academy: Forms of Hedging in Scientific Research Articles. *Written Communication*, *13*, 251–281. doi:10.1177/0741088396013002004

Iser, W. (1974). *The Implied Reader*. Baltimore: Johns Hopkins University Press.

Jauss, H. R. (1982). *Toward an Aesthetic of Reception*. Hemel Hempstead: Harvester Wheatsheaf.

Kärkkäinen, E. (2003). *Epistemic stance in English conversation: a description of its interactional functions, with a focus on I think*. John Benjamins.

Knowlson, J., & Pilling, J. (1979). *Frescoes of the Skull*. London: John Calder.

Lempert, M. (2008). The poetics of stance: Text-metricality, epistemicity, interaction. *Language in Society*, *37*, 569–592. doi:10.1017/S0047404508080779

Levorato, A. (2009). Be steady then, my countrymen, be firm, united and determined. Expressions of stance in the 1798-1800 Irish paper war. *Journal of Historical Pragmatics*, *10*(1), 132–157. doi:10.1075/jhp.10.1.11lev

Martin, J. R. (2001). Beyond Exchange: Appraisal Systems in English. In Hunston, S., & Thompson, G. (Eds.), *Evaluation in Text. Authorial Stance and the Construction of Discourse* (pp. 142–175). Oxford: OUP.

McKenna, C. W. F., & Antonia, A. (2001). The Statistical Analysis of Style: Reflections on Form, Meaning, and Ideology in the 'Nausicaa' Episode of *Ulysses*. *Literary and Linguistic Computing*, *16*(4), 353–373. doi:10.1093/llc/16.4.353

Mosteller, F., & Wallace, D. L. (2007). *Inference and Disputed Authorship: The Federalist Papers (with a new introduction by John Nerbonne)*. Stanford: CSLI.

Ochs, E. (Ed.). (1989). The Pragmatics of Affect. Special issue of Text, 9(1).

Opas, L. L. (1990) *Aspects of Style in Samuel Beckett's Prose Works*. Unpublished DPhil. Thesis. University of Oxford.

Opas, L. L. (1996). A Multi-Dimensional Analysis of Style in Samuel Beckett's Prose Works. In S. Hockey & N. Ide (Eds.), Research in Humanities Computing '92 (pp.81-114). No. 4 in the series Research in Humanities Computing. Oxford: Clarendon Press.

Opas, L. L., & Tweedie, F. J. (1999). The Magic Carpet Ride: Reader Involvement in Romantic Fiction. *Literary and Linguistic Computing*, *14*(1), 89–101. doi:10.1093/llc/14.1.89

Paradis, C. (1997). *Degree modifiers of Adjectives in Spoken British English*. Lund: Lund University Press.

Paradis, C. (2000). It's well weird. Degree modifiers of adjectives revisited: the nineties. In Kirk, J. (Ed.), *Corpora Galore: Analyses and Techniques in Describing English* (pp. 147–160). Amsterdam, Atlanta: Rodopi.

Riddle Harding, J. (2007). Evaluative stance and counterfactuals in language and literature. *Language and Literature*, *16*(3), 263–280. doi:10.1177/0963947007079109

Riffaterre, M. (1978). *Semiotics of Poetry*. Bloomington: Indiana University Press.

Scott, M. (2004). *WordSmith Tools version 4*. Oxford: Oxford University Press.

Selden, R., Widdowson, P., & Brooker, P. (1997). A Reader's Guide to Contemporary Literary Theory. (4th ed.). Hemel Hempstead: Prentice Hall.

Simon-Vandenbergen, A. (2008). Almost certainly and most definitely: Degree modifiers and epistemic stance. *Journal of Pragmatics*, *40*, 1521–1542. doi:10.1016/j.pragma.2008.04.015

Simon-Vandenbergen, A., & Aijmer, K. (2007). The discourse functionality of adjectival and adverbial epistemic expressions: evidence from present-day English. In Butler, C. S., David, J., & Hidalgo Downing, R. (Eds.), *Functional Perspectives on Grammar and Discourse: In Honour of Angela Downing* (pp. 419–445). Amsterdam, Philadelphia: John Benjamins.

Tabata, T. (1995). Narrative Style and the Frequencies of Very Common Words: A Corpus-Based Approach to Dickens's first person and third person narratives. *English Corpus Studies*, *2*, 91–109.

Tabata, T. (2004). Differentiation of Idiolects in Fictional Discourse: A Stylo-Statistical Approach to Dickens's Artistry. In Hiltunen, R., & Watanabe, S. (Eds.), *Approaches to Style and Discourse in English* (pp. 79–106). Osaka: Osaka UP.

Thompson, G., & Hunston, S. (2001). Evaluation: An Introduction. In Hunston, S., & Thompson, G. (Eds.), *Evaluation in Text. Authorial Stance and the Construction of Discourse* (pp. 1–27). Oxford: OUP.

ADDITIONAL READING

Barr, G.W. (2003) Two Styles in the New Testament Epistles. *LLC*, 18, 235-248.

Burrows, J.F. (1992a). Not Unless You Ask Nicely: the Interpretative Nexus between Analysis and Information. *LLC*, 7, 91-109.

Burrows, J. F. (1992b). Computers and the Study of Literature. In Butler, C. (Ed.), *Computers and Written Texts* (pp. 167–204). Oxford: Blackwell.

Burrows, J.F. (2002a). 'Delta': a Measure of Stylistic Difference and a Guide to Likely Authorship. *LLC*, 17, 267-287.

Burrows, J. F. (2002b). The Englishing of Juvenal: Computational Stylistics and Translated Texts. *Style (DeKalb, IL)*, *36*, 677–699.

Burrows, J.F. (2006). All the Way Through: Testing for Authorship in Different Frequency Strata. *LLC*, 22, 27-47.

Burrows, J. F., & Craig, D. H. (1994). Lyrical Drama and the 'Turbid Montebanks': Styles of Dialogue in Romantic and Renaissance Tragedy. *Computers and the Humanities*, *28*, 63–86. doi:10.1007/BF01830688

Clement, R. & Sharp, D. (2003). Ngram and Bayesian Classification of Documents. *LLC*, 18, 423-447.

Craig, H. (1999). Jonsonian Chronology and the Styles of A Tale of a Tub. In M. Butler (Ed.) Re-Presenting Ben Jonson: Text, History, Performance (pp. 210-232). Houndmills: Macmillan.

DeForest, M. & Johnson, E. (2001). The Density of Latinate Words in the Speeches of Jane Austen's Characters. *LLC*, 16, 389-401.

Dillon, G. L. (2007). The Genres Speak: Using Large Corpora to Profile Generic Registers. *Journal of Literary Semantics*, *36*, 159–187. doi:10.1515/JLS.2007.009

Forsyth, R.S., Holmes, D. & Tse, E. (1999). Cicero, Sigonio, and Burrows: Investigating the Authenticity of the *Consolatio*. *LLC*, 14, 375-400.

Fortier, P. (2002). Prototype Effect vs. Rarity Effect in Literary Style. In Louwerse, M., & van Peer, W. (Eds.), *Thematics: Interdisciplinary Studies* (pp. 397–405). Amsterdam: Benjamins.

Fortier, P. A. (1993). Babies, Bathwater and the Study of Literature. *Computers and the Humanities*, *27*, 375–385. doi:10.1007/BF01829388

Hockey, S. (2000). *Electronic Texts in the Humanities*. Oxford: OUP.

Holmes, D. (1994). Authorship Attribution. *Computers and the Humanities*, *28*, 87–106. doi:10.1007/BF01830689

Holmes, D., Gordon, L. & Wilson, C. (2001). A Widow and Her Soldier: Stylometry and the American Civil War. *LLC*, 16, 403-420.

Holmes, D., Robertson, M., & Paez, R. (2001). Stephen Crane and the New York Tribune: A Case Study in Traditional and Non-Traditional Authorship Attribution. *Computers and the Humanities*, *35*, 315–331. doi:10.1023/A:1017549100097

Hoover, D. (2007). Quantitative Analysis and Literary Studies. In Siemens, R., & Schreibman, S. (Eds.), *A Companion to Digital Literary Studies* (pp. 517–533). Oxford: Blackwell.

Hoover, D. L. (1999). *Language and Style in The Inheritors*. Lanham, MD: University Press of America.

Hoover, D.L. (2002). Frequent Word Sequences and Statistical Stylistics. *LLC*, 17, 157-180.

Hoover, D.L. (2003). Frequent Collocations and Authorial Style. *LLC*, 18, 261-286.

Hoover, D.L. (2004a). Testing Burrows's Delta. *LLC*, 19, 453-475.

Hoover, D.L. (2004b). Delta Prime? *LLC*, 19, 477-495.

Laan, N. (1995). Stylometry and Method: the Case of Euripides. *LLC*, 10, 271-278.

Love, H. (2002). *Attributing Authorship: An Introduction*. Cambridge: CUP. doi:10.1017/CBO9780511483165

McCarthy, W. (2007). Knowing...: Modeling in Literary Studies. In Siemens, R., & Schreibman, S. (Eds.), *A Companion to Digital Literary Studies* (pp. 391–401). Oxford: Blackwell.

Opas, L.L. & Kujamäki, P. (1995). A Cross-linguistic Study of Stream-of-consciousness Techniques. *LLC*, 10, 287-291.

Potter, R. G. (1988). Literary Criticism and Literary Computing: the Difficulties of a Synthesis. *Computers and the Humanities*, *22*, 91–97. doi:10.1007/BF00057648

Ramsay, S. (2003). Toward and Algorithmic Criticism. *LLC*, 18, 167-174.

Ramsay, S. (2007). Algorithmic Criticism. In Siemens, R., & Schreibman, S. (Eds.), *A Companion to Digital Literary Studies* (pp. 477–491). Oxford: Blackwell.

Rommel, T. (1995). Aspects of Verisimilitude: Temporal and Topographical References in *Robinson Crusoe*. *LLC*, 10, 279-285.

Rybicki, J. (2006). Burrowing into Translation: Character, Idiolects in Henryk Sienkiewicz's Trilogy and its Two English translations. *LLC*, 21, 91-103.

Spence, M., Bodaleho, B. Robinson, P. & Howe, C.J. (2003). How Reliable is a Stemma? An Analysis of Chaucer's Miller's Tale. *LLC*, 18, 407-422.

Stewart, L. (2003). Charles Brockden Brown: Quantitative Analysis and Literary Interpretation. *LLC*, 18, 129-138.

Waugh, S., Adams, A., & Tweedie, F. J. (2000). Computational Stylistics Using Artificial. *Neural Networks*, *LLC*, 15, 187–198.

ENDNOTES

1 For a discussion on terminology, see Thompson and Hunston 2001: 1-6.

2 The dates in the present text and all the graphs refer to the time the prose works were written. The Appendix is a list of the works with the edition used here and the date of first publication noted. This solution was arrived at since in some cases there is a time lag between the time of composition and the time of publication.

3 *Fizzles 1-6* were written in 1959-1960, *Fizzle 7* was written in 1972 and *Fizzle 8* in 1975.

4 SPSS of course produced similar scores for all texts on all 12 components.

5 The program PAST will do this.

6 The tool was purpose built by Mari Karsikas, Suvi Tiinanen and Tapio Seppänen (University of Oulu) and runs on the MATLAB platform.

APPENDIX

List of works sampled. Note that these are the editions used. The date of first publication has also been recorded.

Beckett, Samuel (1979). *All Strange Away*. [1976]. John Calder. Sample: pp. 12-19.

Beckett, Samuel (1982). *Company*. [1980]. Pan Books Ltd. Sample: pp. 52-60.

Beckett, Samuel (1974). *Enough*. [1965]. In *'First Love' and Other Shorts*. Grove Press, Inc. pp. 57-60.

Beckett, Samuel (1982). *First Love*. [1970]. Penguin Books Ltd. Sample: pp. 27-29.

Beckett, Samuel (1979). *Fizzles 1-8*. [1976]. Grove Press, Inc., New York.

Beckett, Samuel (1982). *Ill Seen Ill Said*. [1981]. John Calder. Sample: pp. 8-15.

Beckett, Samuel (1974). *Imagination Dead Imagine*. [1965]. In *'First Love' and Other Shorts*. Grove Press, Inc. pp. 63-66.

Beckett, Samuel (1979). *Malone Dies*. [1951] Pan Books Ltd. Samples: pp. 222-224, 225-227, 235-237, 239-240, 257-259.

Beckett, Samuel (1979). *Molloy*. [1950]. Pan Books Ltd. Samples: pp. 12-14, 16-18, 47-49, 61-62, 106-108, 128-130, 144-145, 149-151.

Beckett, Samuel (1957). *Murphy*. [1938]. Grove Press, Inc. Samples: pp. 2-6, 20-25, 70-74, 99-104, 199-203, 211-216.

Beckett, Samuel (1979). *The Unnamable*. [1952]. Pan Books Ltd. Samples: pp. 274-276, 277-279, 304-306, 313-315, 351-352, 376-378

Chapter 3
Literary Onomastics and Language Technology

Lars Borin
University of Gothenburg, Sweden

Dimitrios Kokkinakis
University of Gothenburg, Sweden

ABSTRACT

In this chapter, we describe the development and application of language technology for intelligent information access to the content of digitized cultural heritage collections in the form of Swedish classical literary works. This technology offers sophisticated and flexible support functions to literary scholars and researchers. We focus on one kind of text processing technology (named entity recognition) and one research field (literary onomastics), but we try to argue that the techniques involved are quite general and can be further developed in a number of directions. This way, we aim at supporting the users of digitized literature collections with tools that enable semantic search, browsing and indexing of texts. In this sense, we offer new ways for exploring the large volumes of literary texts being made available through national cultural heritage digitization projects.

DOI: 10.4018/978-1-60566-932-8.ch003

INTRODUCTION

Literature can be studied in a number of different ways and from various perspectives, but text analysis – in a wide sense – will probably always make up a central component of literature studies. In this day and age, the computer has become an indispensable tool in many kinds of text analysis, such as in linguistics and in information access, to mention two fields. However, the potential of the computer as a text analysis tool in literature studies is arguably largely untapped (Bradley 2005; Juola 2008).

Literature is now increasingly available in electronic form. Modern literature is born digital as a matter of course (but may not always be available in this form to research), while older literature is being computerized apace as part of national cultural heritage preservation efforts. Thus, there is no shortage of literary works in digital form. We can see this as an opportunity to explore how text analytical tools that have turned out to be useful in other fields could be put to effective use also in literature studies. In our case, we are interested in developing and exploring computer tools based on language technology, which is our primary field of expertise. Here, a reasonable approach would be to identify some particular component or subfield of text analysis in literature studies having requirements which would match the capabilities of some mature language technology, and further see how this could be packaged up in a way that would be of help to literary scholars.

In this chapter, we argue that the field of literary onomastics is part of literature studies. We also point out that there is a mature language technology which can be ancillary to text analysis in this field, namely the technology of named entity recognition.

In the next section, we briefly describe literary onomastics and named entity recognition. In Section 3, we give an account of our recent work on automatically providing a large number of digitized classical Swedish literary works with named entity annotations and making these annotations accessible to users through a search and browsing interface. In this account, we try to cater both to those readers who are mostly interested in the implications of our work for literary and other Humanities scholarship, and to those who are curious about the technology involved. Section 4 outlines some future directions in which we would like to continue our research, specifically intelligent information access as applied to literary and historical texts. Finally, Section 5 offers some conclusions to this chapter.

DEFINING THE AREA

Literary onomastics is a field of inquiry where literature is seen through the names appearing in literary texts. Specific topics may comprise studies of the etymology or symbolism of names, those of how fictional names make the transition into the real world, or of the use and function of names and naming in the works of an individual author, a literary school, genre, or period (Alvarez-Altman & Burelbach, 1987; Svedjedal, 2004; van Dalen-Oskam & van Zundert, 2004; van Dalen-Oskam, 2005).

Literary onomastics is not our field of expertise, but from familiarizing ourselves with the literature in this field we have concluded it is a well-established and lively area of investigation which presupposes that names can be located and recognized with minimum of effort. It is also clear that analysing the use of names requires access to a broad basis of comparison. Ideally, information both within and outside a genre should be readily available, for instance, when studying the use and function of names in late nineteenth-century and early twentieth-century crime fiction. Obviously, it is possible to mark up digital texts manually (as described by Flanders, Bauman, Caton, & Cournane, 1998), but this is a very time-consuming, and consequently costly, endeavor. This is where language technology enters the picture in the form of named entity recognition technology.

NAMED ENTITY RECOGNITION

Named entity recognition (NER) has numerous applications in a number of human language technologies. It has emerged in the context of information extraction (IE) and text mining (TM), which aim at the automatic retrieval of particular kinds of information from texts (IE – McCallum, 2005) or the automatic discovery of new facts in texts (TM – Fan, Wallace, Rich, & Zhang, 2006). In these activities, the automatic recognition and marking-up of proper names and some other related kinds of information – particularly words and phrases referring to human agents, time and measure expressions – has turned out to be a recurring basic requirement. Hence, NER has become of great relevance to numerous applications and a wide range of techniques (Jackson & Moulinier, 2007).

At present, NER systems are geared toward a particular language and genre, and are often fine-tuned to a particular application domain as well. Thus, systems need to be adapted whenever it is to be applied to other languages, genres and/or domains. This adaptation can be automatized to some extent, but it generally involves a fair amount of manual work. This is a one-time effort, however, and having accomplished it, we can then proceed to mark up unlimited amounts of text at virtually no additional cost, as opposed to manual markup, which incurs a cost more or less proportional to the amount of text processed and becomes virtually impossible when the volume of text grows beyond a certain limit.

NER systems have typically been built for application in specialized, often quite technical, fields like biomedicine or financial news and for processing modern language. In our imagined scenario involving crime fiction, we need to adapt a NER system to the language used in fiction around the turn of the twentieth century. However, it should not be fine-tuned specifically to crime fiction, since an important aspect of this kind of study involves the comparison of the use and function of names.

In the following section, we describe our work on a NER system for dealing with Swedish fiction from the 19th and 20th centuries. We also describe how this system has allowed the automatic addition of named entity information to the texts, making the named entities searchable and browsable through a web interface.

THE SWEDISH LITERATURE BANK

Litteraturbanken, the Swedish Literature Bank, (<http://litteraturbanken.se/>) is a national cultural heritage project financed by the Swedish Academy. It aims at making available online the full text of relevant works of Swedish literature, in critical editions intended to be suitable for literary research and for the teaching of literature. There is also abundant commissioned ancillary material on its website, such as author presentations, bibliographies, and thematic essays about authorships, genres or periods, written by experts in each field. The literary works in this resource are available in three different formats:

- e-text, which is a flexible, fully searchable XML format, designed to be compatible with the language corpus format used in *Språkbanken* (see below), but which also contains additional, and specific information used for reproducing the sometimes complex typographical layout of the original printed work;
- electronic facsimiles, that is, high-quality digital images in several sizes, of particularly interesting book editions;
- pdf documents, containing text or sometimes scanned page images.

Similarly to many other literature digitization initiatives, most of the works in *Litteraturbanken* are such for which copyright has expired (under Swedish law this means that more than 70 years must have passed since the death of the author). At present, the bulk of the texts are from the 18th, 19th and early 20th centuries. However, there is also an agreement with the national organizations representing authors' intellectual property rights, allowing the inclusion of modern works according to a uniform royalty payment scheme.

The literary bank described above somewhat followed the model of *Språkbanken*, the Swedish Language Bank, (<http://spraakbanken.gu.se>), which is run by a research unit in the Department of Swedish Language at the University of Gothenburg in Sweden. It was established with government funding in 1975 as a national center with a remit to collect, process and store Swedish text corpora (i.e., large systematically compiled text collections). It also aims at making linguistic data extracted from the corpora and other linguistic resources, such as electronic lexicons and term lists, available to researchers and to the public. Today, this research unit possesses a unique combination of competences in the areas of Swedish text corpora, parallel text corpora, Swedish computational lexicons, and language technology tools for the processing, annotation and presentation of text corpora, coupled with the kind of stable organization required for lasting large-scale corpus processing and presentation. For this reason, *Språkbanken* was chosen as the developer and maintainer of *Litteraturbanken*.

This being the case, we decided to design the technical solutions to be implemented in the project with language technology applications in mind. The rationale for this was that we saw these literary texts not only as representing Sweden's literary heritage, but also as high-grade empirical data for linguistic investigations. Hence, we wanted to build an infrastructure for *Litteraturbanken* which would allow this intended dual purpose of the material to be realized to the fullest, where, say, a 19th-century novel would be available as a literary work as well as a language corpus component. This precluded the use of ready-made digital library software or content management system (CMS) solutions, as we wanted to be compatible with emerging storage and exchange standards for language resources and tools, such as the TEI/(X)CES (Text Encoding Initiative, n.d.; XCES, 2008) and ISO TC37/SC07 (Ide & Romary, 2002), which to our knowledge has never been a consideration in the design of digital library or CM systems. The format of *Litteraturbanken* has consequently been designed with this in mind, and all our language technology processing – including NER – is performed only on e-text. In addition to this double use of the texts, we soon also started to think about possible cross-fertilization – how the kinds of annotations made possible by language technology could be of use to others than linguists, such as literary scholars, historians and researchers in other fields in the Humanities and Social Sciences. In broad terms, this would concern easier access to the *content* of large text materials, for example, what in linguistics and language technology is referred to as *semantic and pragmatic annotation*. This includes annotation of texts according to their topic (as in information retrieval), assignment of words and phrases to semantic fields (similar to what is found in a thesaurus) or semantic type (NER being a special case of this), classification of verb arguments into actors and patients, etc.

TOWARDS A NAMED-ENTITY RECOGNITION SYSTEM

Here, we will focus on named entities (referred to variously as 'names', 'named entities', or simply 'entities' in the following), as automatically recognized and marked-up as such by a NER system. Combined with suitable interfaces for displaying, searching, selecting, correlating and browsing them, we believe that the recognition and annotation of named entities in *Litteraturbanken* will facilitate literary research. We also have reason to believe that historians, for example, could find this facility useful, insofar as these fictional narratives also contain descriptions of real locations, characterizations of contemporary public figures, and so on. Flanders et al. (1998, p. 285) argue that references to people in historical sources are of intrinsic interest since they may reveal "networks of friendship, enmity, and collaboration; familial relationships; and political alliances [...] class position, intellectual affiliations, and literary bent of the author". Regardless of what we think of literature as a historical source, it is easy to see that the same kind of questions could be put by a literary scholar to a work of fiction in order to explore the fictional world developed therein. The questions we ask about the real world and the fictional worlds of literature are often not very different in kind, and it should be no disadvantage if the tools that we develop for the one would be immediately applicable also to the other.

The system we use originates from the work conducted in the *Nomen Nescio* project (Johannessen et al., 2005; Kokkinakis, 2004). This is a multipurpose Swedish NER system, which comprises a number of modules applied sequentially in a pipeline fashion. This system was extended to deal with written 19th-century Swedish language and evaluated on a small number of novels available in *Litteraturbanken*, work which we have reported on elsewhere (Borin, Kokkinakis, & Olsson, 2007). This evaluation prompted a number of modifications of the NER system, and a prototype of the modified system is now being incorporated as a regular feature.

Figure 1. Place name search in Litteraturbanken

Berger Bendel & Co	s. 284	ig och passerades. Bortom **Adams street** street blef den oerhörda avenyen
Berger Bendel & Co	s. 284	street blef den oerhörda **avenyen** mörkare, och vid van Burens hörn
Berger Bendel & Co	s. 284	en loge. - Kommo de till **Paris** i sommar så skulle de köpa ett par
Berger Bendel & Co	s. 284	hon visste en adress vid **Boulevard Males-** Malesherbes, där de såldes i
Berger Bendel & Co	s. 284	elge någonsin har varit i **Paris**, tillade hon. Van Buren var mörk och
Berger Bendel & Co	s. 284	r som - ligt. Från Lister **Building** hade Helge sett några skepnader
Berger Bendel & Co	s. 285	igt och lyfte lätt på sin **panama**, det är som vore vi i gay Paree -
Berger Bendel & Co	s. 286	Reuter, damerna äro från **Norge** eller, nej, hur var det? Sverige,
Berger Bendel & Co	s. 286	eller, nej, hur var det? **Sverige**, tror jag. Men, herre gud, det är
Berger Bendel & Co	s. 291	nda ned till barriären åt **Clark street** street och bekväma liggstolar, s
Berger Bendel & Co	s. 292	rande, svindlande höjder. **Michigansjöns** ofantliga yta mötte österut
Berger Bendel & Co	s. 293	Snedt till vänster syntes **Masonic Temples** Temples takkrön som ett strål
Berger Bendel & Co	s. 293	hvilken var reflexen från **Milwaukee**. Men själfva sjön tedde sig som
Berger Bendel & Co	s. 294	kajmurar, hörde han också **Michigans** brusande andhämtning och därefter
Berger Bendel & Co	s. 296	och se efter - gossarna i **England**. Men några dagar hinner jag alltid
Berger Bendel & Co	s. 296	g öfver Kanalen. Bor du i **Paris** på Grand Louvre som förut? - Ja, svarad
Berger Bendel & Co	s. 296	analen. Bor du i Paris på **Grand Louvre** Louvre som förut? - Ja, svarade
Berger Bendel & Co	s. 298	hvars syster är gift med **Indiens** vicekonung. Jag måste gå. Han
Berger Bendel & Co	s. 298	talade de om den franska **rivieran** och spelbanken i Monte Carlo. -
Berger Bendel & Co	s. 298	rivieran och spelbanken i **Monte Carlo** Carlo. - Jag skall hvila ut där i

All the hundred-plus books currently available as e-text have been processed and the resulting named entity annotations added to the repository. Further, we have built an experimental name search and browsing application on top of the regular search interface as can be seen in Figure 1.

Figure 1 illustrates a search for place names in *Litteraturbanken*. This can be seen as a generalized concordance function, i.e., it offers concordance lines for (types of) names, with links into the text locations themselves where the names appear and can be browsed in the text. We see the concordances for hits 1021-1040 out of 43,126 place names automatically located and annotated by the NER system in the e-texts available in the literary bank.

Figure 2 shows the result of clicking on one of the hits (the sixth from below in Figure 1, or number 1,035), which puts the interface in browsing mode, where you can go back and forth through the e-texts by jumping between place name occurrences.

In the following section we provide a short description of our NER system, highlighting the necessary adaptations made to it in order to reach sufficient coverage on literary texts, especially the older, 19th-century ones. We also describe the further enhancements made to the system, such as gender attribution to person entities.

RESOURCES AND ARCHITECTURE

Our point of departure for the work described here was a Swedish multi-purpose NER system that has been successfully applied in different domains (Kokkinakis & Thurin, 2007). It comprises a number of modules organized into layers and applied

Figure 2. Place name browsing in Litteraturbanken

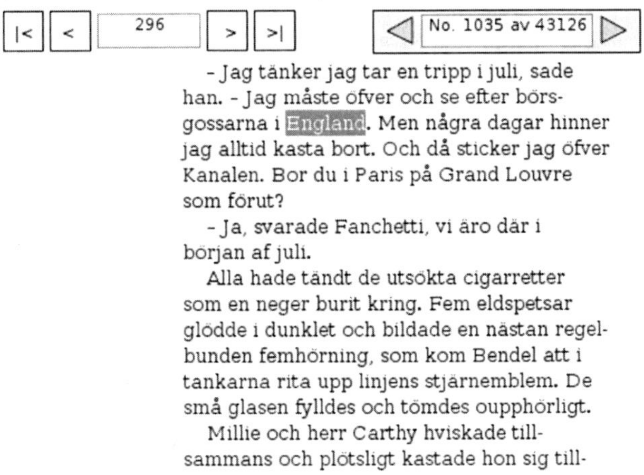

sequentially, in a pipeline fashion. The major components are described below in the same order that they are applied in the automatic processing of text. In the system architecture, following standard procedure in constructing language technology systems, we strive to make a clear separation between the system's lexical, grammatical and processing resources.

Lists of multiword names (approximately 10,000 names), extracted from various types of corpora, are matched directly against the text being processed. Empirical experience proves this to be a reliable resource that can be safely applied in the early stages of NER for any document, since there are rarely ambiguities or conflicts between such multiword entities (some examples include *Adolf Fredriks torg* 'Adolf Fredrik Square', *Fontana di Trevi*, and *Svenska Röda korset* 'The Swedish Red Cross').

The next component applies sets of linguistic rules – grammars – for each type of entity recognized by the system. Each rule in such a grammar defines patterns in the entity itself and its local context (classes of trigger words, designators and modifiers), in order to safely recognize entities displaying largely unambiguous structure or appearing in mainly unambiguous contexts. For instance, '*Institutionen för \S+ska \S+*' (where '\S+' implies any sequence of alphanumeric characters) can successfully recognize entities such as *Institutionen för nordiska språk* 'Department of Scandinavian Languages'.

The annotations produced by the previous component, which has a high degree of accuracy, are then used in a separate module in order to make decisions regarding possible entities in less reliable contexts. This module is based on the labeling consistency principle (that is, the observation that a name will tend to refer to the same entity throughout a given text, as discussed below).

Lists of single-word names (so-called *gazetteers*) collected from various corpora (approximately 120,000 names) are consulted next. Each name in these lists is marked for a major type and in some cases a minor subtype which further specifies the entity in question. For instance, the named entity *Ericsson* is encoded in the gazetteer both as a person and an organization (of subtype corporation). If an entity is annotated during the application of the first two modules above, then it is ignored during the single name lookup process. Thus, if, in an earlier processing stage, an entity has already been assigned the category *X* in a particular document, and the list of single names provide the category *Y* for the same entity or a part of it, category *X* is kept.

Animacy recognition is based on a large set of designators from the person entity grammar. The designators include honorifics, titles and a large set of common nouns denoting professions, family relations, nationalities, etc., as well as gender signaling adjectives such *kvinnlig* 'female' and *manlig* 'male'.

A list of people's first names in which each name is marked with biological gender, male/female (approximately 16,000 names), is one of the resources used for gender attribution (see below). The content of this list has been acquired from Internet sites (such as <http://www.babynames.com> and the corresponding Swedish site <http://www.bebisnamn.se>).

In order to find name variants and misspellings of names that are already in the name lists used by the system, a name similarity calculation module is applied. A candidate named entity identified as such by the name grammar but not found in any of the system lists is compared to each name in these lists using standard string similarity metrics, i.e., a kind of fuzzy matching (see below).

Finally, a theory revision and refinement module reviews the annotated document, in order to detect and resolve possible errors and assign new annotations based on existing ones. This can involve merging compatible annotations, modifying and even deleting partial annotations and fragments, for instance merging a person designator (*herr*, 'Mr') with a person name, as in examples 1a-1b in Figure 3.

This module also applies a set of templates, a kind of local discourse structures for recognizing new entities that are neither in a gazetteer nor recognized by the grammar component and for which the surrounding context provides a reliable clue for recognition. For instance, enumerations that can be located by the presence of named entities separated by punctuation and conjunctions. The system can then infer the label of a potential entity from other available annotations to the left and/or to the right, as in Examples 2a-2c in Figure 3.

Figure 3. Examples of named-entity annotations

(1a) *Merging:*
<ENAMEX ANI="UNM">**Herr**</ENAMEX> <ENAMEX TYPE="PRS" SBT="HUM">**Boman**</ENAMEX>
(1b):
<ENAMEX TYPE="PRS" SBT="HUM" ANI="UNM">**Herr Boman**</ENAMEX>

(2a) *Template:*
Konstantinopel , Alexandria , Antiokia och Jerusalem
... Ovidius , Racine , Voltaire
(2b):
<ENAMEX TYPE="LOC" SBT="PPL">**Konstantinopel**</ENAMEX> , <ENAMEX TYPE="LOC" SBT="PPL">**Alexandria**</ENAMEX> , **Antiokia och** <ENAMEX TYPE="LOC" SBT="PPL">**Jerusalem**</ENAMEX>
...<ENAMEX TYPE="PRS" SBT="HUM" ANI="UNU">**Ovidius**</ENAMEX> , **Racine** , <ENAMEX TYPE="PRS" SBT="HUM" ANI="UNU">**Voltaire**</ENAMEX>
(2c):
<ENAMEX TYPE="LOC" SBT="PPL">**Konstantinopel**</ENAMEX> , <ENAMEX TYPE="LOC" SBT="PPL">**Alexandria**</ENAMEX> , *<ENAMEX TYPE="LOC" SBT="PPL">**Antiokia**</ENAMEX>* **och** <ENAMEX TYPE="LOC" SBT="PPL">**Jerusalem**</ENAMEX>
...<ENAMEX TYPE="PRS" SBT="HUM" ANI="UNU">**Ovidius**</ENAMEX> , *<ENAMEX TYPE="PRS" SBT="HUM" ANI="UNU">**Racine**</ENAMEX>* , <ENAMEX TYPE="PRS" SBT="HUM" ANI="UNU">**Voltaire**</ENAMEX>

NAMED-ENTITY TAXONOMY

The nature and type of named entities vary depending on the task under investigation or the target application. Also, semantic annotation is not as well understood as grammatical annotation, and there is no consensus on a standard tagset and content to be generally applicable. In any case, personal names, location and organization names are found in all proposed named-entity taxonomies. Recently, however, there have been attempts to define and apply richer name hierarchies for various tasks, both specific (Fleischman & Hovy, 2002) and generic (Sekine, 2004). Our current system implements a rather fine-grained named entity taxonomy with eight main named entity types as well as 57 subtypes (Johannesen et al., 2005; Kokkinakis, 2004). The eight main types and some of their subtypes are the following:

- **Person** (PRS): proper nouns – personal names (forenames, surnames), animal/pet names, mythological names, etc. – and common nouns and noun phrases denoting people;
- **Location** (LOC): functional locations, geographical, geo-political, astrological, etc.;
- **Organization** (ORG): political, athletic, media, military, etc.;
- **Artifact** (OBJ): food/wine products, prizes, means of communication, etc.;
- **Work & Art** (WRK): printed material, names of films and novels, sculptures, etc.;
- **Event** (EVN): religious, athletic, scientific, cultural, etc.;
- **Measure/Numerical** (MSR): volume, age, index, dosage, web-related, speed, etc.;
- **Temporal** (TME): no subtypes since the need for subclassifying the temporal expressions has not arisen yet in the problem domains to which the system has been applied.

In Figure 3, we can see what the named entity annotations look like in the underlying XML format. Named entities in the text are automatically identified by our system and marked with surrounding *<ENAMEX>... </ENAMEX>* tags (ENAMEX stands for 'Extended NAMe EXpression'), and the starting tag contains so-called attributes, which indicate the kind of named entity. Thus, *<ENAMEX TYPE='LOC' SBT='PPL'>* in Examples 2b-2c in Figure 3 indicates a named entity of main type *Location* and subtype *Geo-political*.

Although not necessary for onomastic studies, time expressions are important since they allow temporal reasoning about complex events as well as time-line visualization of the story developed in a text. The temporal expressions recognized include both relative (*klockan 8 på morgonen i dag* '8 o'clock in the morning today') and absolute expressions (*i början af tolfhundratalet* 'in the beginning of the thirteenth century'), and sets or sequences of time points or stretches of time (*varje dag* 'every day'). From these examples we see that, in principle, temporal expressions could be sub-classified in much the same way as measure expressions. This may be done in a future version of the system.

Animacy

The rule-based component of the person-name recognition grammar is based on a large set of designator words (mostly common nouns – *läkaren* 'the doctor', *svärson* 'son-in-law' – and a number of gender-bearing adjectival modifiers in noun phrases – such as animate masculine adjective forms ending in *-e*, e.g., *starke* 'strong', *gamle* 'old') and verbal predicates that most probably require an animate subject (*berätta* 'to tell', *fundera* 'to think'). These are used in conjunction with orthographic markers in the text, such as capitalization, for the recognition of person names. Designators provide a highly relevant and reliable piece of evidence that is explored for the annotation of animate instances in literary texts, which is also the first step for gender recognition (Section 3.7). The designators, common nouns and adjectives, are divided into four groups that denote:

1. Family ties and relationships (e.g., *svärson* 'son-in-law')
2. Professions (e.g., *läkaren* 'the doctor')
3. Nationality or the ethnic/racial group of a person (e.g., *tysken* 'the [male] German [person]')
4. An individual who cannot be unambiguously categorized into any of the three other groups (e.g., *patienten* 'the patient').

Besides this classification, inherent characteristics of at least a large group of the designators (internal evidence/morphological cues), also indicate referent (biological) gender (illustrated above by *tysken* 'the [male] German [person]'). In this way, the animacy annotation is further specified for male, female or unknown gender. Unknown in this context means unresolved or ambiguous, such as *barn* 'child'. The unknown cases are to a great extent resolved by the application of simplistic pronoun resolution, which attempts to determine whether two mentions in a document, typically a named entity (a name or a designator) and a personal pronoun, refer to the same thing. If this is the case, then the named entity is assigned the appropriate gender (Section 10). For each designator group, as previously described, the annotation takes the form of an attribute 'ANI' with a value depending on the recognition or not of the designator's gender. Male designators are, for instance, the nouns *kong* 'king', *baron* and *herr* 'Mr', and animate masculine adjective forms ending in *-e* such as *starke* 'strong', *hygglige* 'kind' and *gamle* 'old'. On the other hand, female designators may be illustrated by *tant* 'aunt/lady', *fru* 'wife/Mrs' and *tös* 'girl' (the adjective form contrasting with animate masculine *-e* is the feminine/neuter/inanimate masculine *-a*, which consequently cannot be used for gender attribution). The attribute 'ANI' can take the values FAM, FAF and FAU for FAmily ties, Male, Female and Unknown respectively (*mor* 'mother': FAF); PRM, PRF, PRU for PRofession designators (*herr direktör* 'Mr Director': PRM); NAM, NAF and NAU for NAtionality designators (*amerikanen* 'the [male] American': NAM, as opposed to *amerikanskan* 'the [female] American': NAF); and UNM, UNF and UNU for UNknown / other designators (*värdinna* 'hostess': UNF).

In contrast to English writing practice, compounds in Swedish are written as a single orthographic unit. This fact simplifies the recognition of animacy for a large set of words (common nouns and gender-bearing adjectives) with minimal resources, by the use of a set of suitable headwords, and by capturing modifiers using simple patterns. Approximately 20-30 patterns – mainly suffixes – are enough to identify the vast majority of animate entities in a text. For instance, *-inna* / *-innan* / *-innor* and *-erska* / *-erskan* / *-erskor* are reliable, typical designator suffixes for female individuals, which, when preceded by a set of obligatory strings and followed by a set of optional inflectional patterns, capture a long list of words – most of them compounds – denoting female individuals. Some examples would be *taleskvinna* 'spokeswoman', *lyxälskarinna* 'luxury mistress'; and *fångvakterskor* 'female prison guards', *företräderskor* 'female predecessors', etc.

CHANGING ORTHOGRAPHIC NORMS

Nineteenth-century Swedish spelling is noticeably different from today's orthography. This is because we are seeing two different standards divided by an intervening spelling reform, commonly dated to the year 1906, but actually encompassing a transition period of some decades around the turn of the 20th century (Teleman, 2005). Our NER system was originally based on the modern orthography, and in principle we could have considered devising a new NER system specifically for 19th-century Swedish, thus regarding it as a language system in its own right.

Instead, we have opted for extending the NER system so that it handles both orthographies – the pre-spelling reform orthography and the modern spelling – simultaneously, for three reasons. First, as already mentioned, there was a long transition period in which we will find texts using both spellings. In fact, the change was gradual also in the sense that some aspects of the modern orthography were adopted earlier than others, so that from our viewpoint we even find a mixture of older and newer spellings within the same text. Second, the extension comes with little risk of confusion, as there are few or no ambiguities introduced by allowing such orthographic doublets in our NER system, and consequently, its accuracy will not be compromised. Third, there is intrinsic methodological interest in being able to deal with spelling variation in texts.

The last point requires more detailing. Some earlier periods in the history of the Swedish language are characterized by a marked lack of orthographic standardization, especially the Old Swedish period of the Middle Ages, but this is also largely true of the Modern Swedish period (from 1526 onwards), before a nationwide standard spelling was accomplished in the 19th century (Pettersson, 2005). In order to deal with pre-standardization textual material using modern language technology, we must find viable methods for dealing with the spelling and other variation exhibited in these texts (Borin & Forsberg, 2008), and in order to reuse existing technology, we need principled methods for adapting modern language technology tools, such as part-of-speech tagging, to historical data sources (Pilz, Ernst-Gerlach, Kempken, Rayson, & Archer, 2008; Rayson, Archer, Baron, Culpeper, & Smith, 2007). The calculation of various metrics for measuring the amount of difference between two sequences of symbols, the so-called edit distance or similarity, between different spelling variants is the basic approach for dealing with the problem. This allows systems to cope successfully with the analysis of texts written in different time periods and even in different genres, than the one a system has been designed for. Our approach is thus based on the identification of spelling variants using an ensemble of standard similarity algorithms. After some empirical experimentation with such metrics, we decided on suitable threshold values. New candidate entities that passed such thresholds were manually inspected for the elimination of "false friends" such as *Bosporus* (the location) and *Bespara* the verb 'to save' (as written sentence-initially). In this way, we have complemented the NER lexical component with the addition of a large number of entity variants. This is accomplished by a filtering stage in which the NER lexicons, which to a great extent cover modern Swedish, are compared to extracted lists of unannotated potential entity tokens identified in the historical texts by the application of simple grammar rules. Each named entity in the available name lexicons is pre-classified into one, and sometimes more than one type and subtypes. However, the content of the extracted lists should fulfill a number of appropriate format criteria, particularly orthography and number of characters. Since the electronic material is a digitized, proofread edition of the published original, we anticipate that named entities should be capitalized. Therefore, only tokens that start with a capital letter and which consist of more than four characters (a threshold chosen on the basis of experimentation in order to avoid too many spurious comparisons) are considered. Moreover, named entities recognized during a pre-annotation stage are also excluded since such annotations are considered trustworthy and do not need to be compared with the tagger's lexical resources once again. An alternative strategy is applied for the recognition of time and measure entities, where capitalization is not a criterion for the recognition of such entities, as in the case of person and location entities previously discussed. No gazetteers are used for the recognition of time expressions which is a process that solely relies on grammar rules. Therefore, we chose to manually incorporate spelling variants for a small number of tokens, which are central to the time and measure entity recognition grammars, such as (old spelling/new spelling): prepositions (*af/av* 'of'); numbers (*tolf/tolv* 'twelve'); names of days (*thorsdag/torsdag* 'Thursday'); and other designators (*qväll/kväll* 'evening'). Most of these variants have been found by applying a handful of templates to the historical texts, such as *i ? ? +talet* which extracts time expressions such as *i början af tolfhundratalet* 'in the beginning of the thirteenth century'. The results of the application of such templates were manually inspected and appropriate additions of spelling variants were made to the time and measure grammars.

DOCUMENT-CENTERED APPROACH AND LABELING CONSISTENCY

There is a well-known trade-off in language technology between rule-based and statistical systems. Rule-based, i.e., handcrafted-grammar based systems typically obtain better results, but at the cost of considerable manual effort by domain experts. Statistical NER systems typically require a large amount of manually annotated training data, but can be ported to other domains or genres more rapidly and require less manual work. (Tjong Kim Sang & De Meulder, 2003)

Although the Swedish system is mainly rule-based, using a handcrafted grammar for each entity group, it can also be considered a hybrid system in the sense that it applies a document-centered approach, a term introduced by Mikheev (2000), to entity annotation. For instance, relating person entities across a document is difficult because of the potential many-to-many mappings between names and the entities that they refer to, i.e., name words and name phrases may be ambiguous. However, it has been observed (Ravin & Kazi, 1999) that a document usually defines a single context, in which it is quite unlikely to find that the same name expression refers to more than one entity. This is particularly evident in novels in which a character is introduced unambiguously by designators such as title, affiliation, social status, age, relation to other family members or the society, usually in the very opening paragraphs of the novel. If such a discriminating context can be discovered in a document, then it can be applied for reducing the potential many-to-many mapping between variants to a single entity in other less discriminating contexts. It is common, at least as a rule of thumb, that if the same entity appears more than once in the same document, such entities tend to have the same labels throughout the document. The document-centered approach (henceforth DCA) implements exactly this observation. DCA is a form of online learning from the document being processed where unambiguous usages are used for assigning annotations to ambiguous words, and information for disambiguation is derived from the entire document. In our system, DCA is used in two different tasks. Firstly, it is used for ensuring labeling consistency between named entities (see below) and secondly for labeling consistency regarding gender attribution (Section 10).

Table 1 illustrates this approach with the Swedish Nobel Laureate Selma Lagerlöf's novel *Nils Holgerssons underbara resa genom Sverige*. In the examples, the person names *Klement* and *Akka* are not in the gazetteer lists, but have been introduced by the author using unambiguous designators such as *gubben* 'the old man' for the first entity, and *mor* 'mother' for the second. Most of the subsequent mentions of the same names are given without any reliable clue for appropriate labeling.

However, as already discussed above in this section, subsequent mentions of the same name should be annotated with the same label. Therefore, since the same entity usually appears more than once in the same text, in our case a novel, this procedure guarantees reliable results and better coverage in most cases. Both labeling consistency and the DCA approach rely on the assumption that usage is consistent within the same document by the same author.

The best results in terms of annotation accuracy are achieved when the DCA approach deals with single-word or two-word entities, particularly personal names. But even for these entities there are some exceptions. Table 2 illustrates such a case in H. Bergman's novel *Clownen Jac*.

In this novel, *Sanna* refers to a person, but also to a farm with the same name in a few places in the text, two of which are shown in Table 2. However, our system has annotated almost all single mentions of *Sanna* as a person for lack of a reliable disambiguation context, while a few occurrences of *Sanna* have been annotated as locations, in one case because of the left context *reser till* 'travels to', a typical and reliable context for locations. The labeling consistency hypothesis and the document-centered approach were originally formulated on the basis of the relatively short modern non-fiction texts – typically news items or research article abstracts – which are the normal object of study in NER experiments. A general conclusion to be drawn from cases like the one presented here is perhaps that we should investigate if we can state any useful generalizations about deviations from labeling consistency in texts like the older novels found in *Litteraturbanken*, and subsequently devise appropriate grammar rules in the NER system for dealing with these cases.

Table 1. Positive and ambiguous gender evidence for the person entities (Klement and Akka in the novel Nils Holgerssons underbara resa genom Sverige by S. Lagerlöf)

Animacy label	*Occurrences*	*Text*	*Gloss*	*Gender evidence*
UNU	75	Klement	Klement	ambig.
UNU	10	Klement Larsson	Klement Larsson	ambig.
UNU	1	Klements	Klement's	ambig.
UNM	1	spelmannen Klement Lars-son	folk musician Klement Lars-son	positive
UNM	1	lille Klement Larsson	little Klement Larsson	positive
UNM	1	gubben Klement Larsson	old man Klement Larsson	positive
UNU	144	Akka	Akka	ambig.
FAF	13	mor Akka	mother Akka	positive
FAF	2	gamla mor Akka	old mother Akka	positive

GENDER ATTRIBUTION

Current NER systems are limited to the recognition of a small set of entity types without attempting to make finer distinctions. Our system goes beyond this in the sense that it both deals with a wide range of named entity types and subtypes and also attempts to automatically determine the referential gender of all animate entities. Referential gender relates linguistic expressions, both persons and groups of individuals, to the non-linguistic reality by identifying whether the individual is

Table 2. Data from the novel Clownen Jac by H. Bergman

NE type	*Occurences*	*Text*	*Gloss*
PRS	135	Sanna	Sanna
PRS	13	Sannas	Sanna's
PRS	2	fröken Sanna	Miss Sanna
PRS	1	Sanna själv	Sanna herself
PRS	1	Sannas fästman	Sanna's fiancé
PRS	1	flickan Sanna	the girl Sanna
PRS	1	Caroline och Sanna	Caroline and Sanna
PRS	1	yngsta dottern Sanna	the youngest daughter, Sanna
PRS	1	kusin Sanna	cousin Sanna
LOC	1	Sanna	Sanna
LOC	1	Sanna gård	Sanna Farm

female, male or gender-indefinite (Hellinger & Bußmann, 2001). This is an important piece of information which substantially contributes to better performance in subsequent language processing applications which are based on NER, such as anaphora resolution by filtering out gender-incompatible candidates (Evans & Orasan, 2000). Our approach to gender discrimination is based on applying a combination of the following parameters and observations.

NER has high accuracy in identifying person individuals, person groups as well as animacy designators, a large number of which are assigned gender. In this way, a first distinction is already being made between animate and inanimate entities as well as animate entities that carry gender due to the inherent morphological properties of a large number of common nouns and adjectives. In turn, such annotations can be assigned to other mentions of the same animacy type in a single discourse by collecting gender evidence from the whole document (Table 3).

A pre-classified list containing approximately 16,000 first names is used for assigning gender to known first names. The content of this list has been acquired from various Internet sites. If a person's first name has been assigned gender according to a previous module, then the application of this module does not have any effect on the already assigned gender.

Gender-marked pronouns (grammatical gender) in the vicinity of person entities almost unambiguously refer to an animate entity if certain conditions are fulfilled. This is a form of pronoun resolution in which we try to make simple decisions by matching a person entity or animate common noun denoting, for instance, profession or family relation with the gender-bearing personal pronouns *han* 'he', *hans* 'his', *hon* 'she' and *hennes* 'her'. A number of templates are also applied in this case,

Table 3. Positive and ambiguous gender evidence for the person entity sergeant

Label	*Occurrences*	*Text*	*Gloss*	*Gender evidence*
PRU	54	sergeanten	the sergeant	ambiguous
PRU	41	Sergeanten	the Sergeant	ambiguous
PRU	6	sergeant	sergeant	ambiguous
PRU	5	sergeantens	the sergeant's	ambiguous
PRU	3	Sergeantens	the Sergeant's	ambiguous
PRU	1	Sergeant	Sergeant	ambiguous
PRM	3	*herr* sergeant	Mr sergeant	positive
PRM	3	*herr* sergeanten	the Mr sergeant	positive
PRM	1	sergeanten *Alberts*	the sergeant Albert's	positive
PRM	1	*hygglige* sergeanten	the kind sergeant	positive

such as *hon heter* 'her name is', which assigns female gender to a person named entity following it.

Labeling consistency, discussed in the previous section, which is a technique that operates over the whole annotated text, is also applicable in this case. This module reviews the entire annotated document in order to support animacy and gender attribution of uncertain cases based on unambiguous previous assignments. This is a robust and simple approach that does not rely on pre-compiled statistics of any kind and results in high-speed running performance. In order to capture such consistency we employ a two-stage labeling approach. During the first stage, we note the instances of person entities with unknown gender, and search for a context where the same entity has been assigned gender (male, female) due to a gender-indicating context and for which no other occurrences of the same entity are found in the document with a different gender. If this is the case, then all occurrences of that entity are assigned the same gender throughout the document. Table 3 illustrates this approach with an example taken from the novel *Det går an* by C.J.L. Almqvist.

In this example, the entities *sergeant/sergeanten* 'sergeant/the sergeant' appear in the document either as genderless (ambiguous gender evidence) or as male (positive gender evidence). Many of the subsequent mentions of the same entity are given without any reliable clue for appropriate labeling. However, the entity *sergeanten* is introduced in the document preceded by the adjective *hygglige* 'kind', in which the suffix *-e* signals that the referent of the head noun is of male gender. Since no conflicts are present, i.e., no unambiguously female instances of *sergeant*, all occurrences of *sergeant/sergeanten* are assigned male gender.

During the second stage, the system investigates if there are any conflicting, ambiguous annotations for gender for which the local context and the supporting resources (first name gazetteer) cannot decide the gender attribution. If this is the case and more than one possible annotation for gender is recorded, we choose the most frequent label as that feature for the entity. This is something of an ad-hoc solution – although grounded in the statistics of the text being processed – and in the future we intend to investigate other means for eliminating (possibly marginal) errors caused by this kind of ambiguous use of names in texts. However, we would like to avoid manual disambiguation as far as possible, for reasons given earlier.

RESEARCH DIRECTIONS

As we near the second decade of the 21st century, the sciences have amassed a tremendous amount of digitized information and the task of storing and generating an ever greater volume becomes simpler and more efficient with every passing day. This continuous increase of data in almost every field has afforded individual researchers the unique opportunity of having vast stores of searchable material close at hand. Along with this opportunity, however, comes a further challenge: to create the means whereby they can tap this great potentiality and engage it for the advancement of scientific understanding. The answer lies in eScience – the development of infrastructures, methodologies and designs that enable us to explore this immense repository of data in unprecedented ways, deriving fresh connections and novel facts that may point to the solutions we seek.

Thus far the relatively new notion of eScience has been largely associated with the effort to create a sophisticated architecture that would allow for global collaborations among scientists and the sharing of computational systems, data collections and specialized experimental facilities. Perhaps one of the best known projects is the United Kingdom's *Globus approach to the Grid*, described by its inventors as an infrastructure that enables "flexible, secure, coordinated resource sharing among dynamic collections of individuals, institutions and resources" (Foster, Kesselman & Tuecke, 2001, p. 200).

While this definition of eScience may be wholly applicable to the natural sciences, with their strong reliance upon high-capacity computing facilities and structured data in large databases spread throughout the world, the term must be extended to address the particular challenges faced by researchers in the Humanities, where the general reliance is on textual data and the primary concern is the development of methodologies and tools that will enable the researcher to extract, transform, mine and visualize this type of information in productive ways. To effectively deal with this problem, eScience must include more than infrastructural innovation (the improvement of broad human-to-human collaboration); it must also include fundamental research in Language Technology (LT) and Interaction Design (the improvement of specialized human-to-text and human-to-computer interaction).

The work presented in this chapter represents a modest beginning of such an endeavor, but a necessary first step. The named entity annotations automatically added in *Litteraturbanken*, together with an appropriate search and browsing interface could open new possibilities for literary onomastics studies. For instance, one notes in perusing the literature in this field that studies are generally small-scale (e.g., those presented in Alvarez-Altman & Burelbach, 1987). The strength of the computer lies – here as elsewhere – in its ability to process and correlate large amounts of information and to present this information in ways that make sense to people. Given the right kind of input and the right instructions, computers are capable of producing enlightening bird's eye views of large amounts of data, generalizations, as it were, over massive data sets.

Our work is thus only a very modest first step toward rich new functionality in support of research. One very logical next step will be to provide 'name profiles' for single texts, for authorships, and for whole genres or periods, which could allow literary onomastics research to add an additional level of abstraction in the phenomena studied. An issue in connection with this, however, is to determine which variables are most useful in compiling such profiles, in addition to the entity annotations themselves. Possible candidates would be at least frequency (of individual names and name types), size of onomasticon and distribution of names and name types (interpreted as occurrence in some defined context). Frequency and other empirical quantitative information on linguistic phenomena obtained from language corpora have turned out to offer new interesting insights in linguistics (Ellis, 2002). This could prove to be the case in literary studies as well. We cannot know the answer for sure, unless we actually attempt to produce such quantitative data in a form that makes sense to literary scholars.

Another natural next step would be to add map coordinates to the geographical name annotations. This would then be possible to link geographical names in the text to some mapping application such as Google Maps or GIS (Geographical Information System), for showing where the locations mentioned in text are, either in absolute terms or in relation to one another, on the map. Thus, it would add functionality to the *Litteraturbanken* user interface (cf. Jessop, 2004; van der Sluijs & Houben, 2008).

Like other automatic language technology-based annotation processes, NER is not foolproof. In other words, there will be errors among the named entity annotations, some spurious and rare, and some systematic and irritating to the user, as when, for instance, the name of a main character of a novel is erroneously classified as a place name. We probably need to include in the user interface a means for allowing the user to override system annotations, and possibly even to modify the system gazetteers. This would allow us to experiment with approaches in which the NER system learns from interaction with its users, thereby extending research on self-learning systems in language technology (Olsson 2008) into a partly new problem area and a new user category.

As we have seen, our NER system does not pick out only proper names of people, but actually endeavors to locate and annotate all human entities in the texts. Information about entities gathered in the course of analysis of the full text of a single literary work by combining entity mentions facilitates the collection and aggregation of entity profiles, for instance person profiles of the main characters. In the same way, identification of place and time expressions allows us to locate the characters in time and space. Working towards the integration of richer entity descriptions in the form of identifying and attaching meta-labels to entities in the text will allow more semantically-oriented exploration of texts by computer. This means that not only the proper names as such but also pronoun mentions and other linguistic indicators (cf. Bontcheva, Dimitrov, Maynard, Tablan, & Cunningham, 2002) closely related to an entity such as family mentions (*hennes make* 'her husband') can be identified and integrated into structured formats that will allow a user exploration of, e.g., social networks of characters.

In short, our results are important for:

- improving information access to the content of texts, enabling semantic querying of the texts;
- supporting advanced and more sophisticated indexing, searching and browsing;
- allowing automatic metadata enhancement of literary texts;
- enhancing the performance of various corpus processing tools – such as concordancing software – through the added value provided by named entities;
- allowing cross-searching and linking between characters of the same author and even other information sources of that time.

As already mentioned, we believe that such functionality will enable literary scholars to add a level of abstraction to studies of literature, by allowing them to work comfortably with the much larger text materials that are now being put online in digitization endeavors in a number of countries. Moreover, *Litteraturbanken* and the language technology tools used in processing it are being built to conform to emerging international standards and best practices in language technology (Section 3.1), as well as to be compatible with emerging Grid infrastructure (see above). As similar goals are being pursued in a number of countries, this will in the long run make it comparatively easier than at present to construct multilingual systems. Such systems will make it possible, for instance, to compare name usages in a number of national literatures in Europe. Correspondingly, other kinds of linguistic annotation would allow further comparisons across literary traditions.

CONCLUSION

In this chapter, we have tried to argue that language technology in the form of named entity recognition and annotation systems can be usefully applied for building computer applications to support literary research and also other kinds of text-based scholarship. We are aware that the increasing availability of literary texts in large numbers in digital form holds the potential for extending and expanding this kind of text study, which so far normally has been conducted on single texts or even text fragments. We have argued that given the right kind of technical support – automatic named entity recognition and annotation technology in this case –, this potential can begin to be tapped in fruitful ways. Using these resources, we are able to automatically mark up literary works with information about the named entities appearing in them, at the same time as these works are added to the online repository of classical Swedish literature described in this chapter. This information in turn forms the basis for computer tools that researchers could utilize for investigating the uses of names in literature from a number of different angles. The first tool that we have implemented is a basic named entity search and browsing facility. Other tools are in the pipeline, as are other additional kinds of annotations, but in both cases they will of course need to be developed in close cooperation with literary scholars. It is our belief that the large-scale automatic entity annotations described in this chapter will allow new kinds of qualitative and quantitative exploitations of literary and historical texts, contributing an important building block to the emerging field of the digital Humanities.

On a final note, it is necessary to stress that what we have described in this chapter is an aid for *locating* and partly *classifying* names and other entities in Swedish literary texts. It cannot help – in any other than the most superficial way – in the literary *analysis* of names and name usages in literary texts. Instead, we see its role as taking some of the mechanical drudgery out of this work for the human scholars, allowing them to devote the time thus freed to ultimately more rewarding analytical research activities conducted on much larger text masses than has traditionally been the case, thus allowing more encompassing generalizations to be formulated.

REFERENCES

Alvarez-Altman, G., & Burelbach, F. M. (Eds.). (1987). *Names in literature: Essays from Literary Onomastics Studies*. Lanham, MD: University Press of America.

Bontcheva, K., Dimitrov, M., Maynard, D., Tablan, V., & Cunningham, H. (2002). Shallow methods for named entity coreference resolution. In *Proceedings of Traitement Automatique des Langues Naturelles*. Nancy: TALN.

Borin, L., & Forsberg, M. (2008). Something old, something new: A computational morphological description of Old Swedish. In *LREC 2008 Workshop on Language Technology for Cultural Heritage Data (LaTeCH 2008)* (pp. 9-16). Marrakech: ELRA.

Borin, L., Kokkinakis, D., & Olsson, L.-J. (2007). Naming the past: Named entity and animacy recognition in 19th century Swedish literature. In *Proceedings of the ACL Workshop: Language Technology for Cultural Heritage Data (LaTeCH)* (pp. 1-8). Prague: ACL.

Bradley, J. (2005). What you foresee is what you get: Thinking about usage paradigms for computer assisted text analysis. *TEXT Technology*, *2*, 1–19.

Ellis, N. C. (2002). Frequency effects in language processing. *Studies in Second Language Acquisition, 24*(2), 143–188.

Evans, R., & Orasan, C. (2000). Improving anaphora resolution by identifying animate entities in texts. In *Proceedings of the DAARC 2000*. (pp. 154-162). Lancaster, UK.

Fan, W., Wallace, L., Rich, S., & Zhang, Z. (2006). Tapping the power of text mining. *Communications of the ACM, 49*(9), 77–82. doi:10.1145/1151030.1151032

Flanders, J., Bauman, S., Caton, P., & Cournane, M. (1998). Names proper and improper: Applying the TEI to the classification of proper nouns. *Computers and the Humanities, 31*(4), 285–300. doi:10.1023/A:1001066508011

Fleischman, M., & Hovy, E. (2002). Fine grained classification of named entities. In *Proceedings of the 19th International Conference on Computational linguistics* (pp. 1-7). Taipei: ACL.

Foster, I., Kesselman, C., & Tuecke, S. (2001). The anatomy of the Grid: Enabling scalable virtual organizations. *The International Journal of Supercomputer Applications, 15*(3), 200–222. doi:10.1177/109434200101500302

Hellinger, M., & Bußmann, H. (Eds.). Gender across languages: The linguistic representation of women and men.: *Vol. 1. IMPACT: Studies in Language and Society 9*. Amsterdam: John Benjamins.

Ide, N., & Romary, L. (2002). Standards for language resources. In *Proceedings of the Third Language Resources and Evaluation Conference (LREC)* (pp. 839-844). Las Palmas: ELRA.

Jackson, P., & Moulinier, I. (2007). *Natural language processing for online applications: Text retrieval, extraction and categorization*. Amsterdam: John Benjamins.

Jessop, M. (2004). The visualization of spatial data in the humanities. *Literary and Linguistic Computing, 19*(3), 335–350. doi:10.1093/llc/19.3.335

Johannessen, J. B., Hagen, K., Haaland, Å., Björk Jónsdóttir, A., Nøklestad, A., & Kokkinakis, D. (2005). Named entity recognition for the mainland Scandinavian languages. *Literary and Linguistic Computing, 20*(1), 91–102. doi:10.1093/llc/fqh045

Juola, P. (2008). Killer applications in digital humanities. *Literary and Linguistic Computing, 23*(1), 73–83. doi:10.1093/llc/fqm042

Kokkinakis, D. (2004). Reducing the effect of name explosion. In *Proceedings of the LREC Workshop: Beyond Named Entity Recognition – Semantic Labeling for NLP*. Lisbon: ELRA.

Kokkinakis, D., & Thurin, A. (2007). Anonymisation of Swedish clinical data. In *Proceedings of the 11th Conference on Artificial Intelligence in Medicine (AIME 07)*. Amsterdam.

McCallum, A. (2005). Information extraction: Distilling structured data from unstructured text. *Queue*, *3*(9), 48–57. doi:10.1145/1105664.1105679

Mikheev, A. (2000). Document centered approach to text normalization. In *Proceedings of the 23rd ACM SIGIR Conference on Research and Development in Information Retrieval* (pp. 136-143). Athens.

Olsson, F. (2008). *Bootstrapping named entity annotation by means of active machine learning: A method for creating corpora*. Data linguistica 21. Department of Swedish Language, University of Gothenburg. Retrieved from http://spraakdata.gu.se/publikationer/datalinguistica/DL21.pdf

Pettersson, G. (2005). *Svenska språket under sjuhundra år: En historia om svenskan och dess utforskande*. Lund: Studentlitteratur.

Pilz, T., Ernst-Gerlach, A., Kempken, S., Rayson, P., & Archer, D. (2008). The identification of spelling variants in English and German historical texts: Manual or automatic? *Literary and Linguistic Computing*, *23*, 65–72. doi:10.1093/llc/fqm044

Ravin, Y., & Kazi, Z. (1999). Is Hillary Rodham Clinton the President? Disambiguating names across documents. In *Workshop on Coreference and Its Applications*. Maryland.

Rayson, P., Archer, D., Baron, A., Culpeper, J., & Smith, N. (2007). Tagging the Bard: Evaluating the accuracy of a modern POS tagger on Early Modern English corpora. In *Proceedings of Corpus Linguistics 2007, University of Birmingham, UK*. Retrieved September 14, 2008 from http://www.corpus.bham.ac.uk/corpling-proceedings07/index.htm

Sekine, S. (2004). Definition, dictionaries and tagger for extended named entity hierarchy. In *Proceedings of the Language Resources and Evaluation Conference (LREC)*. Lisbon: ELRA.

Svedjedal, J. (2004). Almqvist och namnen. En studie i litterär onomastik. *Samlaren*, *125*, 52–77.

Teleman, U. (2005). Language cultivation and language planning II: Swedish. In Bandle, O. (Eds.), *The Nordic languages: An international handbook of the history of the North Germanic languages* (*Vol. 2*, pp. 1970–1983). Berlin: Walter de Gruyter.

Text Encoding Initiative. (n.d.). Retrieved September 13, 2008, http://www.tei-c.org

Tjong Kim Sang, E., & De Meulder, F. (2003). Introduction to the CoNLL-2003 Shared Task: Language-independent named entity recognition. In [Edmonton, Canada: ACL.]. *Proceedings of CoNLL, 2003*, 142–147.

van Dalen-Oskam, K. (2005). Comparative literary onomastics. Retrieved September 6, 2008, from http://www.huygensinstituut.knaw.nl/index.php?option=com_content&task=view&id=197&Itemid=118

van Dalen-Oskam, K., & van Zundert, J. (2004). Modelling features of characters: Some digital ways of looking at names in literary texts. *Literary and Linguistic Computing, 19*(3), 289–301. doi:10.1093/llc/19.3.289

van der Sluijs, K., & Houben, G.-J. (2008). Metadata-based access to cultural heritage collections: The RHCe use case. In *Proceedings of the 2nd International Workshop on Personalized Access to Cultural Heritage (PATCH'2008)*. (pp. 15-25). Hanover.

XCES. (2008). *XCES: Corpus encoding standard for XML*. Retrieved September 13, 2008, from http://www.xces.org

ADDITIONAL READING

Adolphs, S. (2006). Introducing electronic text analysis: A practical guide for language and literary studies. Abingdon: Routledge.

Anderson, J. M. (2007). *The grammar of names*. Oxford: Oxford University Press. doi:10.1093/acprof:oso/9780199297412.001.0001

Eichler, E., Hilty, G., Löffler, H., Steger, H., & Zgusta, L. (Eds.). (1996). *Namenforschung/Name studies/Les noms propres: Ein internationales Handbuch zur Onomastik/ An international handbook of onomastics/Manuel international d'onomastique* (*Vol. 1–2*). Berlin: Walter de Gruyter.

Hockey, S. (2000). *Electronic texts in the humanities: Principles and practice*. Oxford: Oxford University Press.

Lendvai, P., & Borin, L. (Eds.). (2009). *Proceedings of the EACL 2009 Workshop on Language Technology and Resources for Cultural Heritage, Social Sciences, Humanities, and Education (LaTeCH -- SHELT&R 2009)*. Athens: ACL. Retrieved from http://www.aclweb.org/anthology-new/W/W09/#0300

McCrank, L. J. (2002). *Historical information science: An emerging unidiscipline*. Medford, NJ: Information Today, Inc.

Mitkov, R. (Ed.). (2003). *The Oxford handbook of computational linguistics*. Oxford: Oxford University Press.

Nadeau, D., & Sekine, S. (2007). A survey of named entity recognition and classification. *Lingvisticæ Investigationes, 30*(1), 3–26. doi:10.1075/li.30.1.03nad

Nerbonne, J. (2005). Computational contributions to the Humanities. *Literary and Linguistic Computing, 20*(1), 25–40. doi:10.1093/llc/fqh041

Chapter 4
Collocation as Instrumentation for Meaning: A Scientific Fact

Bill Louw
University of Zimbabwe, Zimbabwe

ABSTRACT

Until fairly recently, linguistics has been classified as a 'science' by definition, averral, and ideology rather than because of the uniformity of its practices across its many schools of thought. It is seldom the case in any discipline that a particular phenomenon begins to question that discipline's raison d'etre, *withdraw the option and luxury of its often directionless and eclectic practices and proceed to force unwelcome and sweeping changes upon the discipline by beginning to dictate its method. This paper re-states its author's earlier proofs as* claims *that collocation as instrumentation for meaning is a scientific fact. The burden of this proof has acquired renewed urgency of an interdisciplinary nature that makes this paper both timely and necessary. The claim for collocation as science is reinforced by a number of new discoveries: the fact that all* devices *are brought about by* relexicalisation *as a* marked form *rather than the purported markedness that is mentalist and hence, merely averred.*

DOI: 10.4018/978-1-60566-932-8.ch004

INTRODUCTION

J.R. Firth wrote that scientific facts do not exist until they are claimed (in F.R. Palmer ed., 1968: 43) according to scientific criteria. This chapter sets out to claim scientific status for collocation as multi-purpose instrumentation for language. In doing so, it will demonstrate the power of collocation as a single, reliable form of instrumentation for language as: (1) the main linguistic source of empirical access to the context of situation and culture (Firth, 1957; Malinowski, 1935; Sinclair, 2006); (2) the primary empirical means for data-assisted reading in general, such as the detection of spin. This almost invariably involves the reading of suasive texts for what is missing from them physically but remains instantiated empirically and recoverably in their collocates (Louw, 2004; Mahlberg, (Chapter 7, in Hoey et al, 2007: 196). Corpus stylistics uses the same techniques (Louw, 2007a); (3) the determinant of verbal art (Louw, 2007b) and the sketcher of literary worlds (Louw, 2007b; 2008a); (4) the source of markedness (Enkvist, 1973) of all literary devices, including humour through relexicalisation (Louw, 2008a; 2008b), all other mentalist theories, such as that of lexical priming (Hoey, 2005) being only purportedly (Louw, 2007c) rather that recoverably marked; (5) semantic prosody (Louw, 1993; 2000); and (6) the means for automating or falsifying literary, linguistic and stylistic theories (Louw, 2008c; 2010, forthcoming).

The major concern of this paper will be to explain collocation as a scientifically respectable instrument and to demonstrate and integrate its use in the digital automation of deeper forms of reading, criticism, methodology and the automation or falsification of linguistic and stylistic theories.

SCIENCE, COLLOCATION AND THE QUESTION OF METHOD

Paradigm shifts in science invariably require for their successful occurrence either new discoveries or the irrational replacement of one paradigm with another as science begins to 'prefer' a new paradigm to an existing one (Bullock and Trombley, 2000: 755). But for the signal absence of the computer, the worlds of philosophy, linguistics and science might have been ready for momentous changes leading to linguistic instrumentation as early as 1921. However, the synergy created by the scholarship of Frege (1884), Wittgenstein (1922), Carnap, (1928), Russell (1946), Firth, (1957)Malinowski (1935) and Markoff (1913) has remained temporarily both analogue and end-stopped because of the absence of the computer at that time. The possibility of all factors necessary for a scientific revolution coming together has always fired the imagination of theorists. For example, Caspi (1998) speculates on the forms of deliberation that might have taken place between distinguished scholars in the rooms in Cambridge of C.P. Snow on the eve of the creation of the first computer. Snow's fictional list of invitees included Alan Turing (1912-1954), who is generally acknowledged as the inventor of modern computing. British Prime Minister, Gordon Brown recently apologized to Turing's family for the manner in which Alan had been treated on account of his gender orientation. Brown did not mention the extent to which Turin's 'thinking machine' had been seen as a threat to security.

However, this paper proposes a more scientific alternative based upon the manifest ability of collocation to falsify or automate not only the theories of philosophers, linguists and stylisticians, but also its ability to falsify fake institutions. These are the intellectual (*sic*) products of spin doctors in collaboration, often secretly and with the direct assistance of qualified professionals within the law and the unspoken support of governments. British Prime Minister, Gordon Brown declared that spin was dead, but as recently as April, 2009, it was discovered that the spin section based at 12 Downing Street was still in place. Among the issues apparently dealt with by this organization were the Truth and Reconciliation Commission of South Africa (Louw, 2003) and the Weapons of Mass Destruction Report [WMDR] that went missing shortly before the invasion of Iraq. The invitation back into government of Lord Mandelson may well turn out to be a related event.

The advent of collocation as instrumentation for language (Louw, 2007a; 2007b; 2008a), will involve the removal of huge obstacles within the discipline of linguistics. These include inter alia the demotion of syntax, the disappearance of word-meaning, the dismissal of concepts and the demise through their direct falsification of intuitively-derived theories (Louw, 2007d). The fact that this move is already under way may sound unsettling, but there is nothing about it that J.R. Firth had not foreseen in 1957 as he wrote the lines below that formed the impetus of John Sinclair's research on collocation and culminated in the OSTI Report (Krishnamurthy, 2004).

Meaning by collocation is an abstraction at the syntagmatic level and is not directly concerned with the conceptual or idea approach to the meaning of words. One of the meanings of ***night*** *is its collocability with* ***dark****. (Firth, 1957:181) (emphasis added)*

The scientific facts to which this paper lays claim have already been set out (Louw, 2000; now also kindly reprinted by Professor Francois Rastier: http://www.revue-texto.net/index.php?id=124) but, at the time, that paper was written only in the expectation that the community of linguists would accept it as science. This did not occur. These same scientific claims will now be pursued more vigorously in this chapter.

As a direct result of the automation, by digital collocation of Firth's remarks above, we are likely to find in future that an absence of empiricism within a theory will come to be synonymous with the presence of intuitively-derived and hence falsifiable elements (Popper, 1959; see also Chateau: 2007; Preston, 2008).

It may be the case that the scientific revolution involving collocation as instrumentation for language will need to be dealt with, at least initially, *not* by linguists, but by representatives of those sections of scholarship that possess better-established conventions for dealing with both the nature and advent of paradigm shifts. In other words, it may be better to involve *philosophers* (who deal with uncertain knowledge) and *scientists* (to whom philosophers hand over knowledge once they can prove that its status has become 'settled') (Russell, 1960: 11). Sadly, linguists and stylisticians continue to cling to 'schools of thought' with such a high degree of sentimentality that it is likely to place them in danger of clouding their own scientific judgment (Louw, 2003).

But, when John Sinclair used the term 'trust the text' for the first time at a conference on Systemic Functional Linguistics in July 1990 and later as the title of a book, was he motivated by a sense of ecumenism alone? His motive was to see the corpus as a form of truth within theory that was so compelling as to be converting, and this to the point that his readers might abandon their existing theories for new ones: 'It is impossible to study patterned data without some theory, however primitive' (Sinclair, 2004a: 10). There *is* theory here. No filing cabinet is implied. The corpus was to be accorded the respect or primacy due to it. No linguists responded. Russell (1948) had the same intention. He was appalled when his readership failed to notice the scientific power that he had brought to logical positivism by refining it in the direction of logical atomism. Apparently responsible academics sailed blithely on into the future of scholarship in the absence of the scientific rigour that Russell had provided. As a result, knowledge that was fairly settled remained with philosophy. It was not handed over to science, as convention within philosophy demands. The machinery has become 'stuck' and the belated handover needs now to be prompted.

The Decision to Involve Philosophy and Science

Some appreciation of the evidence involved is to be found routinely in the appearance and content of a simple KWIC (Key Word in Context) concordance (See also, Sinclair, 2004b). A concordance may be a better vehicle for explaining the paradigm shift than any exposition merely written in prose. Just as Sinclair uses the term 'chunking' (1991: 124; Sinclair and Maurenen, 2006: *passim*) to refer to the way in which readers break texts up into meaningful units, so digital collocation, 'abstracted from syntax' (Firth, 1957: 196) 'chunks' experience into the facts, states of affairs or *Sachverhalten* that comprise the world. Wittgenstein (1922: 7) effectively described the world with great economy about 73 years before the second edition of the *Cobuild Dictionary* marked the advent of corpora large enough for the present tasks of automation and falsification (Sinclair, 1995).

1. The world is all that is the case

1.2 The world is the totality of facts not of things (Wittgenstein, 1922: 7)

Seen today from a Wittgensteinian perspective, the frequency lists that accompanied the creation of the first corpus-based dictionaries dealt mostly with things (produced as 'thin' word lists), whereas the collocates of those 'things' chunk the context of situation and culture into facts or *Sachverhalten* (Sinclair, 2006) (produced as 'fat' concordances) and force us to recognise the moment at which collocation automates Wittgenstein's (1922) Picture Theory of Meaning. This means that if collocates that are *co-selected*, are capable between them of chunking a repeatable state of affairs or *fact (Sachverhalt)*, that fact will correspond to the first of two theses that Wittgenstein proposed in the *Tractatus*: (1) the propositions of factual language are pictures; and, (2) the propositions of logic are tautologies (Mautner, 2000: 602). Wittgenstein was convinced that the latter might be dropped in favour of what he termed 'the logic of our own language'. Tautologies picture nothing (Urmson, 1956). The computer is capable of demonstrating that apparent tautologies, such as *business is business* when taken from corpora of natural language are, *facts* or *Sachverhalten* (states of affairs). We can only speculate about how Russell might have reacted to the fact that the phrase is uttered by persons to anyone whose requests threaten profitability.

Wittgenstein's (1922) definition of facts or what Russell (1946: 298) later terms events (see also, Louw, 2008c) have much in common. This is doubtless the product of their acrimonious but deep collaboration at Cambridge. Wittgenstein not only defines facts as states of affairs, but he locates them within logical space, an issue that is at the centre of his vision for 'natural language philosophy' in both his early and later work.

An example of instrumentation in action is in order at this point. (Source: *The Times,* 1995)

```
MicroConcord search SW: untenable CW: position
80 characters per entry
Sort: 2L/SW    unshifted.
1  alternative to what has become an untenable position over Bosnia.   Russia has
2 s position has become increasingly untenable. As chief executive of securities t
```

3 8, said his position had been made untenable. He added: "I am taking legal advic

4 n, M Juppe's position could become untenable. Last night M Juppe dismissed the r

5 res could make Mr Davis's position untenable; he submitted a report to the Natio

6 hat Mr Lewis's position had become untenable when the Parkhurst trio escaped: Ju

7 y regulator's position had become "untenable". After that meeting with his cha

8 o sterling, she found her position untenable. She recalls her embarrassment when

9 Mr Crawford had found his position untenable after the Princess gave the intervi

10 n. Mr Banks, 58,found his position untenable after his constituency party voted

11 ions that could makes his position untenable. The Editor of the News of the Worl

12 a cover-up will make his position untenable. MPs believe he should have found

13 evelations would make his position untenable. Jack Cunningham, Labour's Shadow N

14 saying that he finds his position untenable. "It is no longer possible for me t

15 M Juppe's position awkward, if not untenable. The Government's embarrassment was

16 failed, leaving the company in an "untenable position". Fay was sent back to Bri

17 bsidiaries found "themselves in an untenable position". The failure of the com

18 ways instruct her. But she's in an untenable position now. They'll have to make

19 Shell Group find themselves in an untenable position and feel it is not possibl

20 r. Such a position is increasingly untenable and will culminate in a humiliating

21 r post as her position is becoming untenable. She has sold her Washington house

22 governments had made its position untenable. It would now seek permission to di

23 tions, to make Mr Major's position untenable. This theory does not stand up. The

24 Date> <Headline>Easby moves into untenable position</headline> <byline>By Da

25 cribed Claes's position in Nato as untenable. "The highest court does not lightl

26 ip described London's position as "untenable and unobtainable". The statement ca

27 rce: Pennant-Rea's position became untenable not so much because it was immoral

28 on-event". But his position became untenable when Judge Jean-Marie d'Huy, in cha

29 old Mr Lewis that his position was untenable and discussed a statement that coul

30 r Foster, but that position became untenable when the nominee shone at his confi

31 at the SIB's present position was "untenable". The directors gave their "full su

32 hat the SIB's present position is "untenable". He and his fellow frontline reg

33 chael thought Lewis's position was untenable," said an aide. "There was no way h

34 ite rare. If someone's position is untenable, they usually resign." Anyone fac

35 lead to Mr Li's position becoming untenable, despite the protection he has from

36 to make his position increasingly untenable." Alan Williams, Labour member of

37 y "pro-choice" position completely untenable. Many Republicans would probably

38 the Home Secretary's position was untenable. Downing Street reiterated, however

39, realised that their position was untenable. Therefore, they invoked force maje

40 n. In the end, the position became untenable. "Margin calls have been made and

41 uld make their position absolutely untenable. However, Malcolm Rifkind, the Defe

42 to make his position increasingly untenable." Much of the questioning by Mr P

43 said that Mr Aitken's position was untenable. "The unavoidable fact is that he w
44 ead him to believe his position is untenable. Nobody with the good of the Engl
45 ake the Prince of Wales's position untenable," said Lord St John of Fawsley. "He
46 ritain's position was increasingly untenable. "While that case runs, the other c
47 d Lord Mackay's position would be "untenable" if his divorce reforms, which have

In the example above, the output of the concordancer indicates that the node *untenable*, **co-selected** with the context word *position*, no more than 4 words apart, occur 47 times as collocates in the continuous newspaper corpus of 44 million words (one calendar year's worth of newspaper, kindly supplied to the author by the late Tim Johns) from which they were drawn. This means that they occur almost once every million words, or once every 948,881 words to be precise. The co-selected expression marks with great precision a particular state of affairs or *Sachverhalt* in Wittgenstein's (1922: 7) terms that could not be isolated by any other form of digital instrumentation available to us, apart from a collocator with a co-selection facility.

Other forms of technology provide only a partial picture. For example, a frequency list for the language that informs us of the frequency ranking of the term *position* would be of no use to us at all. Such a list, as mentioned earlier, concentrates on what Wittgenstein would have classified as *things* rather than *Sachverhalten* or facts. It is only because the two co-selected terms together constitute a fact in Wittgenstein's terms, i.e. a combination of function and argument (*Fa*) in Frege's (1884) method or a Russellian event (Russell, 1948: 97), that the empiricism of the concordance is helpful to the point of providing us with an accessible, respectable, scientific extract from the vast empiricism of experience captured within a corpus.

Notice that this concordance represents a fairly common event that appears in no dictionary, but is, nonetheless instantly recognisable. Collocation automates Frege's (1885) distinction between *Sense and Reference* well as the theories of Firth (1957) and Malinowski (1935). Futhermore, proof that the philosophers were thinking along the lines of differentiating items such as events and occasions is to be found in the following quote from the philosopher A.J. Ayer. Note how accurately it describes the content of a concordance such as the one above, long before such concordances became available. As we read it, we appreciate the disservice that linguistics has done philosophy by failing to point out, on an interdisciplinary level, the fact that settled knowledge has arrived.

"What we are seeking is a difference in type, a difference in the way the respective ranges are constituted, and I think that I can see what this difference is, though I have not been able to find a very satisfactory way of describing it. In the case of a predicate, the ground which we have for saying that the different occasions to which it applies exemplify the same situation, namely the situation which the predicate signifies, is the situation of qualitative resemblance." (Ayer, 1954: 13)

No 'Event' Dictionary Exists: Instrumentation Makes it Unnecessary

The event set out above is instantly recognisable to all adult readers, some of whom may have experienced the phrase both at first hand and poignantly, immediately prior to the request for their resignation on account of some misdemeanour, purported or real. These '*misdemeanours'* mostly occur linguistically to the *left* of the component words of the co-selected expression. To the *righ*t we may expect the outcome or result of finding one's position untenable (e.g. lines 20 and 34). Note how the concordance acts as an instrument of event-analysis: the node (which effectively divides the page in half down the middle) declares the cessation of tolerance for the misdemeanour to the left of it and points to the resolution of the problem or attitudes of defiance to the right.

If the phrase *position+untenable* does not fall within the direct experience as sense-data (Russell, 1912) of reader/hearers, such reader/hearers are still likely to be aware of this type of event because it may have affected their colleagues or acquaintances in the past. Within Bertrand Russell's (1948) work, the term *sense-datum* is gradually replaced during its development by the better-elaborated term *event.* Each concordance line is likely to represent a separate instance of a similar event. We saw this desire earlier also in the passage quoted from the pre-computational work of Ayer. This apparently unremarkable fact accounts for the huge effort of standardisation that we witness in other disciplines: the creation of laboratory conditions required for an experiment.

So, where, we may ask, is the philosophical and scientific power in what we are witnessing as we stare at this concordance? The answer to this question would have induced a sense of shock in the pre-computational mind. However, the post-computational mind may already, today, find the explanation banal, even where an explanation has never before been attempted. Much of the power is to be found in the fact that co-selection concentrates upon a particular type of event and upon no other. The 'logic of our own language' as Wittgenstein ([1953] 2005: 93, section 345) termed it, is easily spotted if and only if a particular state of affairs is isolated by and as the product of collocational co-selection. All the other events of human life except the one being observed are of no concern unless they share the same collocates as those that have been co-selected.

Within the space of the calendar year of a newspaper corpus, all the other intervening states of affairs of daily life are, as it were, lost between the individual citations or concordance lines. The concordancer, by co-selection, selects facts from life and simultaneously keeps the empiricism pure by trimming away all other factual experience. The procedure and method are their own Petri dish (Louw, 2008b; 2008d).[1]

The time gap between two contiguous concordance lines may be of significance to any future science that chooses to deal with the nature of events. For example, *untenable positions* may occur only a matter of weeks apart, while events such as military activity carried out by mercenaries may occur only once every seven years (Louw, 2008c)[2]. Events such as the appearance of Halley's Comet may rate a mention more frequently than the comet appears physically, but the time between different appearances of the comet may be isolated by co-selecting dates such as 18* or 19*. However we proceed, only the co-selected facts will appear. All other events in a 44 million-word corpus or even a 550 million-word corpus are held in abeyance until they become material to the picture embodied in a separate search. Once a co-selection has been made, all other events are shut out by the instrumentation and are shown the door (Pears, 1971: 70), because Wittgensteinstein's method not only identifies the properties of states of affairs, but it shows us, simultaneously, what states of affairs are *not*. This accords with John Sinclair's dual vision (1991: 25) of *life* being sampled by a corpus of natural language that is itself a *living* document 'of no final extent'. Everything else is relegated to the background while the concordancer focuses upon one event alone that has been singled out for consideration. One powerful aspect of the instrumentation is that all other potential distractions from the stream of experience are shut out while a single event is dealt with (Louw, 2008b).

The process allows us particularly powerful findings as we open each context for closer reading: men whose position is untenable often refuse to resign and do not do so. Women in the same position may refuse to resign but are ultimately generally removed from office *by men*. Thus, when we next encounter the expression *position+untenable*, our question as reader/hearer will no longer be: 'What was the offence?' but 'Is the accused male or female?' Intuition has literally become data-driven by the empiricism of the example (Tognini-Bonelli, 2001: 44).

COLLOCATION AND SEMANTIC PROSODY

Further scientific proof for collocation as instrumentation is to be found in the fact that events are shaped probabilistically and logically (Carnap, 1956). Each event carries with it a predictable coterie of accompanying collocates. Many of these determine its precise nature and structure as a fact. For example, an event that involves the formation of an untenable position may not solidify overnight. The situation may develop and deteriorate progressively over a period of time. Collocates will mark this within the event and verifiably across other corpora of natural language. The forms *increasingly*, *become* and *became* testify to this in the concordance above.

A similar profiling of collocates characterizes other events, for example where the term events is itself metalingually involved in a reversal. In the case of the node *turn+of+events,* the collocates combine to offer a semantic prosody (Louw, 1993; 2000) of unexpectedness and shock. Note how the ontological meaning of the semantic prosody is found to subsist more vividly in the disruption of expectation caused by a *turn of events* rather than anything inherent in the contextual situation to the left or to the right of the node within particular instances. These collocates of surprise and shock are set out in bold type in the concordance below. Items that appear in bold, italics and underlined are candidates for being considered ironic or insincere as turns of events. Exceptions to a semantic prosody are at the heart of their scientific respectability because the exceptions have their own descript structure (Bacon, 1605). Some turns of events manifestly operate to the advantage of others, especially where they have been engineered (Louw, 1993). Those who find a turn of events delightful, positive or amusing are themselves 'read' morally by the event itself. Such instances indicate the availability of empiricism for carrying out ethical evaluations of situations using natural language, an issue hitherto deemed virtually impossible by modern philosophers, but always included by ancient Western philosophy as a component of its four-part syllabus: metaphysics, epistemology, ethics and aesthetics. An example from the Bank of English records that Adolf Hitler, upon hearing that Japan had joined the war on the side of Germany '...was delighted by this turn of events.'

We find in the concordance below that the sense of shock is often most keenly felt where the narrative takes the form of averral as testimony in the first person; for example, by someone who has just realized that he/she is being *framed.* (Source: The Times, 1995)

MicroConcord search SW: turn of events

80 characters per entry

Sort: 1L/SW unshifted.

1 things **suddenly** got **worse** with a turn of events so **improbable** that I still can't

2 shareholders, be party to such a turn of events"? The answer is simple. There is

3 **osing** his wicket to Salisbury, a turn of events not at all to the young man's ta

4 ecause, last week, in an **amazing** turn of events, I found myself nodding in agree

5 ment of **defeat.** This **astonishing** turn of events was the **result** of several factor

6 when Asprey unveiled the latest turn of events in its colourful history. The

7 yers were **dismayed** by the latest turn of events, which **interrupted** a critical ph

8 xpress my **distress** at the recent turn of events (report, February 13). I can u

9 s much **frustration** at the second turn of events as he did pleasure over the firs

10 o bowl his off-spin. A **strange** turn of events, which had everything to do with

11 re Italy invaded. The subsequent turn of events there meant that his pictures we

12 e UN forces is very **upset** at the turn of events, there being no intention to cau
13 wever, reasonably ***happy*** with the turn of events this season. They may not be dom
14 n Britain, are **astonished** at the turn of events. Cantona began this year in such
15, to save the government. "The turn of events had left me in a **distraught stat**
16 We are frankly **astonished** at the turn of events. We were used to living rough an
17 opponent and were **aghast** at the turn of events. In America, from where the in
18 ters, are hugely ***relieved*** by the turn of events, keeping the player Ferguson des
19 Sanderson was **devastated** by the turn of events and later left Bovis, as the pro
20 Oxford's **disappointment** at this turn of events was allayed to some extent by Ca
21 Brian were full of hope and this turn of events was totally **unexpected** for them
22 in a gay disco. Crucially, this turn of events **threatens** the lifelong friendshi
23 them again after September. This turn of events will, I am sure, ***inspire*** Donald
24 st have been a further **unnerving** turn of events for Spring. Spring had led the L

It is worth noting that these levels of determinism satisfy Berofsky (1971) rather less than they might Malinowski (1935), Russell (1946) or Sinclair, (2006). However, there is no doubt that we are witnessing converting levels of scientific attainment within attempts to make contextual and co-textual studies reliable empirically, just as Firth had envisaged and often well beyond the realm of syntax alone.

Meaning by collocation is an abstraction at the syntagmatic level and is not directly concerned with the conceptual or idea approach to the meaning of words. One meaning of night is its collocability with dark [...](in Palmer, 1957 [1968]: 197)

Futhermore, Russell (1946) makes a key concession that enables philosophy to effect the handover of settled knowledge to science. What follows below is of key importance to the claiming of a scientific fact and upon it our case rests. Almost all of Russell (1948) is devoted to deduction. The fact that it received very little attention from his readership may our best indication of why the handover to science has become a grey area.

Induction is an independent logical principle, incapable of being inferred either from experience or from other logical principles, and that without this principle science is impossible. (Russell, 1946:. 647)

A key criterion of science is versatility of application. This paper continues by offering examples associated with the domains set out in the introduction. The illustrations that follow are all in the nature of applied studies in digital collocation.

Literary Worlds as Collocation

Wittgenstein (1922:7) may have envisaged the possible existence of Frege's (1884) *subsets* of *that* world that is the set of all sets. Some of these might well be termed fictional worlds (Sinclair, 1987), although they might be deemed by philosophers to subsist with another branch of philosophy: aesthetics. Either way, this would constitute further proof that collocation is instrumentation for literary or fictional worlds and is fairly easily supplied, both within corpora of a writer's work and by comparing it with the world as sampled by large corpora of natural language (Louw, 2008a). Differences of quality would be recoverable in the lexical fabric of the corpus. One might hypothesise that a corpus of fiction is likely to be more strongly lexicalised. The world of a literary artist such as a poet will be characterized not by its things, but by its facts or states of affairs. If we study the descending word frequency list for the collected poetry of Philip Larkin, we find that by the time that we reach the first fully lexicalised words in his poetry, we are immediately thrown back upon collocation to deal with our discovery through empiricism of such a major insight into his literary world. The pair of words to be examined usually comes as a surprise to readers and is not attested by their intuition as we shall see below. In the case of Larkin, these terms are *day* and *night*. Note how the former is tinged with the latter within the poet's world-view in the sample concordance that follows. (Source: *The Collected Poetry of Philip Larkin,* edited by Anthony Thwaite, 1988, Faber and Faber, London and Boston.)[3]

```
MicroConcord search SW: day
80 characters per entry
Sort: 1R/SW    unshifted.
1 ng I got up and it did not. The first day after a death, the new absence Is alwa
2 oss for half the night, but find next day All's kodak-distant. Easily, then (tho
3 s thunderstorms, Holds up each summer day and shakes It out suspiciously, lest s
4 With shovel and spade; That each dull day and each despairing act Builds up the
5 d for her own attending, And there by day and night With her blithe bone mending
6  6 May 1977 [ 207 ] Aubade I work all day, and get half-drunk at night. Waking a
7 ss of night Swamps the bright nervous day, and puts it out. In other times, when
8 e time, Half-past eleven on a working day, And these picked out of it; see, as t
9  her getting away Now she's there all day, And the money he gets for wasting his
10 es. Wedding-Wind The wind blew all my wedding-day, And my wedding-night was the
11 ing and the dark is sleep And twice a day before their gate We kneel between the
12 s in our summer wear Brother, and the day Breathes coldly from fields far away A
13 ing provides for. What can it do each day But hunt that imminent door Through wh
14 osite) won't achieve. That's clear as day. But come back late at night, You'll h
```

```
15 rotics No one gives you a thought, as day by day You drag your feet, clay-thick
16  to join us? In a pig's arse, friend. Day comes to an end. The gas fire breathes
17 ess faces: Gold surf of the sun, each day Exhausted through the world, gathers a
18 ld mingle, and the night would not Be day's exhaustion; there would drift about
19 ghs up failure, Carries the night and day, fetches Profit from sleep, from skies
20 winds crying for that unbroken field, Day having lifted) Black flowers burst out
21 tempt of good and bad; But one Spring day his land was violated; A bunch of hors
22 -lifting arms. She was slapped up one day in March. A couple of weeks, and her f
23 al memory. So it was stale time then, day in, day out, Blue fug in the room, not
24 lways there: Unresting death, a whole day nearer now, Making all thought impossi
25 y. So it was stale time then, day in, day out, Blue fug in the room, nothing to
26 Above the sea, the yet more shoreless day, Riddled by wind, trails lit-up galler
27 ents, naturally. Thereafter night and day She came both for the sight Of his slo
28 xx 'Sinking like sediment through the day' Sinking like sediment through the day
29 lither - Creatures, I cherish you! By day, sky builds Grape-dark over the salt U
30 r's impressive lie - Upon whose every day So many ruined are May could not make
31 omething is always approaching; every day Till then we say, Watching from a bluf
32 ay' Sinking like sediment through the day To leave it clearer, onto the floor of
33 like long hills, a range We ride each day towards, and never reach. 17 November
34 nripe day you bore your head, And the day was plucked and tasted bitter, As if s
35 g to catch my Comet One dark November day, Which soon would snatch me from it To
```

This selection of concordance lines above allows us to see that the term *day*, in spite of its empirical prominence, is almost entirely swamped by and at the mercy of night and those related forces that between them constitute the most empirically prominent semantic prosody within the private symbolism of Larkin's world. The collocates *dull, nervous, day in day out, all, sinking, bitter, night, grape-dark* begin to taint the term *day*, causing it to contain more of the blatant menace we associate with *night.*

The insights gained from this type of analysis have the further advantage of allowing us to develop and bring to fruition in the digital era, Enkvist's (1973) notion of markedness in stylistics. Enkvist was unable to state the source of that markedness as clearly as has now become possible using collocation. The collocates of day in Larkin's poetry enable us to hypothesise that all literary devices are marked by means of the relexicalising agency of collocation (Louw, 1991; 2007b; 2008a). This operates within the 9-word window of collocative power identified by Sinclair (1991, 2004a: 181). It is optimally identified using a ***co-selection*** facility and a 4+4 span to the left and right of the node. Hence, all semantic prosodies are potential backdrops for ironic or insincere reversal. All literary and non-literary (such as humour) devices share the phenomenon of relexicalisation. 'All As are B' is a universal scientific proposition. In the context of this paper, 'All devices *relexicalise* through the power of collocation.' (Louw, 2010, forthcoming)

The Implications of Collocation for Stylistics

This paper concludes with an example so compelling that the renowned poet Herbert Williams kindly offered the author permission for the use, in this paper, of the entire poem. The author first used this example in a class of second-year undergraduates. The philosopher under discussion in class was Rudolph Carnap (1891-1970). The proof that follows was offered as part of a detailed refutation of Hoey's (2005) and Whitsitt's (2005) rejection of semantic prosody and was circulated in a one-day workshop (June 2008) on semantic prosody at the University of Bologna Forli, to which the author had not been invited by the organiser, Guy Aston. Second year students at the University of Zimbabwe were interested in verifying Carnap's (1928) theory of the logical construction of the world. Mauthner (2000) believes that Carnap's theory was 'too daring'.

He writes as follows:

Carnap proposed one framework constructed on a very slender basis consisting of one relation, 'remembrance of similarity', and basic data. The basic data are occurrences of total immediate experiences, and so-called sense-data are logical constructions based on those. A sensory quality is in turn defined on that basis. It did, however, become clear to critics, and to Carnap himself, that this construction project was too daring. (Mauthner, 2000: 86)

The example below takes this further. The poet informs us that the protagonist in the poem set out below is dishonest and insincere. The string in bold print: ***a heart made bleak by sacrifice*** ought to be sufficient to trigger Carnap's 'remembrance of similarity' if it exists: it would take the form of *'a+blank+made+blank+by.* A simple wildcard search *a * made * by* was used to trace in the British National Corpus precisely what the similarity that might have been be remembered might be. Carnap's pre-computational prediction was that it would occur in the form of a sense-datum. The highest scoring collocate ('possible') is our guide to experience and hence is the string's inductive counterpart within corpus-based empiricism (see also Chapman, 2008: 168). Our intuition is incapable of recovering it. Only the computer can do this for us and modern software is often rather less able than Tim Johns's prototype concordancer, *MicroConcord* in carrying out simple wildcard searches. The reason why the co-selection on modern search engines is often syntax-bound is difficult to fathom. *WordSmith* allows co-selection, but Lookup (Bank of English) and CHAB (The Corpus Hub at Birmingham) do not. The power of collocation ought eventually to get rid of skip-search based models that require more ponderous forms of search instruction and are bound by the linearity of text in the way in which they function.

The result allows us to rest our case: The subtext (note how we have verified that old critical notion literally, see Cudden, 1980: 665) of the poem is that the protagonist through 'a knack of lies' has lived a comfortable life made possible by deception.

Daughter of the House[4]

It is not love that keeps her here, tending
The stubborn enterprise of age. Her hands
Are clinical expressions of **a heart**
Made bleak by sacrifice, *her eyes*
Neutralise her therapeutic smile.

Love is an easy master, but her guile
Springs from more terrible demands.
It is the blood's dictatorship, bending
Her uninvited kinship to the part,
Masking indifference with a knack of lies.

(Herbert Williams)

```
MicroConcord search SW: a * made * by
80 characters per entry
Sort: 1R/SW    unshifted.
1 requiring the giving of reasons, a point made explicitly by Megarry V.C. in McIn
2 d set up in Threadneedle Street, a move made possible by his marriage on 9 Janua
3 law, since the damage must be of a kind made likely by the characteristics known
4 ural rights even more important, a point made cogently by Lord Wilberforce in Ma
5 t was a profession in name only (a point made indirectly by my lecturer who stud
6 ee what it would cost me to have a tank made up by the local chap that most enth
7 d guilty. The youths were black, a fact made clear by the relatively unusual use
8 urseries and botanical gardens – a trip made possible by the award of the first
9 ting seated events last year, in a move made possible by new developments in dem
10 ical equipment in the workplace, a task made compulsory by the UK's 1990 Electri
11 t he would have to do in 1962 is a leap made only by Gaullists predisposed to el
12 curing the reasons for doing so: a task made easier by his tortuous prose style.
13 Iranian revolution) on March 16, a loan made possible by the US decision to rema
```

14 ited impatiently, ill at ease in a room made noisome by vats and bubbling beaker

15 und up between low, stark trees. A path made dangerous by loose stones and snow.

16 ed to Shelley, and began to sing a song made famous by Miguelito, giving her a p

17 always been played at both ends, a fact made significant by Robson's assertion t

18 only really produce themselves, a fact made clear by Billy Nicholls' dire Would

19 n policies. More research is not a call made usually by conservationists – quite

20 icle of romance, gliding through a night made mysterious by more than fog. </p>

21 iving far above the Sussex norm, a situation made clear by the accounts of the l

22 ite the Leyton House team having a weekend made difficult by and act of sabotage

23 y sea from one State to another, a point made explicit by the Visby amendments.

24 of Israel's amen corner – to use a phrase made famous by a conservative columnis

25 group of acacias, standing above a village made golden by the late sun, blazed w

26 the mask of the temporal that is a facade made hideous by the graffiti of desire

27 man, M. Ghiglion-Green rest upon a primitivism made permissible by the pre-World

28 rovision was included based upon a recommendation made earlier by Mr. Leathart.

29 reat house in a very short time, a transaction made easier by Browne's use of th

30 The country is in the depths of a recession, made worse by the worst drought in

31 ssion of necessary propositions, a discussion made necessary by Copleston's desi

32 relevant contextual assumptions (a point made nicely by Gumperz (1977) who calls

33 is which some journalists, using a phrase made popular by A.M. Klein, have refer

34 mble to the constitution itself, a blindness **made possible** by the ideological di

35 is concentrated in the cabinet, a situation **made possible** by a weak legislature

36 reach 100 megabits per second – a capacity **made possible** by France's planned sw

37 that now carry only one channel, a marvel **made possible** by digital compression.

38 humour: Surrealist objects like a tea-cup made useless by fur; and a pair of wh

(Source: The British National Corpus)

Apart from the negative semantic prosody on the string ***'made bleak by sacrifice'*** that can only be disclosed through access to the corpus, readers of the poem are offered no earlier hint than this line of the poem's concerns: the *duplicity* and abuse of power of the daughter of the house. This is reminiscent of the line in Philip Larkin cited in Louw (1993: 162): 'Days are where we live…' that led to the first use in corpus stylistics of the predictive power of semantic prosody. This approach is taken further into the question of literary worlds in Louw (2010, forthcoming).

During his career, Carnap (1928) set about concentrating upon the language of science for the reason that he felt it was likely to bring scholarship closer to truth. It is worth concluding with the following expanded context from which the same string was extracted in a small scientific corpus.

*Such **a** system, **made realistic by** the rapid advances in VLSI technology, is said to be linearly connected if each processing element can only communicate directly with its two nearest neighbours (Source: Association for Computational Linguistics Data Collection Initiative.)*

The term *realistic* arguably offers a more scientific perspective, perhaps, than the term *possible.* Science seems to favour truth over the manipulation of events to make them possible. The power of collocation in literary studies arises from the fact that collocates, whether they occur in the target text or in the reference corpus, *all* qualify for inclusion in the act of data-assisted reading.

In a recent volume by Watson and Zyngier (2007; Louw, 2007e) second language learners are offered insights into the value and power of corpus-based approaches to corpus stylistics. However, the concordance lines were ruined because they were not in 8 point Courier font and they spilled over the line ends and caused a new line to enter between each citation. The result has the valuable heuristic effect of demonstrating how easily the instrumentation works, but ***only*** in 8 point Courier. The instrumentation is completely ***neutralized*** by larger fonts. Sabotage in such cases cannot be ruled out. In a recent volume by Ron Carter and Peter Stockwell purporting to offer essential readings in stylistics, no papers on corpus stylistics were included. Carter has been aware of the approach since 1987, as Louw's (1989) first ever paper on corpus stylistics, using large Cobuild corpora, was presented in his presence at St Hilda's College in April 1987 (shortly *before* the publication of the first edition of the Collins Cobuild English Language Dictionary). In Watson and Zyngier (2007), Carter refers in its introduction to the 'awesome power' of the corpus, but seems not to have checked that the final version of Louw (2007e) contained the concordances in 8 point Courier. Watson and Zyngier (2007) was missing from the Palgrave table at PALA in Sheffield in July 2008. Copies that were promised by the representative did not arrive. In the case of Louw (1989), Carter, who edited the collection, apparently and inexplicably omitted Louw's concordance lines from the COBUILD Reserve Corpora.

CONCLUSION

Instrumentation for language is at hand. Most countries in the world are signatories to the International Covenant on Economic, Social and Cultural Rights (as at 1 August, 1993, 122 countries had ratified it). This convention entitles all the peoples of the world to the benefits of scientific advancement. Whatever our discipline, it is time to ask what the corpus and collocation can bring to it, rather than enjoy the precarious nature of a dated and unaltered discipline 'made possible by censorship and denial'.

The Human Rights aspect is readily satisfied by the sheer versatility of digital collocation as instrumentation for language. The claim that collocation is instrumentation for meaning needs to be made using an appropriate speech act verb rather than a mere constative. This article needs to be seen as its *hereby* test.

The arguments are clear. Collocation is diagnostic. It corrects intuitive mismatches and imposes the condition upon intuitively derived theory and data that it should be checked. It dismisses the mind-set of schools of thought. It is non-political, scientific and truthful. It falsifies mentalist theories and fake institutions. It dismisses untruth and shows it the door (Pears, 1971). It uses set theory to create the subset of literary worlds within stylistics. Its markedness withstands all tests. All devices use the 9 word window of collocative power (Sinclair, 1991) to relexicalise. No other theory is as descriptly marked as collocation and semantic prosody. It reinforces the injunction of John Sinclair (whose collocation dictionary and project LUCID, both based upon collocation, were apparently censored). Sinclair (2004a) insists that we *trust the text* by entrusting all textual applications, both literary and civic, to collocation as *instrumentation* for meaning.

REFERENCES

Ayer, A. J. (1954). *Philosophical Essays*. London: Macmillan.

Bacon, F. [1605] (1985). The Advancement of Learning. Harmondworth: Penguin.

Berofsky, B. (1971). *Determinism*. Princeton: PUP.

Bullock, A., & Trombley, S. (Eds.). (2000). *The New Fontana Dictionary of Modern Thought*. London: HarperCollins.

Carnap, R. (1928). *Der Logische Aufbau der Welt.* Berlin-Schlagtensee: Weltkreis-Verlag.

Carnap, R. (1956) Meaning and Necessity: A study in Senmantics and Modal Logic. Chicogo: University of Chicago Press.

Caspi, J. L. (1998). *The Cambridge Quintet: A work of scientific speculation*. London: Abacus.

Chapman, S. (2008). *Language and Empiricism: After the Vienna Circle*. New York: Palgrave. doi:10.1057/9780230583030

Chateau, C. (2007). Drift and shift: How "continental" moves in geological English. Dijon: mimeo.

Cudden, J. A. (1980). *A Dictionary of Literary Terms*. Harmondsworth: Penguin.

Enkvist, N. E. (1973). *Linguistic Stylistics*. The Hague: Mouton.

Firth, J. R. (1957). *Papers in Linguistics 1934-1951*. Oxford: OUP.

Frege, G. (1884). *The Foundations of Arithmetic: A Logico-Mathematical Enquiry into the Concept of Number (J.L. Austin, Trans., 1974)*. Oxford: Blackwell.

Hoey, M. H. (2005). *Lexical Priming: A New Theory of Words and Language*. London: Routledge.

Hoey, M. H., Mahlberg, M., Stubbs, M., & Teubert, W. (Eds.). (2007). *Text, Discourse and Corpora: Theory and Analysis*. London: Continuum.

Krishnamurthy, R. (2004). *English Collocation Studies: The OSTI Report*. London: Continuum.

Louw, W. E. (1989). Sub-routines in the integration of language and literature. In Carter, R. (Ed.), *Literature and the Learner: Methodological Approaches*. London: MEP/British Council.

Louw, W. E. (1991). Classroom concordancing of delexical forms and the case for integrating language and literature. In Johns, T., & King, P. (Eds.), *Classroom Concordancing, ELR Journal 4*.

Louw, W. E. (1993). Irony in the text or insincerity in the writer? The diagnostic potential of semantic prosodies. In Baker, M. (Eds.), *Text and Technology: In Honour of John Sinclair*. Amsterdam: John Benjamins.

Louw, W. E. (2000). Contextual Prosodic Theory: Bringing Semantic Prosodies to Life. In Heffer, C., & Sauntson, H. (Eds.), *Words in Context. In Honour of John Sinclair*. Birmingham: ELR.

Louw, W. E. (2003). Dressing up waiver: a stochastic-collocational reading of the Truth and Reconciliation Commission (TRC). Harare: mimeo. Also available in the *Occasional Papers dei Quaderni del CeSLIC*. Retrieved from http://www.lingue.unibo.it/ceslic/e_occ_papers.htm

Louw, W. E. (2004, May 20). Unravelling the ideological from the authentic. *Guardian Weekly*. Retrieved August 2006 from http://www.guardian.co.uk/education/2004/may/20/tefl4

Louw, W. E. (2007a). Truth, literary worlds and devices as collocation. Closing Keynote presentation at TaLC6 on 7th July 2004. In E. Hidalgo, L. Quereda, & J. Santana (Eds.), *Proceedings of the Sixth Conference on Teaching and Language Corpora.* Amsterdam: Rodopi.

Louw, W. E. (2007b). Collocation as the determinant of verbal art. In Miller, D., & Turci, M. (Eds.), *Verbal Art Re-Visited* (pp. 149–180). London: Equinox.

Louw, W. E. (2007c). Corporibus Phlogiston: A Gentle Refutation of Michael Hoey's Theory of Lexical Priming. Harare: mimeo.

Louw, W. E. (2007d). *Are literary texts and their worlds 'thrown together' as collocation?* Keynote presentation to ACORN Symposium, in Honour of John Sinclair, on 4th May 2007. Retrieved from http://www.aston.ac.uk/symposium.htm

Louw, W. E. (2007e). Literary worlds as collocation. In Watson, G., & Zyngier, S. (Eds.), *Literature and Stylistics for Language Learners: Theory and Practice.* Basingstoke: Palgrave.

Louw, W. E. (2008a). Consolidating empirical method in data-assisted stylistics: towards a corpus-attested glossary of literary terms. In Viana, D., & Zyngier, S. (Eds.), *Directions in Empirical Literary Studies. In Honour of Willie van Peer.* Amsterdam: John Benjamins.

Louw, W. E. (2008b). Two chapters in D. Hoover, et al (Eds.), Approaches to Corpus Stylistics. London: Routledge.

Louw, W. E. (2008c). Establishing a historiography for corpus-events from their frequency: a celebration of Bertrand Russell's (1948) five postulates. Harare: mimeo.

Louw, W. E. (2008d). What is a homogenized corpus? Harare: mimeo

Louw, W.E. (2010). Automating the extraction of literary worlds. *Textus*, special edition on stylistics. Genoa: Tilgher.

Malinowski, B. (1935). *Coral Gardens and their Magic.* London: Allen and Unwin.

Mauthner, T. (2000). *The Penguin Dictionary of Philosophy.* London: Penguin.

Palmer, F. R. (1968). *Selected Papers by J.R. Firth 1952-1959.* London: Longman.

Pears, D. (1971). *Wittgenstein.* London: Fontana Collins.

Popper, K. R. (1959). *The Logic of Scientific Discovery.* London: RKP.

Preston, J. (2008). *The Structure of Scientific Revolutions.* London: Continuum.

Russell, B. (1912). *The Problems of Philosophy*. London: RKP.

Russell, B. (1946). *The History of Western Philosophy*. London: Routledge.

Russell, B. (1948). *Human Knowledge: Its Scope and Limitations*. London: Routledge.

Russell, B. (1960). *Bertrand Russell Speaks his Mind*. London: Arthur Baker.

Sinclair, J. M. (1987). Fictional Worlds. In Coulthard, R. M. (Ed.), *Talking about Text* (pp. 43–60). Birmingham: ELR.

Sinclair, J. M. (1991). *Corpus, Concordance, Collocation*. Oxford: OUP.

Sinclair, J. M. (1995). *Collocation on CD-ROM*. Glasgow: HarperCollins.

Sinclair, J. M. (2004a). *Trust the Text*. London: Routledge.

Sinclair, J. M. (2004b). *Reading Concordances*. London: Longman.

Sinclair, J.M. (2006). *Phrasebite*. Pescia: TWC.

Sinclair, J. M., & Maurenen, A. (2006). *Linear Unit Grammar: Integrating speech and writing*. Amsterdam: John Benjamins.

Tognini-Bonelli, E. (2001). *Corpus Linguistics at Work*. Amsterdam: John Benjamins.

Urmson, J. O. (1956). *Philosophical Analysis: Its development between the two World Wars*. Oxford: Clarendon Press.

Watson, G., & Zyngier, S. (Eds.). (2007). *Literature and Stylistics for Language Learners*. Basingstoke, New York: Palgrave.

Wittgenstein, L. 1922. Tractatus Logico-Philosophicus. (D.F. Pears & D.F. McGuiness, Trans., 1960). London: Routledge and Kegan Paul.

Wittgenstein, L. (2005). *Philosophical Investigations*. Oxford: Blackwell.

ADDITIONAL READING

Louw, W. E. (2010, forthcoming). Automating the extraction of literary worlds. *Textus*, special edition on stylistics. Genoa: Tilgher.

Toolan, M. (2009). *Narrative Progression in the Short Story*. Amsterdam: Benjamins.

Zyngier, S., et al. (Eds.). (2008). *Directions in Empirical Literary Studies*. Amsterdam: Benjamins.

ENDNOTES

1. Naturally, there are exceptions to this co-occurrence, but very often they form part of the relexicalisation common to all devices. For example, data-assisted copy-writing in an advertising agency may have been involved in a competition promotion showing a young woman opening a container of yoghurt and cutting to a shot of the same girl, much more scantily clad on a sunny beach. The text stated: 'Peel the top off of an X brand yoghurt and you could be peeling your top off on a tropical island!'
2. This paper formed part of a presentation at *Corpus 2009* in Liverpool in July 2009.
3. This research was first reported by the author at the annual conference of The Poetics and Linguistics Association in Birmingham in 2002.
4. The author is grateful to the poet Herbert Williams (copyright holder of this poem) for his generous permission to use 'Daughter of the House' in its entirety and for his encouragement in the area of research being developed. Details of the book by Herbert Williams in which this poem appears are as follows: *Wrestling in the Mud: New and Selected Poems*, published by Cinnamon Press in 2007.

Section 2
Education

Chapter 5
tEXtMACHINA:
Or How to Account for the Methodological Particularities of the Humanities in the E-Learning Field

Stefan Hofer
University of Zurich, Switzerland

René Bauer
University of Zurich,Switzerland

Imre Hofmann
University of Zurich, Switzerland

ABSTRACT

The Humanities and cultural studies in particular have traditionally been distinguished by the specialty of their scientific practices. Since the object of their analyses can be broadly considered as meaningful texts, they usually emphasize hermeneutical, qualitative and discursive analytical procedures such as reading, text-analysis, interpretation and comparison. The new media offer fresh possibilities in this field of research by permitting web-based discursive text-interpretation for a community of scientists. In this chapter, the authors focus on the e-learning environment tEXtMACHINA by exploring the question of how these methodological particularities of the Humanities can be accounted for adequately with the new technical facilities. The didactic e-learning concept of tEXtMACHINA is based on the virtual simulation of scientific practices in class. By offering a set of techniques, such options as highlighting text-passages, communication tools or the flexible

DOI: 10.4018/978-1-60566-932-8.ch005

combination of different media, which allow for the collaborative, discursive and analytical interpretation of texts, students may be able to acquire the practical and theoretical scientific competencies for their field in a blended learning setting.

INTRODUCTION

In the early days of the emerging new technology, online environments were developed predominantly for pre-structured learning-processes. The web-based e-learning tool tEXtMACHINA (http://www.textmachina.uzh.ch) discussed in this paper goes in another way. It has been designed to satisfy the need for a digital learning tool which is adequate for the field of literature. It is our opinion that the Humanities, and literary studies in particular, distinguish themselves from the natural sciences not only in their object but also in certain procedural respects. These distinctions become clearest if one takes into account the specific object with which the Humanities deal: meaningful texts. This implies that cultural studies rely to a high extent on qualitative, hermeneutical and discursive procedures that need to be considered by developers of e-learning environments.

tEXtMACHINA aims at taking into account the particularities of the Humanities by focusing on the interpretive and discursive practices in this field. The software enables its users to qualitatively analyze a given text and to discuss its interpretation online. Its open and flexible technical implementation allows for an individualized problem-based simulation of these discursive practices by offering a set of easy-to-use functions. A few concrete examples of best practice will illustrate these features.

SETTING

In 2001, when tEXtMACHINA was developed at Zurich University, we intended to address an epistemological problem that seemed not to have drawn much attention: the question of how to adequately account for the particularities of the Humanities in the e-learning field. The challenge which this starting point posed for the development of a new e-learning tool was therefore that of combining a specific and a universal approach. On the one hand, it was our aim to take into consideration the specificities of the Humanities. On the other hand, teachers had to be allowed to insert their own material. This implied that a certain universality or formality of the approach had to be reached by abstracting it from any concrete content of study. The resulting product in the end aimed at enabling a group of students to easily collaborate on a shared text-basis of their or their teacher's choice, in an individualized and flexible use of the tool.

EPISTEMOLOGICAL AND METHODOLOGICAL PRELIMINARIES

The requirements of an e-learning environment for the Humanities have to be based on a thorough understanding of scientific practices. In this respect, we consider the application of a specific methodological approach appropriate to the particular object of study as a crucial epistemological condition for successful research. This does not mean that we contest the rational and nomothetic – as well as idiographic (Windelband, 1894) – character of scientific research in the Humanities. This field aims at nomothetic knowledge about regularities and laws as does any other science, and at the same time it tries to establish idiographic interpretations of singular objects such as poems. Latter characteristic entails its particular translation of scientific rationality into adequate meaning (Albert, 2000).

The Humanities are by no means homogeneous in themselves. In this chapter, the term is applied to cultural sciences such as literature, art, history, popular culture, etc. The common feature of these sciences, as opposed to other disciplines such as psychology or sociology, is their shared object of research. This object is usually referred to as a text – or sign, by which we mean any cultural or meaningful object that is open to interpretation (Plett, 1979, p. 38-40; Eco, 1964).

Now, there seems to be little doubt that the adequate approach to these kinds of objects lies in their systematic analysis and interpretation. These processes originate from seemingly simple everyday practices. We have to read signs all the time and usually we are quite successful at doing so. Yet, beneath the surface, these practices involve a very complex combination of different skills. Scientific reading is the endeavor to methodologically improve the results of interpretation and to avoid mistakes. The most successful results in this regard stem from efforts in hermeneutics, semiotics and linguistic text and discourse analysis.

These efforts have made it clear that the systematic interpretation of texts (and signs) consists of different complementary processes. Scientific reading involves: drafting a hypothetical assumption of the meaning of a text as a whole and of its underlying code; verifying or disproving this and other assumptions by contextualizing the text in a wider referential environment as well as by comparing these assumptions with smaller units of meaning in the text; revising these assumptions if they cannot be upheld any longer in light of the context or inconsistent text elements and modifying them by selecting and combining relevant elements and relations; and so on (Eco, 1964; Hirsch, 1967; Dilthey, 1970). This process of holistic and systemic feedback between different levels of meaningful (and meaning-relevant) units is also known as the hermeneutical circle, even though its dialectic dynamic should rather be perceived as a spiral. The goal of the interpretive process is the construction of a coherent and consistent explanatory code and interpretation which achieves maximum plausibility and comprehensiveness.

In order to accomplish this interpretive task, readers have to be able to analyze an existing text into its meaning units as well as to relate it comparatively or contextually to other texts and facts, and finally, to comment on it. These techniques are commonly part of hermeneutical, qualitative or discursive practices. The last point gives rise to two other essential characteristics of literary studies: since interpretations of texts generate new texts, object (language) and meta language have the same ontological state – both being meaningful signs (Peirce, 1932). The Humanities work not only on, but also with, texts. Scientific practice in this area therefore takes place in the same medium as the object of study: text in a broad sense. It thus follows that scientific comments on a primary text (source) can eventually become an object of research themselves. This raises another crucial issue to be considered: systematic scientific interpretation of texts takes place as regulated social practice in a concrete historical context. This practice is designed and normatively organized as a collaborative and consensus-oriented rational dialogue (Habermas, 1973) within the interpretive community of the different object fields (Fish, 1980). The interpretive process therefore results in the genesis of a virtually endless dialogue which manifests itself in an ongoing discourse constituted by observable intertextual references (Kristeva, 1969; Barthes 1973; Maingueneau, 1991). This collaborative process consists not only of a steady construction of new knowledge by settling on canonical interpretations, but also of an agreement on criteria and standards regarding how new knowledge is to be established (Foucault, 1969).

However, the criteria of scientific text production also depend on the technological possibilities of a certain historical situation (as well as of the prevailing political framework). It is by now a truism that the Gutenberg revolution of letterpress printing has had massive effects on the scientific standards of text production, and there can be no doubt that the digital revolution of the media world will have an even more profound impact on observable scientific practice (Giesecke, 2002; Flusser, 2004). It has not yet been possible to gain a clear overview of this impact in the current situation, which is still defined by the printing paradigm. To get an idea of this potential, one should merely consider the new perspectives offered by the capacity to draw formerly excluded contents such as sound and video into scientific discourse as well as to relate primary texts much faster and more easily – with a click of the mouse – to their secondary comments in the hyper-referential web. The possibilities of the new media not only affect the production of scientific literature but also extend to techniques of text and discourse analysis which, so far, have been virtually limited to marking passages in a book with a pen. Digital software nowadays enables a group of users to collaboratively do the same on a shared text basis. The processes of scientific reading and writing are virtually fusing into one activity.

Therefore, the massive consequences of the digital media for what Friedrich Kittler (1985, 1992) called the scientific discourse network (the term focuses on the technical and media-based conditions of production and reception of a discourse) also need to be explored in the context of the sciences by experimentally adapting the new technologies for research purposes. As we will show, tEXtMACHINA also allows one to do so by offering a set of text-centered tools for collaborative text-analysis and interpretation, which can be used for teaching as well as for research.

EDUCATIONAL IMPLICATIONS: PROBLEM-BASED SIMULATION OF SCIENTIFIC DISCOURSE

Knowledge in the Humanities cannot be accounted for adequately without considering the aforementioned epistemological and methodological particularities of its genesis. It is therefore a basic requirement for students in this field to acquire the cognitive capabilities and the standards necessary to participate in this scientific practice.

Given these text-focused and discursive conditions – holistic interdependence of meaning relations, ontological identity of object and meta language, structured intertextual reference in the production of scientific discourse –, the question arises as to how to implement them adequately with a didactic approach that takes advantage of the opportunities that new media, and the World Wide Web in particular, provides. Stockmann (2005) emphasizes that "different disciplines make entirely different demands on the new forms of teaching and learning" (p. 62, our translation), and Schulmeister (2004) observes a lack of e-learning in those sciences that struggle with the "hermeneutical method" (p. 361).

The principal didactic aim of a scientific formation in the Humanities is to acquire practical competence and theoretical knowledge necessary to deal professionally in a discursive scientific community. Students on their way from novices to experts (Bransford, Brown & Cocking, 2000) should therefore be able to analyze and interpret documents systematically, be aware of methodological criteria, rules and standards, be acquainted with the fundamental theoretical concepts underlying their interpretive work and show the dialogical and collaborative competencies necessary to participate in academic discourse. It seems to us that the interactive and communicative possibilities of the World Wide Web suggest a didactic model based on the idea of simulating the discursive interpretive practice found in the Humanities. By trying to do what scientists actually do, students not only learn about the canonical content of their subjects but also understand how this content was produced in a process of knowledge construction. In addition, they realize how arguments have to be verified and analytical standards need to be established in collaborative dialogue.

It follows that the didactic approach must aim at virtually simulating the quasi-public discourse of a scientific interpretive community by enabling and forcing students to become aware of the rational and standardized procedures of text interpretation. Students have to learn how to make use of the analytical, comparative and referential techniques as well as know how to discuss in academic settings where texts are discussed.

One relevant advantage of this approach lies in the fact that it can be implemented smoothly with the model of competence-oriented learning (Bransford, Brown & Cocking, 2000) as well as with that of problem-based learning (Boud & Feletti, 1997). Both models focus on students' individual learning processes and are based on the constructivist assumption that practical exercise facilitates successful learning. In competence-oriented and problem-based learning environments, students are typically prompted to solve specific scientific problems or questions in individual learning groups and to compare and contrast their findings with the findings of experts. Teachers supervise their effort (Oser, Achtenhagen & Renold, 2006), aiming at supporting students' development from novices to experts. According to these models, it is not as important to find the only solution to a problem as it is to work together in order to develop creative and plausible solutions.

During this process of problem-solving, students have to draw on existing knowledge, search for further relevant information and dialogically generate and agree on new insights. The appraisal of the different solutions takes place according to as authentic or realistic criteria as possible. The whole process from problem analysis to evaluation of the solution can be negotiated in the interpretive community and objectified in their (written) discourse. By assigning students specific scientific social roles and immediately applying new competencies, the normative as well as the factual discursive practice of the scientific community can be illustrated in step with their actual practice. In the Humanities, problem-based and competence-oriented learning can draw from a wealth of canonical case studies in order to furnish concrete courses with relevant content.

With regard to different possible e-learning concepts, it seems reasonable to implement the favored didactic approach according to the blended learning setting (Sauter, Sauter & Bender, 2004). This integrative and complementary form of instruction combines traditional attendance teaching with the adoption of the new media, trying to profit from the advantages of both while avoiding the disadvantages of each. For the educational scenario up for discussion, this means above all to achieve the necessary social dynamics, group organization, scheduling and result evaluation by periodic classroom teaching while benefiting from the technical potential of the new media in the online simulation of the interpretive discourse. Interpretations, exercises and short papers can be compiled and published by the students online, individually or in groups. Using the medium of a quasi-public e-learning environment, students learn to observe each other and themselves to demonstrate their thoughts systematically and traceably for others. For the teachers, the online environment makes it possible to continuously follow the students' learning process. For attendance teaching, there is more time and scope to intensify the discussion on certain selected issues as well as to clarify problems that have appeared during the problem-based collaboration.

To summarize these didactic approaches, educational aims in the Humanities could efficiently and successfully be achieved by means of problem-based strategies in a blended learning context. The technical perspectives of the new media and in particular the World Wide Web can be adopted to set up a virtual learning environment that makes it possible to simulate the scientific construction and rational negotiation of practical and theoretical knowledge in an interpretive community. The utilization of the e-learning environment in a blended learning setting should help sensitize students to the discursive features of scientific practice, to boost their awareness of methodical standards and theoretical issues, to inspire critical reflection, to reveal and improve existing competencies and to support them in attaining further skills. This means that such a scenario should be easily adaptable to meet the demands that have been raised recently concerning the so-called key-competencies, such as interactive appliance of the new media, interaction in heterogeneous groups and independent acting (Weinert, 2001). All in all, such an application should make it possible to improve the quality and efficiency of a course as well as to increase students' participation and performance by inspiring them to engage in written debates.

tEXtMACHINA has therefore been designed to facilitate the simulation of scientific discourse by providing the infrastructure and the tools necessary to implement exercises based on the didactic concept of problem-based and competence-oriented learning. We therefore consider it as a contribution to the applied research in the field of literary e-learning. Its tools focus on the analysis of and commentary on a given text and enable a group of students or researchers to work together in the process of its interpretation. In order to allow individual course scenarios as well as the implementation of other didactic settings, its functions were designed as rather abstract techniques that are independent of all content and impose hardly any structural constraints.

TECHNICAL IMPLEMENTATION: WEB-BASED COMMENTING AND ANALYZING OF TEXTS

We discuss tEXtMACHINA as an attempt to implement the aforementioned didactic concept of a competence-oriented and problem-based simulation of a scientific discourse. We take into account the particularities of the Humanities, enabling problem-based blended learning courses and taking advantage of the possibilities of the new media. Its conceptually drafted features centering on a collaborative discourse led to it becoming a typical Web 2.0 platform at a time when the expression had yet be coined. The term Web 2.0 stresses the fact that people increasingly use the World Wide Web not only to retrieve information but also to contribute to it with their own content (cf. wikis, blogs, video-sharing and social networks). In this sense, tEXtMACHINA is not just another tool in the common paradigm of e-learning platforms but an integrated medium. The following principles govern its implementation:

a) Use of the platform and its tools is easy to learn. The barrier to the first active steps is kept very low and no additional technical skills – such as programming – is therefore needed. This concern for usability often gets lost when considering technical and theoretical issues.
b) Work on and with actual texts is the focus for all tools. The term 'text' in this context is meant in a very broad sense, including any kind of multimedia, such as image, sound or movie.
c) Structure has to allow varying discursive and intertextual relations. It allows commenting other texts as well as to generating links between texts.
d) Users must be able to interact and collaborate online. The platform has therefore to be programmed as a dynamic web-application that allows real-time interaction.
e) Tools must make it possible to construct dynamic and flexible structures that can be freely adapted to the needs of a community. A set of tools which can be applied and combined individually is needed in order to keep the structures flexible.
f) Written discourse is open and transparent to observation and critical review. Open visibility is the default status; closed areas have to be generated intentionally.
g) Evolving structure enables dialogical activities such as discussions, negotiations, agreements.
h) The given tools shall make it possible to build and to organize knowledge as an observable discourse in a group.

The combination of these aspects allows an individualized simulation of the central processes of systematic analysis and interpretation in the collaborative dialogue of a scientific community. Since tEXtMACHINA was developed for use at the University of Zurich and at other universities in Switzerland and Germany, such as University of Duisburg-Essen and Zurich University of Arts, its user interface has been kept in German, but this could easily be translated into another language.

The concrete implementation of these principles in tEXtMACHINA is based on the above-mentioned ontological identity of literary object and meta language. Absolutely every entry – from the shortest poem to the most elaborate course – is considered as a so-called 'text-object'. This ontological commitment, combined with the condition that every new entry has to be related ('added') to an existing entry, has the fundamental consequence that in discursive terms every entry has to be a 'comment' on another text-object. In turn, it can be commented on itself. These two elementary features – that everything is a text and every text is a comment on another comment – enable the creation of an open and flexible discourse. Thus, the basic unit of this discourse – the text-object – is a text which relates to other texts or parts of texts and is the tie for further text-objects.

Every discourse in tEXtMACHINA begins with a primary text-object, which is generated by default and which is at the same time the opening entry of the relevant platform. Further content has to be added to this root-entry or to any later entry. This means that the elementary operation consists of adding a new comment. Most of the time what one actually does in tEXtMACHINA is exactly that. Of course, an existing entry is not restricted to one single comment; the number of potential comments is unlimited. In this way, out of the root-entry there sprouts a tree of comments with a flexible hierarchical structure (see Figure 1Figure 1). Yet this chronological hierarchy can easily be crossed and transformed into a rhizomatic fabric by subsequently linking a text-object to other internal reference points. The following illustrates the implementation of this technical scheme step by step; later on we will show some examples of courses carried out.

A simple plain text comment can be added with two mouse clicks. In order to add a new comment to an existing entry one has to click on the 'add' icon for the designated entry. In the second step, the new comment can be entered and then added. The new entry is displayed below the previous one, a slight indent illustrates the new hierarchical level (see Figure 1).

However, this simplicity becomes more differentiated when it comes to deciding what kind of text-object one wants to add. By allowing its registered users to choose from a wide range of different types of text-objects, tEXtMACHINA combines the ontological identity of literary object language and meta language with the 'multimediality' of the new media and the multimodality of dialogical interaction. Whereas the default text-object is plain text and can be added by everyone, including anonymous visitors, registered users can also add different document (i.e..doc or.pdf) and multimedia formats (i.e..jpg,.avi,.swf). In order to do so one has to choose the designated text-object-type and to add the necessary content (i.e. an image).

There is not only a wide choice of different formats but also a large number of text-object types which are specific to tEXtMACHINA. These general types of text-objects allow for the specific implementation of individual didactic purposes by providing text-objects for the creation of exercises and for the organization and structuring of discourse. Since discourse will very soon become too long and complex to fit into a single page, it can be subdivided into smaller units, which are available

Figure 1. The development of a discoursal hierarchical structure

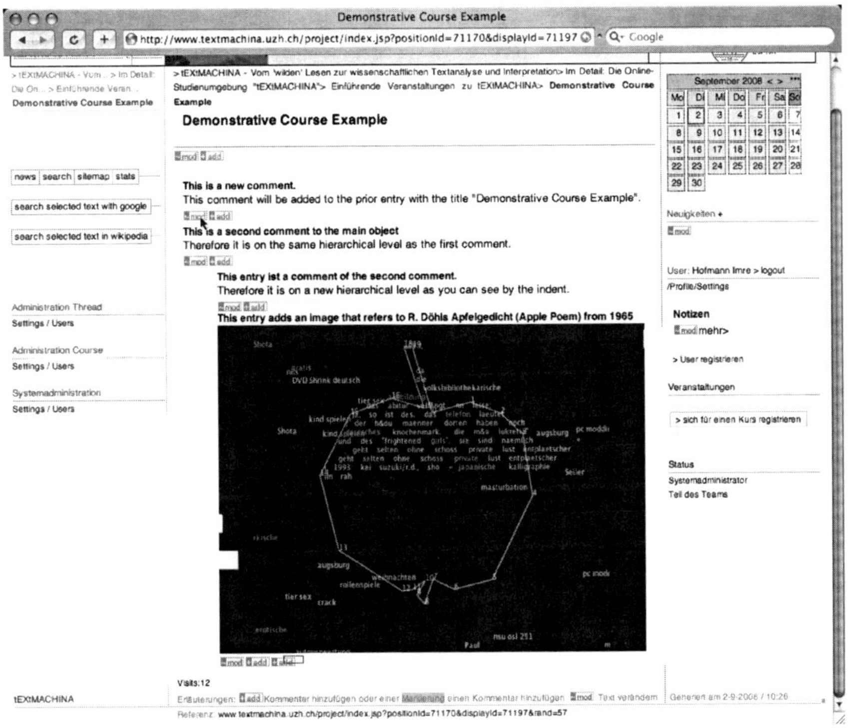

to all users, called threads. A small group of visual text-objects make it possible to visually design and arrange the view of the actual page. Analogous to academic status differences, the choice of available types of text-objects depends on the status of the user and ranges from plain text entries to complex courses. Once a new comment is added it can be modified in a second step. This secondary modification allows one to delete, modify, copy a text-object; transfer its position in discourse or change its rights, visibility and other properties, even its future commentability and modifiability. This broadens the range of individual uses for the collaborative and discursive practice of an interpretive community further.

Whereas single entries are defined by the available types of text-objects, it is the combination of different text-objects that allows maximum flexibility regarding the structure and the design of exercises, courses or the platforms/discourses as a whole. This means that users can define the structure by themselves and do not depend on a rigid and hierarchical structure. Yet this formal and elementary character of the text-object-types implies that the meaning and value of the tool are defined to a great extent by its successful application. In order to judge adequately the technical infrastructure of tEXtMACHINA, one has to look at best practice examples.

Since the scientific practice of interpretation not only consists of commenting online on existing primary texts (sources) as a whole but also on specific segments, tEXtMACHINA allows one to comment on an extract of a text as well, which in this case means a plain text (or an image), using the text-highlighting option. The reference to the marked passage can be generated in different ways: the excerpt itself has somehow to be made visible. This can be done by using a color or a different font trait (see Figure 2). If working with colors, the repeated marking of a certain extract leads to a more intense color.

But not only does tEXtMACHINA offer different marker options, it also provides different types of reference from the new comment to the marked extract. The new comment may be added below the text commented on; in such a case the reference is marked by a number as with a footnote. The in-text comment can also be laid in a layer over the previous text (see Figure 2) as if it were stuck on with a note. Since this type of display can make it difficult to read the text to be analyzed, the new layer can also be displayed 'invisibly' as long as its correlating mark has not been clicked on by a visitor. This referencing technique also works with images where the comment can be moved to a specific position in the image. Alternatively, the comment also can be written in-between the previous text by splitting it, or it can be written at the border of the text like the traditional side notes in a book. No matter which type of reference is chosen, the new comment remains available by itself for further commenting.

Figure 2. Using different highlighting to comment an image and a text

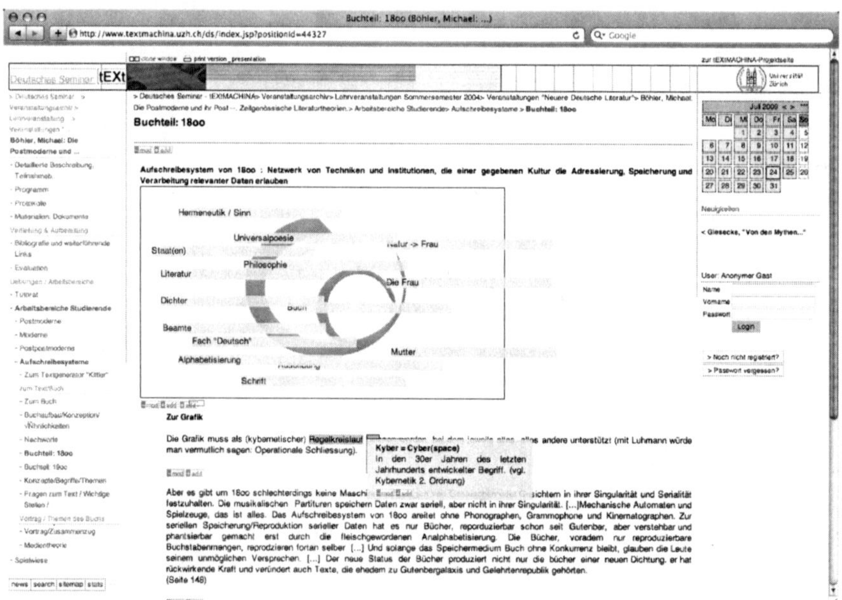

These marker features allow a group to systematically analyze a given text into meaningful subunits. By choosing different marker displays, the analysis can also be codified according to different questions. A sophisticated exercise with the marker feature can therefore display a visual illustration of the intertextual references of the interpretive collaboration.

While the presentation of the different techniques of tEXtMACHINA may provide an overview of its technical possibilities, its true didactic and scientific potential can only be conceived of and assessed when one bears in mind that these techniques can be applied and combined individually for specific teaching scenarios. To make this clear, the next section will describe a few examples of how the tools can effectively be used in a creative and successful manner.

FIELD REPORT

tEXtMACHINA was funded and primarily developed with the practical aim of providing progressive e-teaching in literary studies. Yet it can and has always been considered by its developers as a practical contribution to the e-learning discussion. This e-learning environment allows implementing literary key concepts crucial to the Humanities (such as discourse, intertextuality, hermeneutical interpretation, etc.) to the new media, which so far has not been possible.

Since 2003, the application has been in use at the University of Zurich. The first teachers to make use of the tool were members of the developer team who were familiar with the aims and the conceptual framework of tEXtMACHINA. Therefore, it was easy for them to apply it and to implement exercises according to the decisions discussed above. Apart from initial technical problems (such as server reliability), the observable learning results proved to sustain the claimed need for a specific literary e-learning environment. The following examples demonstrate a selection of successful implementations.

One of the earliest and most common findings is that, despite its clear methodological stance, the e-learning application as such is too under-determined in its functions. As it was one of the design principles that the flexible and formal character of most of the functions should also allow for other educational scenarios than the one we had in mind, and as we had derived the technical implementation from quite general theoretical and methodological considerations, this led to a considerable gap between the conceptual background and the concrete features of tEXtMACHINA. Obviously, the open structure of the available operations did not necessarily prompt teachers to design their courses according to the underlying concepts. It was therefore only slightly surprising that what teachers actually did with tEXtMACHINA varied widely and sometimes deviated considerably from the initially outlined scenario. In this respect, it has to be mentioned that the use of tEXtMACHINA was offered to any interested teacher at the Humanities institutes at the University of Zurich without preliminary introduction and that many teachers were probably not sufficiently acquainted – if at all – with the theoretical and didactic background to the application to be able to use it accordingly (for example in 2007, there were 20 courses at the German Department of Zurich University which made use of tEXtMACHINA; about 12 used it as mere fileserver). Obviously, a new technology does not entail a new form of e-learning inevitably.

This unexpected lack of didactic e-learning ambition on the part of certain academics appears to be a fundamental difficulty of the chosen approach. It seems as if the gap between the conceptual design and the concrete technical implementation of the e-learning environment has been neither truly perceived nor used as an invitation to an individualized and creative use of the application. It has therefore to be concluded that sufficient provision was probably not made for the transfer of the didactic scheme to the actual teachers by the developers at the time of the initial planning of the application. This flaw was probably caused by the fact that the first teachers to use the platform were part of the developer team and therefore did not need to be introduced to the conceptual background. Present efforts of the developer team are aimed at resolving this problem by offering teachers examples of best practices of how tEXtMACHINA can be used in order to stimulate their didactic ambitions and creativity.

This may explain why our recent endeavors concentrated on trying to determine how tEXtMACHINA can or has to be applied in order to actualize the claimed concepts in a manner which is as realistic as possible. Where these efforts resulted in successful teaching, they could at least be taken as evidence for the plausibility of the underlying concepts and the necessity of considering them in the didactic design.

It is therefore necessary to distinguish between the actual platform itself and the individual course with its didactic setting that has to be appraised. The examples below demonstrate that best learning results can be achieved in a problem-based blended learning setting where the use of web based e-learning technologies is an integral part of attendance classes. They illustrate additional educational benefits that cannot be achieved in a traditional offline setting. These positive results were also confirmed by the perception of the students, who expressed their surprise about the potential and efficiency of tEXtMACHINA. Students who had invested a certain degree of time into learning to use the tools began to explore its functions in a playful and enthusiastic manner, sometimes even going beyond the required efforts.

A similar but still quite rare effect is teachers familiarizing themselves with tEXtMACHINA when developing ambitious new ideas for creative course settings. Such observations show that, if communicated and well applied, work with a tool like tEXtMACHINA brings additional benefits simply by being fun. When students experience a high level of self-determination in the process of learning, the quality of their performance demonstrably increases (Deci & Ryan, 1993).

In these examples, the examination of the subject matter was intensified by forcing students to observe themselves and to continuously construe their knowledge in the subject. The fact that students learned the systematic rules and criteria they will need in order to participate in the interpretive discourse of the Humanities in the future can be considered even more important than the amount of canonical knowledge gained, since the metacognitive awareness caused by such a reflection on their own practice will improve their future learning.

We will now discuss five didactic scenarios in line with the conceptual background which proved to be successful: (a) a two-stage exercise consisting of an interpretation and an evaluation task; (b) an interpretive and collaborative group exercise; (c) the creation of a standardized format for exercises labeled as 'tEXtIVITÄT' ('tEXtIVITY'); (d) the focused preparation of a text for discussion in class with the text-marker tool; (e) the collaborative development of the text genre 'hyperfiction' and the writing of a hyperfictional text. Since the examples stem from courses in Switzerland, the texts in the screenshots are in German.

The first illustrative example was taken from the introductory course '*Vom 'wilden' Lesen zur wissenschaftlichen Textanalyse und Interpretation*' ("From 'unaware' reading to scientific text analysis and interpretation", University of Zurich, Prof. Dr. Michael Böhler; 2004). In this course, 27 students of modern German literature had to spontaneously write an interpretation of a poem in the first face-to-face session before any methodological or epistemological issues had been addressed (http://www.textmachina.uzh.ch/ds/index.jsp?positionId=35432). They had to write their interpretation online in a computer room. This exercise makes use of the composite question, which is the most complex text-object type of the dialogical elements. Whereas the other dialogical elements allow a user to prompt later visitors to answer a question, e.g. an evaluative question or a multiple choice question, the composite question facilitates a two-staged interaction with students. In the first step, all users are invited to answer a question, usually by writing an interpretation of a given text. In the second step, all students are given the task of mutually assessing these interpretations by giving a critical comment and a quantitative evaluation (see Figure 3).

In this case report, the second step was assigned as homework: students were asked to read their classmates' interpretations and to assess them both qualitatively and quantitatively (http://www.textmachina.uzh.ch/ds/index.jsp?positionId=37899). The results formed the basis for deepening discussion in class about the clarification of unsolved problems and about those methodological and theoretical issues that were shown to be relevant and disputable during the individual exercise.

This transparent and traceable procedure forces students to observe each other and themselves in the interpretation process and, by doing so, to reflect on their

Figure 3. An example of an answer and its evaluation by fellow students

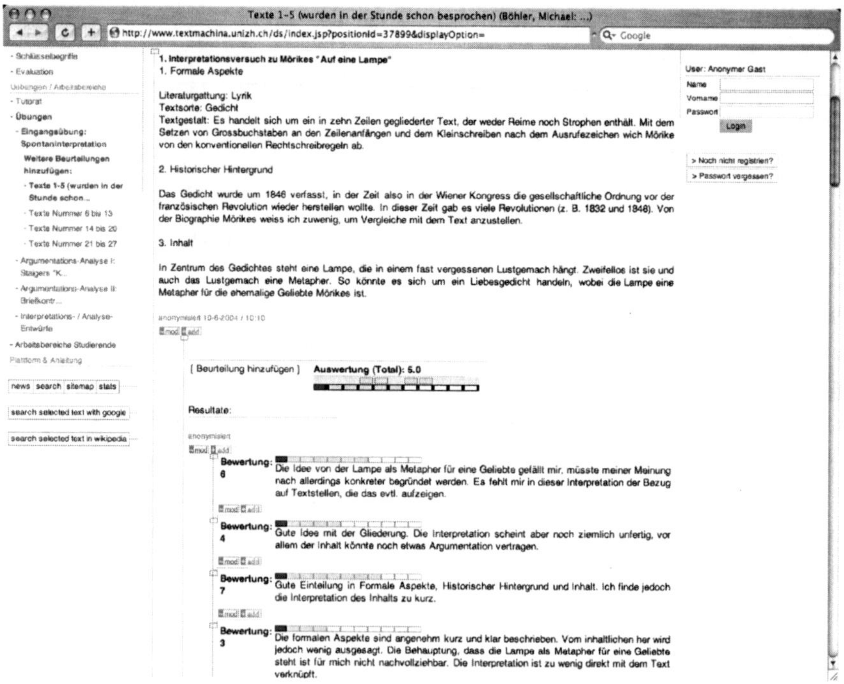

present level of competencies and knowledge (Beck, Guldimann & Zutavern, 1994; Willke, 2000). The following sessions were dedicated to strengthening these processes under the teacher's guidance. The combination of individual work on the platform with the discussion of some exemplarily extracts of student work in class and the comparison of the results to theoretical stances promote students' awareness of the relevant theoretical issues and the methodological criteria which control interpretive practice. This way, they can experience by themselves the dialogical argument and assessment that takes place in a scientific community (Willke, 2001).

Of course, the tool 'composite question' for the mentioned exercise can also be implemented in other ways, e.g. by changing the tasks or the time schedule. It is thus also conceivable that the first task be solved at home over several weeks by using other resources such as secondary literature. It could also be quite revealing if the academic would participate in the task, i.e. by assuming a pseudonym to discuss on equal grounds. Since all entries in tEXtMACHINA are saved by default it might also be interesting to compare the results of solutions to the composite question at the beginning of a term with those to a second exercise at the end of term in order to observe progress in the students' research skills.

The second example is not based on a specific tool in tEXtMACHINA, neither does it claim to be a very innovative scenario. It consists rather of the implementation of a quite well-known didactic concept, the constructive controversy, which allows for discussion of a subject in a small group of learners from diverse perspectives (cf. Johnson & Johnson 1992). Therefore, it is highly appropriate to be used for the collaboratively solving of a specific text-centered problem. While the exercise has a similar purpose to the previously described one – to practice scientific dialogue –, it permits a more individual implementation by using and combining well-known procedures such as discussions in small groups, collecting and exchanging material, finding a shared thesis and preparing a final presentation in class.

The constructive controversy is a paradigmatic exercise according to the idea of collaborative and constructive knowledge acquirement. This scenario aims at reproducing the scientific processes of rational debate and dialogical consensus-building; it is therefore the appropriate implementation of the intended simulation of the scientific practice. The exercise serves to teach students elementary knowledge about the discursive practices and procedures of the Humanities in problem-based debates and makes it possible to achieve two aims at once. On the one hand, students gain specific knowledge about the present topic; on the other hand, the collaboration and the debate on proper texts and statements incites their reflection on the meticulously regulated production and construction of new knowledge in the academic interpretive community. In order to increase simulative authenticity, the exercises can use role-play situations by dividing participants into different groups with specific discursive positions and tasks. In such an arrangement, students may have to argue for their position regardless of their actual convictions. In doing so, they learn to stand aside from their own opinion and to take into account the necessary standards in order to achieve intersubjective plausibility for their position as well as to observe their rational strategies with distance (Beck, Guldimann & Zutavern, 1994; Bransford, Brown & Cocking, 2000).

Of course, the actual design of the didactic arrangement can be varied to correspond to individual needs. This also makes it possible to avoid a difficulty that confronts collaborative educational models which rely on intensive discussions between the participants. Usually, these kinds of model are considered to be unsuited to handling high numbers of students. Yet, by dividing the attendance into small self-organized groups and by delegating certain control tasks to groups or tutors, teachers can be freed up to a considerable degree and manage higher numbers than usually assumed to be possible.

Since the collaborative research process of students is essential for this exercise, it is important that it can be easily documented in tEXtMACHINA. This allows random attendance and assistance by the teacher during the process. The work done online in the groups is then assessed in the plenary sessions when students have to present the result of their studies. By construing and reproducing a scientific controversy, students are forced to give an account of their present level of knowledge and to reach a consensus on a certain issue as well as to settle on unsolved questions which must be taken up again in the plenary discussion.

In order to create a constructive controversy in tEXtMACHINA, one needs the basic operations of adding new threads and modifying the ownership and visibility of these workspaces for the groups accordingly. An example of such an arrangement has been worked out in another introductory course in Modern German Literature in 2004 by Stefan Hofer (http://www.textmachina.uzh.ch/ds/index.jsp?positionId=36539). The exercise was carried out at the beginning of the course when the discussion centered on the question of how to define the limits of literature. The setting consisted of five short texts or extracts which were displayed online and had to be discussed by students online in their group-specific workspaces. Students had to argue in small groups about the question of whether and why these texts can or should be considered as literature (http://www.textmachina.uzh.ch/ds/index.jsp?positionId=36856). Half of the group had to take on the pro position, the other half the contra position. These subgroups had a closed thread at their own disposal where they could prepare by collecting arguments and exchanging findings to be brought into the debate. In so doing, they had to analyze the five texts and to collaboratively construe an interpretation of them.

All of the five primary texts had some reference to music: the first one was a music review in a newspaper, the second was a experimental text entitled "Die japanische Hitparade vom 25. Mai 1968" by the Austrian writer Peter Handke, the third was an extract from the novel "Musica Leggera" by the Swiss writer Franco Supino. The two other texts were hypertexts: "tango rgb – colours of passion" by the German Internet artist Oliver Gassner, an installation that tries to transfer tango in movements of colors, and a hypertext by the Swiss Internet artists Beat Suter and René Bauer which refers to Gassner's project intertextually by alienating it.

The collaborative debate took two weeks and ended with a written summary from every subgroup which then was evaluated by the other students. These results were finally transferred to the plenary session for a concluding discussion. The learning effects seemed to be very positive even though some students tended to be overstrained by the handling of the tEXtMACHINA functions. In order to realize the full potential of such a constructive controversy, students need a certain degree of familiarity with the application. It might therefore be wise not to start with such a task at the beginning of a term.

The formal and flexible character of the techniques offered in tEXtMACHINA demands a certain degree of creativity from of its academic users when they want to implement their didactic concepts. The following example illustrates the potential for an individualized design that lies in this characteristic of the platform. In order to standardize the weekly exercises in his literary courses at University of Zurich,

Stefan Hofer developed a general structured format that made it easy for students to orient themselves in the new tasks during the progression of the course. He labeled this standardized format as tEXtIVITY, which adopts and develops Gilly Salmon's (2002) "E-tivities" concept. This concept, which combines the terms 'activity' and 'electronic', is meant to give a traceable structure to any exercise in virtual learning. Salmon (2002) suggests a precise depiction of the task in question, the aim and the timeframe of an exercise. The formal structure or 'frame' of a tEXtIVITY therefore reproduces a conceptual scheme of exercise that is organized by its type of exercise, the intended purpose, the specific task and its timeframe (http://www.textmachina.uzh.ch/ds/index.jsp?positionId=36539). In practice, these aspects need to be specified with precise information which presupposes a clear conception of the exercise by the teacher. By doing so, a tEXtIVITY can be used in a blended learning setting as well as in strictly online teaching, Beginning with exercises which combine issue-related questions with tasks that improve technical familiarity with tEXtMACHINA has been shown to be quite useful.

It is essential to understand that the structure of a tEXtIVITY is not a programmed entity. It was designed by its academic user and built out of different text-object types which are combined into a more complex structure (contained in a table). Since tEXtMACHINA allows the recursive duplication of its entries, any complex structure can be used as a template and easily copied. This standardized design therefore allows the consistent and repeated implementation of exercises during a whole term.

In the context of the blended learning approach, one of the main challenges is to closely combine attendance sessions with online working. A very simple but efficient way to make sure that this combination works consists of providing exercises whose completion is indispensable for the preparation of the attendance session. This procedure takes advantage of e-learning for the intensification of the preparatory work and leads to an optimization of the attendance discussion, since it can immediately focus on the debatable and relevant issues that need to be reconsidered.

This goal can be reached with different types of exercises. The aforementioned composite exercise is one possible and very structured option. Another much simpler way would be to ask all students to post their questions concerning a given text and explore corresponding hypotheses online and collaboratively before the text is discussed in class. This way everybody would be informed about all the questions and proposed answers before class. This procedure furnishes students with the knowledge and deliberations of their fellow students and allows a teacher to identify students' level of knowledge as well as their problems in understanding.

A very similar procedure capitalizes on the potential of the text-marker tool in tEXTMACHINA. When the preparation for a class consists of analytical work on and the close reading of a text, this function can be very helpful in objectifying this process. Since the tool allows users to mark and to comment on a specific word or extract of a text, teachers can prepare the discussion by asking their students to read and analyze a given text with respect to a specific question. The marks then leave a visual and observable trace of their reading on the text and can therefore be used as a starting point for further discussion. When working with the color marker, visualization also makes it possible to display a kind of collective and intersubjective reading: passages that have been marked several times will appear in a more intense color and therefore tend to be more relevant. For a teacher, such an exercise usually takes more effort to prepare because it often means that the text to be analyzed online has to be scanned or entered manually. Yet this effort may be compensated for by the positive results of more intensive preparation for the attendance class.

This setting of analytical close reading can be refined by the option of using the different marker and reference types of the marker function to codify the text analysis with respect to different questions (i.e. questionability, relevance, pro/contra a specific thesis, etc.). This makes it possible to construct more sophisticated exercises that produce new insights into the structure of a text up for discussion. The example shown in Figure 4 is taken from the aforementioned introductory course by Stefan Hofer. It makes use of this option by asking students to read an important section of Roland Barthes' "Death of the Author" and then to mark passages with respect to two different issues (questionability and importance). The chosen reference types either split the given text in order to add a new comment or produce a new layer that only shows when the marked text extract is mouse-clicked. Students were invited to read their fellow students' comments. The visual traces of the exercise can still be observed online (http://www.textmachina.uzh.ch/ds/index.jsp?positionId=11736).

The last example demonstrates the gradual acquisition of competencies on the topic of hyperfiction (based on the model of competencies from Keller, 2008) in a course for 26 high- school students at the Kantonsschule Baden in 2007. The goal of the teaching unit was to acquaint students with the text genre hyperfiction in order to enable them to write such a text on their own, by combining words, graphics, sound and other digital media without any knowledge of programming languages such as HTML, just using the possibilities of tEXtMACHINA. Since students were not only asked to acquire new knowledge but also had to engage in creative writing, the examples illustrate that tEXtMACHINA can also be used to carry out creative writing projects as well as scientific ones. The conceptual scheme of the application and its technical implementation makes it easy to put into practice recent discoveries in writing research and didactics which place the emphasis on collaborative and staged writing exercises (Baurmann, 2002). This procedure aims to improve students' writing competencies by letting them write regularly online. As their knowledge increases they can reuse their earlier contributions for more advanced tasks (cf. Baurmann, 2002).

Figure 4. A section of students' collaborative analysis of Barthes' text

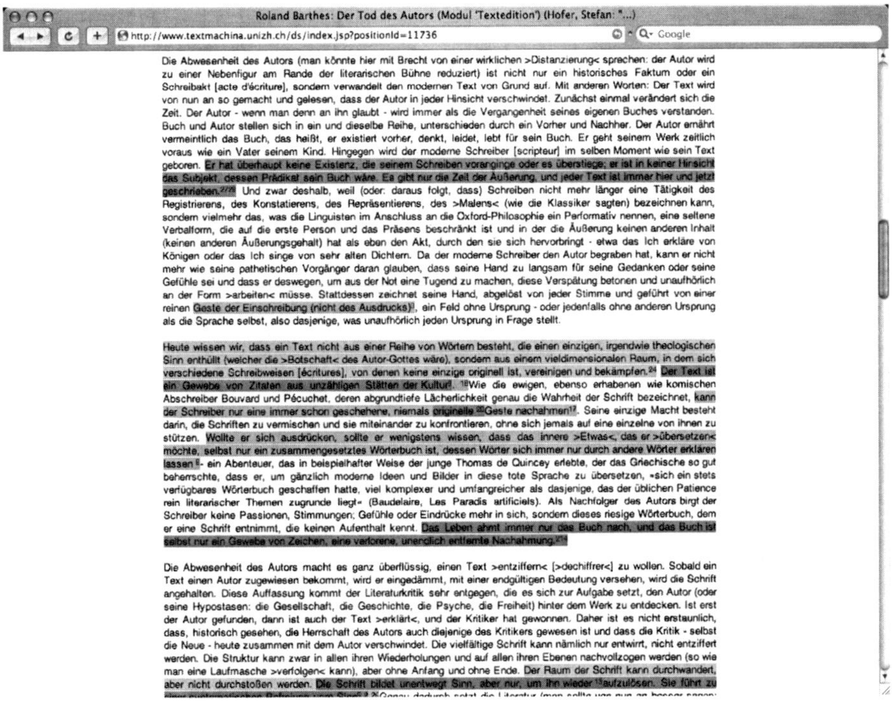

Students were first confronted with the text genre hyperfiction with which they had not been familiar before. After being introduced to previous non-linear writings such as Julio Cortázar's novel "Rayuela" they were presented with a wide range of hyperfiction online. They were invited to read and explore these texts and then to discuss their impressions and finally to coherently reflect on them online in their first written text. After that, the discussion was continued in the attendance session where students also learned the theoretical definitions of the concept of hyperfiction. Once they had become acquainted with it, students were then asked to compose their own hyperfictional text by just using the potential of tEXtMACHINA in as versatile a way as possible. The task was therefore to create a complex hyperfictional text without necessarily applying html or any other programming language.

The given subject of their texts was 'living/dwelling', a subject which had been discussed before. Students had to read a text by Franz Kafka ("Der Bau") and to transform it collectively in a collaborative hyperfiction. A second task consisted in reading another fictional text, "Im Hause enden die Geschichten" by Paul Nizon, and to write a hyperfiction individually starting from some extracts of this novel, using it as a structure for their own hyperfiction composition.

All of the resulting hyperfictions made use of the possibilities of the Internet in their individual ways just with the aid of tEXtMACHINA. Many of them used the functionality of the Web to comment on specific positions of an image and then to continue via hyper-references into further intertextual relations. By doing so, students generated non-linear texts with multiple connections and ramified ways of reading. Some of them experimented with sound while two of them even employed their programming knowledge for the production of their texts (http://www.textmachina.uzh.ch/hofer/index.jsp?positionId=11871; see Figure 5).

After finishing this creative task, students had to write a last text reflecting on the subject 'hyperfiction – literature of the future?' as they were by this time considered as relative experts on the topic of 'hyperfiction' and on the potential and constraints of this relatively new genre.

The five examples of best practices are a brief selection of what has been realized in tEXtMACHINA in order to give something of an idea of what could actually be done if a teacher approached the tool with a clear didactic concept and the necessary imagination for creative course design and implementation.

RESEARCH PERSPECTIVES

As one of the principal results of the practical application of tEXtMACHINA was that its tools were shown to be too under-defined and too formal to actualize the

Figure 5. An immersive hypertext by student Lukas Renggli made of complex visual and textual relations

underlying educational concepts without further explanation, future endeavors should attach more importance to getting academics using the platform. The development and collection of new creative exercise designs will therefore be one of the main tasks for the near future.

The development of tEXtMACHINA integrated findings from the early courses into its design; these included optimizing user administration and rights management, a variety of the dialogical elements, and the semantic indexing of existing entries. The theoretical discussion has therefore always been channeled back into the practical findings and vice versa. This means that, alongside the development of new exercises, the platform itself has also to be developed with the implementation of new features, i.e. upgrading the evaluation techniques or differentiating the discursive roles.

Another focus of future research has to lie on the transition from literary education to real scientific practice to meet the objective of the platform to be both useful in didactic settings and in scientific practice. However, a didactic approach that aims at simulating real scientific practices raises the question of where the border between real practice and its simulation can be drawn. It also raises the question why simulated practice should not also be considered as real practice, given the fact that the only difference lies in the status and the experience of the persons involved (novices or experts).

The tools provided by tEXtMACHINA can be used not only for education but also for research in the Humanities, especially if it is meant to be collaborative, since it offers new technologies for working with texts. Groups of researchers could, for example, discuss their readings and interpretations of a given text online, by commenting on their suggestions and proposals directly in the text. This might be helpful in ongoing research processes like editing work, and could, at least partly, replace the pricey, time-consuming and, in an ecological sense, questionable habits of scientific symposia all over the world. So far, tEXtMACHINA has been adopted for a few small research projects, or projects which span the boundary between education and research; an evaluation of these projects has, however, not yet been forthcoming.

By applying the techniques of a collaborative online environment the scientific practice itself might discover new ways of how its work can be done. Therefore, future attractions for researchers of new applications like tEXtMACHINA might also lie in its changing effects on scientific work as such. The future researcher might consult colleagues on textual problems constantly online, so that the scientific research in the Humanities evolves gradually from the solitary study in the privacy of one's office to the collaborative discussion and interpretation of given texts. In this respect, only three possible perspectives shall be mentioned. The integration of multimedia makes it possible to work analytically with data that has so far been neglected and excluded in literary studies (Giesecke, 2002). tEXtMACHINA with its inherent multimodality shows how graphics, audios, videos can be integrated into the scientific discourse They can be added as comments and therefore do not need to be described. Graphics can also be commented online and collaboratively with the comments lying over a certain position of a graphic. This makes it possible to establish direct intertextual references to a specific part of an image and, by doing this, to visually analyze it online or integrate it into a discourse on a specific issue. As tEXtMACHINA actualizes the discussion on a text, the distinction between the individual texts becomes blurred and one endless and intertextual discourse begins to form and grow. The formerly stable original text is affected by the new comments which impose their particular reading of it, and the original text itself may be changed at a later time by its owner if no other provisions are made. Thus, the cultural perception of a text might eventually also be modified, as it becomes floating and collective (Bauer & Maier, 2003). However, it is not only the border between the original source and comment and its authors that seems to blur: in tEXtMACHINA, the simplicity of the act of writing and the way it is coupled with analytical reading using the marker function leads to the traditionally separated roles of the reader and the writer fusing into something like a "wreader" (Bergermann, 1997).

Developments such as these will press scientists to reflect on the perspectives of their practice under the conditions imposed by the new media in the digital age. tEXtMACHINA will be just a small piece in the jigsaw puzzle of the future.

REFERENCES

Albert, H. (2000). *Kritischer Rationalismus. Vier Kapitel zur Kritik illusionären Denkens*. Tübingen: Mohr Siebeck.

Barthes, R. (1973). *Le plaisir du texte*. Paris: Editions du Seuil.

Bauer, R., & Maier, J. (2003). Schwebendes Schreiben. Vom Schreiben an/in kontextualisierenden Medien wie nic-las.com. In Fehr, J., & Grond, W. (Eds.), *Schreiben am Netz. Literatur im digitalen Zeitalter* (pp. 164–171). Innsbruck: Haymon.

Baurmann, J. (2002). *Schreiben – Überarbeiten – Beurteilen. Ein Arbeitsbuch zur Schreibdidaktik*. Seelze-Velber: Kallmeyer.

Beck, E., Guldimann, T., & Zutavern, M. (1994). Eigenständiges Lernen verstehen und fördern. In Reusser, K. (Ed.), *Verstehen* (pp. 207–225). Bern: Huber.

Bergermann, U. (1997). *'Verkörpert' Hypertext Theorien vom Schreiben?* Retrieved December 18, 2007, from http://www.uni-paderborn.de/~bergerma/texte/zmm.html

Boud, D., & Feletti, G. (Eds.). (1997). The Challenge of Problem-Based Learning (2nd ed.). London, Stirling (USA): Kogan Page.

Bransford, J. D., Brown, A. L., & Cocking, R. R. (2000). How Experts Differ from Novices. In Bransford, J. D., Brown, A. L., & Cocking, R. R. (Eds.), *How People Learn: Brain, Mind, Experience, and School* (pp. 31–50). Washington, DC: National Academy Press.

Deci, L. E., & Ryan, R. M. (1993). Die Selbstbestimmungstheorie der Motivation und ihre Bedeutung für die Pädagogik. *Zeitschrift fur Padagogik*, *1*(39), 223–238.

Dilthey, W. (1970). Der Aufbau der geschichtlichen Welt in den Geistewissenschaften. Frankfurt/M.: Suhrkamp.

Eco, U. (1964). *Apocalittici e integrati*. Milano: Bompiani.

Fish, S. (1980). *Is There a Text in This Class? The Authority of Interpretive Communities*. Cambridge, MA: Harvard University Press.

Flusser, V. (2004). *Writings. Electronic Mediations*. Minneapolis, MN: University of Minnesota Press.

Foucault, M. (1969). *L'Archéologie du savoir*. Paris: Gallimard.

Giesecke, M. (2002). Von den Mythen der Buchkultur zu den Visionen der Informationsgesellschaft: Trendforschung zur aktuellen Medienökologie. Frankfurt/M: Suhrkamp.

Habermas, J. (1973). Wahrheitstheorien. In H. Fahrenbach (Ed.), Wirklichkeit und Reflexion. W. Schulz zum 60. Geburtstag (pp. 211-265). Pfullingen: Neske.

Hirsch, E. D. (1967). *Validity in Interpretation*. New Haven, London: Yale University Press.

Johnson, D. W., & Roger, T. Johnson (1992). Encouraging Thinking Through Constructive Controversy. In D. W. Davidson & T. Worsham (Eds.), Enhancing Thinking Through Cooperative Learning (pp. 120-137). Teachers College Press: New York City.

Keller, S. (2008). 'I Have A Dream!' – mit dialogischem Lernen in Englisch eine gute Rede schreiben. In U. Ruf, S. Keller & F. Winter (Eds.), Besser lernen im Dialog. Dialogisches Lernen in der Unterrichtspraxis (pp. 70-82). Seelze-Velber: Klett/Kallmeyer.

Kittler, F. A. (1985). [München: Fink.]. *Aufschreibesysteme*, *1800*, 1900.

Kittler, F. A. (1992). *Discourse Networks 1800/1900*. Palo Alto, CA: Stanford University Press.

Kristeva, J. (1969). Le mot, le dialogue et le roman. In J. Kristeva, Sémiotiké: recherches pour une sémanalyse (p. 82-112). Paris: Seuil.

Maingueneau, D. (1991). *L'Analyse du discours. Introduction aux lectures de l'archive*. Paris: Hachette.

Oser, F. K., Achternhagen, F., & Renold, U. (2006). *Competence Oriented Teacher Training. Old Research Demands and New Pathways*. Rotterdam, Taipei: Sense.

Peirce, C. (1932). Collected Papers of Charles Sanders Peirce: *Vol. 2. Elements of Logic*. Cambridge: Cambridge University Press.

Plett, H. (1979). *Textwissenschaft und Textanalyse. Semiotik, Linguistik, Rhetorik*. Heidelberg: UTB für Wissenschaft.

Salmon, G. (2002). *E-tivities – The Key to Active Online Learning*. London: Kogan Page.

Sauter, A., Sauter, W., & Bender, H. (2004). Blended Learning: effiziente Integration von E-Learning und Präsenztraining (2nd extended ed.). Neuwied: Hermann Luchterhand.

Schulmeister, R. (2004). Didaktisches Design aus hochschuldidaktischer Sicht – ein Plädoyer für offene Lernsituationen. In Rinn, U., & Meister, D. M. (Eds.), *Didaktik und neue Medien* (pp. 19–39). Münster: Waxmann.

Stockmann, R. (2005). Die Erfindung des Rades – universitäres E-Learning aus Sicht der Nutzenden. In C. Thimm (Ed.), Netz-Bildung – Lehren und Lernen mit neuen Medien in Wissenschaft und Wirtschaft (pp. 51-73). Frankfurt/M.: Peter Lang.

Weinert, F. (2001). Concept of Competence: A Conceptual Clarification. In Rychen, D. S., & Salganik, L. H. (Eds.), *Defining and Selecting Key Competencies. Theoretical and Conceptual Foundations* (pp. 45–65). Göttingen: Hogrefe & Huber.

Willke, H. (2000). *Systemtheorie I: Grundlagen*. Stuttgart, Jena: Gustav Fischer UTB.

Willke, H. (2001). *Systemtheorie III: Steuerungstheorie. Grundzüge einer Theorie der Steuerung komplexer Sozialsysteme*. Stuttgart: Lucius&Lucius.

Windelband, W. (1894). *Geschichte und Naturwissenschaft. Rektoratsrede. Rede zum Antritt des Rektorats der Kaiser-Wilhelms-Universität Straßburg*. Strassburg.

ADDITIONAL READING

Bradley, J. (2008). Thinking about Interpretation. Pliny and Scholarship in the Humanities. *Literary and Linguistic Computing, 23*(3), 263–279. doi:10.1093/llc/fqn021

Breen, R., Lindsay, R., Jenkins, A., & Smith, P. (2001). The Role of Information and Communication Technologies in a University Learning Environment. *Studies in Higher Education, 26*(1), 95–113. doi:10.1080/03075070120043206

Crane, G., Bamman, D., & Jones, A. (2008). ePhilology: When the Books Talk to Their Readers. In S. Schreibman & R. Siemens (Eds.), *A Companion to Digital Literary Studies*. Oxford: Blackwell. Retrieved August 24, 2009, from http://www.digitalhumanities.org/companionDLS

Darby, J. (2001). Networked Learning in Higher Education: The Mule in the Barn. In Steeples, C., & Jones, C. (Eds.), *Network Learning: Perspectives and Issues* (pp. 17–26). London: Springer.

Dennis, A., & Valcich, J. (1999). *Rethinking Media Richness: Towards a Theory of Media Synchronicity*. Retrieved August, 24, 2009, from http://www.doktus.de/dok/38631/3-dennis-valacich.html

Fehr, J., & Grond, W. (Eds.). (2003). *Schreiben am Netz. Literatur im digitalen Zeitalter*. Innsbruck: Haymon.

Gervais, B. (2008). Is There a Text on This Screen? Reading in an Era of Hypertextuality. In S. Schreibman & R. Siemens (Eds.), *A Companion to Digital Literary Studies*. Oxford: Blackwell. Retrieved August 24, 2009, from http://www.digitalhumanities.org/companionDLS

Giesecke, M. (1992). *Sinnenwandel, Sprachwandel*. Frankfurt am Main: Kulturwandel.

Grudin, J. (1994). Computer-supported Cooperative Work: Work, its History and Participation. *IEEE Computer, 27*(5), 19–26.

Hoover, D. (2007). The End of the Irrelevant Text: Electronic Texts, Linguistics, and Literary Theory. *Digital Humanities Quarterly, 1*(2). Retrieved August 24, 2009, from http://www.digitalhumanities.org/dhq/vol/3/1/index.html

Idensen, H. (2001). Kollaborative Schreibweisen – virtuelle Text- und Theorie-Arbeit: Schnittstellen für Interaktionen mit Texten im Netzwerk. In Gendolla, P., Schmitz, N. M., & Schneider, I. (Eds.), *Formen interaktiver Medienkunst* (pp. 218–265). Frankfurt am Main: Suhrkamp.

Kearsley, G., & Shneiderman, B. (1998). Engagement Theory: A Framework for Technology-Based Teaching and Learning. *Educational Technology*, *38*(5), 20–23.

Lancashire, I. (2008). Cybertextuality and Philology. In S. Schreibman & R. Siemens (Eds.), *A Companion to Digital Literary Studies*. Oxford: Blackwell. Retrieved August 24, 2009, from http://www.digitalhumanities.org/companionDLS

Mayes, J., Dineen, F., McKendree, J., & Lee, J. (2002). Learning from Watching Others Learn. In Steeples, C., & Jones, C. (Eds.), *Network Learning: Perspectives and Issues* (pp. 213–227). London: Springer.

Pohl, M., & Purgathofer, P. (2004). Hypertext Writing Profiles and Visualisation. *Computers and the Humanities*, *38*(1), 83–105. doi:10.1023/B:CHUM.0000009226.51168.47

Rockwell, G. (2003). What is Text Analysis, Really? *Literary and Linguistic Computing*, *18*(2), 209–219. doi:10.1093/llc/18.2.209

Schreibman, S. (2002). Computer-mediated Texts and Textuality: Theory and Practice. *Computers and the Humanities*, *36*(3), 283–293. doi:10.1023/A:1016178200469

Siemens, R. G. (2002). A new Computer-assisted Literary Criticism? *Computers and the Humanities*, *36*(3), 259–267. doi:10.1023/A:1016134426453

Suter, B. (2006). Das Neue Schreiben – Von den Widerständen des Schreibwerkzeugs bis zum "fluktuierenden Konkreatisieren". In Giuriato, D., Stingelin, M., & Zanetti, S. (Eds.), *System ohne General* (pp. 167–187). München: Wilhelm Fink.

Trentin, G. (2004). Networked Collaborative Learning in the Study of Modern History and Literature. *Computers and the Humanities*, *38*(3), 299–315. doi:10.1007/s10579-004-1110-8

Unsworth, J. (2005). *Scholarly Primitives: What Methods do Humanities Researchers Have in common, and how might our Tools reflect this?* Retrieved August 24, 2009, from http://jefferson.village.virginia.edu/~jmu2m/Kings.5-00/primitives.html

van Pelt, T. (2002). The Question Concerning Theory: Humanism, Subjectivity, and Computing. *Computers and the Humanities*, *36*(3), 307–318. doi:10.1023/A:1016160114582

Wenger, E. (2000). Communities of Practice and Social Learning Systems. *Organization*, *7*(2), 225–246. doi:10.1177/135050840072002

Wilkerson, L., & Gijselaers, W. H. (1996). *Bringing Problem-Based Learning to Higher Education: Theory and Practice*. San Francisco: Jossey-Bass Publishers.

Wilks, Y. (2004). On the Ownership of Text. *Computers and the Humanities*, *38*(2), 115–127. doi:10.1023/B:CHUM.0000031184.28781.47

Chapter 6
Plays Well with Others: The Value of Developing Multiplayer Digital Gamespaces for Literary Education

Jon Saklofske
Acadia University, Canada

ABSTRACT

The purpose of this chapter is to discuss issues and solutions surrounding the incorporation of interactive video games into university-level literary education. A comparative use of participatory games alongside more traditional texts and critical ideas in the classroom will encourage engaged learning, promote multiple literacies, and facilitate awareness of the nature of reading and the operations of narrative across media forms. While obstacles and challenges to the use of digital games in the university classroom include technology, programming ability, time, budget and platform longevity, the author will demonstrate how, by heavily customising enCore Xpress, an open-source, web-based, multi-user database and constructing two interactive fictions based on Romantic period novels, he has been able to circumvent these difficulties, engage students as lucid players and builders, and support metacritical reflection.

DOI: 10.4018/978-1-60566-932-8.ch006

INTRODUCTION

The intersection between modern digital technologies and literary education is fertile ground for pedagogical innovations and evolutions. Digital Humanities, however, require more than just discussing the newest trends in critical theory and discourse. They necessarily involve technologies that alter perceptions and practices on the most fundamental levels. How we organize, sort, navigate through, relate to and locate meaning within textual information is no longer heavily influenced by the form and functions of book technology. This shift has generated opportunities for evolutions in research and teaching methodology. Teaching and research are not independent entities, but are co-dependent, operating as a feedback loop in which the systems and paradigms that inform each affect both. The effects of digital technologies are thus compounded by this reciprocity. The almost-instantaneous access to and retrieval of scholarly information, which faculty and students in most universities now take for granted, along with new tools for the organization and processing of such information (such as the tools available via TAPoR, the Collex interface for NINES and the ZOTERO addon for Firefox),[1] have changed the nature and character of research, writing and scholarly exchange and dialogue. Temporal and spatial limitations have been largely transcended, resulting in increased research depth and breadth, an opportunity for much more immediate feedback and discussion, and new options for presentation, demonstration and communication. The comparatively cumbersome research practices of just 20 years ago seem archaic: faculty members and students relied on card catalogues, printed journal indexes, and restrictive interlibrary loan programs for secondary research material, and required a substantial budget for travel, time and assistance to locate primary textual material dispersed through the archival holdings or the special collections of many remote libraries. Some scholars might mourn the loss of the discipline and patience required to gather and process resources in this way. However, the opportunities for increased productivity associated with an improved access to information, and the refusal to treat these changing practices as mutually exclusive leads to a new 'best practice' model for embracing this unique historical moment of media in transition.

As a result, the nature and character of many higher-education classrooms are changing. At MIT's Comparative Media Studies Program, students and faculty members work collaboratively and in multiple media technologies to explore and concretize their ideas. At Acadia University, several courses require students to bring their required laptops to each class in order to fully participate, and some science classrooms use survey software to collect immediate feedback from students relating to the current topic of study. Individual experts lecturing to (or performing in front of) silent groups of note-taking students, requiring students to produce assignments using the critical essay's strict paradigms, and encouraging the regurgitation of accurate information during lengthy, comprehensive final exams are certainly not extinct, but have been de-naturalized by scholars who have been nurtured on participatory forms of multiple mediations and digital technologies that extend the forms, perceptions and practices engendered by the book.[2]

It is true that the page and the authoritative, authorial voice, due to their time-tested efficiency will persist as viable traditions of and models for scholarship and anachronistically continue to inform our conceptual understandings of digital mediation. However, their pre-digital erosion via semiotic, reader-response, deconstruction, feminist, cultural studies and post-structural theoretical approaches have already confirmed that new conceptual arenas and a redefinition of participation as playful interaction are not only possible, but available through these new technologies. One such alternative involves the reconceptualization of the printed text as a game-space and as a site of linguistic play. This perspective has already been distinctively theorized and anticipated in relation to literature and culture by Mikhail Bakhtin's (1981) notion of carnivalesque spaces and functions, Jacques Derrida's (1980) acknowledgement of the ideological and ontological tensions and disruptions associated with interpretive freeplay, and Roland Barthes' (1978) pre-digital experimentations with playtexts.

The benefits of participatory mediation for education have been recognized since Plato's promotion of philosophical play as a primary way of knowing and educating a just citizenry (Krentz, 1998). Recently, the importance of play to social, cultural, political and critical practices has been reaffirmed and theorized further by a number of writers. Johan Huizinga (1971) suggests that it precedes culture and is a voluntary activity which lies outside morality, but preserves an essential perspective toward ethical concerns via its resistance to seriousness and its sacred qualities. For Huizinga (1971), play signifies the capacity for irrationalism, freedom, disinterestedness and secludedness. Roger Caillois (2001) resists Huizinga's (1971) universal approach by offering a typology that includes competition, chance, simulation and vertigo after defining it as an pure "waste of time, energy, ingenuity [and] skill" (p. 5) that still remains indispensible for human development. This typology is diversified further in the work of Brian Sutton-Smith (2001) in an effort to reflect on the overall ambiguity of the term. Finally, and controversially, McKenzie Wark's (2007) 'networked book' that initially involved collaborations between the author and web-based readers prior to the publication of its print version (http://www.futureofthebook.org/gamertheory), redefines contemporary Western culture as an imperfect copy of digital gamespace, replaces the conventional subject and citizen with the figure of the gamer, and explores the implications of this reality through comparisons with specific digital games. Wark's (2007) ideas demonstrate the extent to which these concepts can serve as conceptual models for social and political understanding.

While these authors may not all see play as a serious activity, they take its arenas and its cultural effects very seriously. This sociological and theoretical attention, along with the increasing popularity of computer-based interactive narratives, justifies a classroom-based inquiry into the functions, parallels and disparities between interactive digital fictions and literary narratives, and demands pedagogical evolutions in literary education to account for multiple literacies and mediations. At the very least, the mutual illumination afforded through a comparative consideration between books and these computer-based sites of contest and cooperation will clarify and extend students' understanding of the generic nature and functions of literary writing. At most, in a time of media in transition and the erosion of contextual and communal metanarratives, this approach recognizes the importance of comparative media studies and the relationships between mediation, culture, perception and participation.

In this chapter, I explore the pedagogical opportunities and problems that accompany the use of digital games in university-level literary education and comment on the necessary future of such integrations by sharing the results of my own research and practice over the past three years. Using a highly-modified version of the open-source enCore Xpress MOO database,[3] I have produced Acadia's Higher Education Learning Portal (HELP), a flexible, cost-effective and web-based alternative to single-purpose software that is designed to make the creation and modification of interactive scenarios easy and intuitive. These environments generated through HELP's accommodating toolkit are not based on 3-D graphic engines and do not feature the graphic prowess of many recent commercial video games. However, the multimedia gamespaces enabled through the HELP platform appropriately support multiple literacies and cultivate an understanding of the functions of textuality relative to other media. This media awareness is essential for students of literature who are learning strategies for active reading and critical writing. I will illustrate the advantages and challenges of using this software to increase participation in and reflection upon social computing, collective intelligence practices and other Humanities research and teaching assumptions by referring to two of HELP's interactive fictions that were collaboratively constructed for use in my university literature classroom.

BACKGROUND

It is no longer a controversial contention that video games are unique forms of cultural expression that deserve serious critical consideration (Bogost, 2006; Wardrip-Fruin and Harrigan, 2004, 2007; Wark, 2007; Galloway, 2006; Jenkins, 2006, 2008; Jones, 2008; Salen and Zimmerman, 2004; Juul, 2005). Along with this, the idea that they have the potential to be highly rewarding pedagogical tools is no longer a marginal one (see Prensky, 2004). Yet their use in education has largely been limited to information delivery opportunities for pre-university age students. Many elementary-school classrooms in North America often contain at least one computer and students use interactive game software to learn math, spelling, social studies and science concepts. However, computer-based interactive narratives can do more than this: they can invite users to critically examine rhetorical, social and ideological processes that are often interrogated within higher education. For this reason, the creation of digital game environments and narratives for use in university literature classrooms involves more than merely using creative ways to communicate concepts to students. Such initiatives have the potential to serve as invaluable and accessible pedagogical devices that enhance the study of literature by providing a foundation for comparative media studies and conclusions. If approached and applied in a conscientious and lucid manner, the dissonance and convergences created between bookspace and gamespace, between these narrative paradigms, enrich classroom practice through mutual illuminations.

Many recent Humanities computing initiatives, such as NINES and IBM's Many Eyes, are based on a fundamental commitment to a culture of collaborative knowledge creation. Indeed, these models amplify and speed up the kinds of interaction that already take place through the aggregation of bibliographical sources that populate essay spaces like this one. As a consequence, the relative immediacy of their exchanges and their temporally compressed dynamism differentiate them from what has come before.

Despite this growing interest in research methods and practices that look to a social computing model for inspiration, a romanticized paradigm of individualism, self-reliance and self-determination continue to constitute academic practice and performance in university Humanities sectors. As such, the primary means used in Humanities classes to assess undergraduate student capability is still the analytical research essay, which anachronistically establishes the continuing importance of rhetorical monologues in an age of digitally-enabled dialogues. Graduate students in literature programs expand these skills through larger-scale thesis projects which demand increasing specialization and isolation, and professional, competitive academic scholars are indirectly pressured by promotion and tenure criteria to continue the practice of independent, autonomous scholarship and publication of articles and books. These traditional forms of study are collective acts that already, but less immediately, interact with a diverse community of accumulated research and debate. Many of us ignore this in favor of highlighting the validity and value of individual work when instructing our students. In this case, we pass on exclusive print culture values that informed our own scholarship to students who currently exist in a plural space between print and digital cultures. Further, although classrooms are perfect environments for social learning initiatives and for employing a bottom-up model of community-based learning through shared experiences, our individual evaluation of students tends to de-emphasise these criteria in favor of a criterion of private mastery and competition.

Expanding traditionally individualist paradigm of Humanities work by embracing a greater sense of collaborative play, discovery and exchange can be encouraged via the use of digital games *in tandem* with more traditional classroom practices and assignments. Here I rely on Katie Salen and Eric Zimmerman's (2004) definition of 'play' as "a free space of movement within a more rigid structure" (p. 304), and Ian Bogost's (2008) approach to defining video games as interactive, expressive, rule-based systems that do not necessarily involve contest and conflict, but which have the potential to engage players in procedural rhetoric. Both the collaborative design of and multi-user engagement within digital environments can be used to promote and teach social computing practices in Humanities scholarship. A variety of games can be used to generate a sense of community, encourage students and faculty members to actively and equally expand beyond an exclusive model of independent and autonomous scholarship. They can also promote a culture where collaborative knowledge, cooperative decision making and collective, networked intelligence are valued just as much as individual capability and competitive achievement. Games offer a unique opportunity for instructors to minimize their role as a delivery mechanism, to shift from established hierarchies of mastery ('you will learn from me') to an invitation to and facilitation of collaborative achievement ('let's play to learn together').

This potential to reflect on traditional and transformational notions of community, self and their educational interaction is introduced in Gee (2003). In his book, he reviews a number of commercial examples to identify and promote 36 learning principles that video games can variously feature. Here, I wish to highlight the further potential that well-thought-through interactive digital narrative experiences can offer for instructors and students involved in university-level literary education. As mentioned above, video games are already successfully used in a variety of educational environments, but their potential for post-secondary education has not yet been adequately explored. For example, traditional examples aimed at younger children have presented content to users via a participatory and often multi-media environment while encouraging them to exercise basic problem-solving skills. Simulation software has also been used to train and assess adult learners in industry, aeronautics and military fields. However, university itself is a metagaming environment where students are ideally encouraged to learn by critically scrutinizing various paradigms, their associated principles and relative issues of self and subjectivity. By being persuaded to play lucidly while being interpellated by and immersed in the performative demands of digital "possibility spaces created by processes" (Bogost,

2008, p. 42), university-level digital narratives have the potential to drastically evolve our understanding of the functions and operations of the political and social systems that are already interrogated in the classroom. Bogost (2008, p. 9) points out that video games (which he defines as examples of procedural representation and expression) can self-reflexively explain process via playful processes rather than through written or spoken representation. He also suggests that an effectively designed experience can "make the symbolic underpinning of [its] rhetorical context manifest in the rules of the game itself" (Bogost, 2008, p.108). In other words, promoting critical awareness during game development in post-secondary classrooms allows one to fully explore and comprehend the relationship between procedural systems, performative demands and narrative content.

In addition, the unique advantage of bringing such experiences into the higher education classroom is that they can engage students as builders and programmers. In this sense, students can scrutinize the ways that the game framework relates to real-world processes. As Wark (2007) suggests, the increasing prevalence and popularity of digital games "speaks to changes in the overall structure of social and technical relations [...] Games are our contemporaries, the form in which the present can be felt and, in being felt, thought through" (225). These interactive, immersive experiences can thus be learning tools that impart certain strategies and knowledge through rule-based play but also need to be critically understood as processes through which rules and process-based learning can be comparatively interrogated and unveiled. Just as Alice grows from the curious explorer in Lewis Carroll's (2003)*Alice's Adventures in Wonderland* to a more self-aware, mature and critical player in *Through the Looking Glass*, well-constructed interactive digital narratives should encourage a willing and decidedly un-romantic interruption of belief or immersion.

PLAYING TO LEARN IN HIGHER EDUCATION

Issues, Controversies and Problems

Textual studies represent a branch of literary study that promotes a critical awareness of the formal aspects of mediation via the history of the book. If the book is a technology, how does its formal features influence or calibrate our perceptions? This type of formal awareness is also an essential part of Digital Humanities studies, for "if we only look through the interface, we cannot appreciate the ways in which the interface itself shapes our experience" (Bolter and Gromala, 2005, p. 11). The key difference between accessing such awareness through the critical use of digital games and traditional literary narratives is that computer-based interactive narratives marry literary and theatrical modes of representation and participation. Players are not just involved in comprehension and interpretation activities from a distanced vantage point, they are also directly involved in the formative performance of the narrative itself. The participatory and process-based aspect of this kind of experience allows students to initially interrogate the implicitly seductive rhetoric of social and cultural models. It is also crucial, though, that students discuss such experiences via presentations, seminars or formal essays. By encouraging students of literature to participate in the creation of and to play through carefully designed gamespaces, we can more generally support a comparative interrogation of the nature of reading and the ways that the interfaces of the book and printed text choreograph the experiences of the reader. We can also ask them to engage with the integrated use of produce/consume/share philosophies in new media environments, and promote participation in and reflection upon the necessity and value of responsive learning. Finally, participating in comparative media studies using multiplayer narratives will expose them to collaborative knowledge creation and analysis and promote the comparative evaluation of this kind of collective intelligence in relation to independent research, analysis and writing.

Ideally, virtual interaction outside the classroom can be used to encourage exchange and in-person interaction and critical reflection while in class. Not only do shared experiences, accomplishments and frustrations within interactive digital narratives provide the foundation for in-class conversations and discussions in the same way that traditional narratives can, but multi-user computer-based environments support interactive and co-operative play. Unlike the shared experience of reading the same novel, then, mutual participation in games that feature social networking components allows students to work together in unique ways before reuniting in the classroom. Instead of talking about individual interpretations, students can converse about a shared experience, continue earlier dialogues, and reflect on the narrative as well as the experience of acting within that narrative. Further, we can also multiply student literacies and rhetorical strategies by highlighting their actions and reactions within narrative space, discussing user experiences, and exploring differences and similarities between reader and player functions. Further, students can be involved in a process-based interrogation of various subject positions and ideological frames, both reinforcing and extending the features of traditional literary studies.

However, commercially available video games not specifically created for post-secondary applications present problems for praxis and pedagogy. They are certainly as useful as any other 'text' in the arena of critical reflection and cultural analysis. However, they are not intended to take full advantage of university-level subject matter or critical methods and remain limited in their functional potential. While many examples of interactive digital fictions have facilitated a continuous debate as to whether this type of narrative can be considered 'art,' most products are still considered 'entertainment' and are thus created to maximize enjoyment, sales and profits. While nothing necessarily should prevent higher-education gaming experiences from being 'fun,' this should not be a primary motivation for the creator. Software made for use in university literature classes that ask their users to experience the story of a slave in the Middle Passage from a first-person perspective, to become a jury member in a life-or-death trial full of unreliable narrators, or to role play within a familiar literary narrative as one of its protagonists or antagonists (to name a few possible examples) need to be interesting, serious, memorable, accurate and thought-provoking rather than escapist.

This is not to say that for-profit examples are completely devoid of learning opportunities or experiences that promote critical or self-reflexive activities. While one of the critical battles that initiated the academic study of gaming involved a polarized debate between the importance of story versus gameplay, many of the most critically celebrated commercial products in recent years rely heavily on a narrative basis that users are responsible for activating, negotiating and interpreting as they progress through the experience. Also, over the last 30 years, as computer users have matured and technology has improved, digital games have developed as well, both in their subject matter and in the increased complexity and opportunity offered through their experiences. Some recent examples include *Mass Effect* in which racism and prejudice are confronted, foreign policy theories and practices are questioned, and moral choices are made in a science-fiction setting. Another illustration is *Grand Theft Auto IV* (GTA IV), condemned for its criminality, sexuality and violence in the same way that moral majority groups used to condemn rock and roll music. What the critics often forget is that each new version of the game satirically and unrelentingly exposes the hypocrisies and ironies of the American Dream. GTA IV does so quite effectively and poignantly from the perspective of a disillusioned immigrant.

An alternative to tailoring one's literary syllabus or planned research outcomes to the inherent limitations of software is to plan and program one from scratch. However, the increased demand for resources that a ground-up initiative would demand can exacerbate the issues that interfere with a successful and flexible utilization of available gaming platforms in university teaching and research, such as budget, time, technology, and platform longevity/obsolescence. One possible alternative would be to make use of features and tools that urge users to creatively modify content (rather than just play through pre-rendered environments and narratives). However, the time-consuming nature of the learning required to effectively use such graphic and scripting tools becomes somewhat prohibitive for faculty with limited research funds and programming experience or for students who are taking a single-term course. Although full-year courses might allow for deeper student expertise with such toolkits, technological requirements, accessibility, compatibility and longevity continue to pose problems.

Those who design any piece of software need to have a clear idea of the ways in which it is going to be used and to anticipate exactly what functions and abilities the program will have. Nothing promotes efficiency in software development like a comprehensive preliminary idea of what the program needs to achieve. Even a 'sandbox' type of environment requires a crystal-clear developmental philosophy. This necessity is certainly made more difficult by the lack of applicable and successful models for higher education, though a number of different examples are emerging. Titles like *Global Conflict: Palestine*, *Peacemaker*, *Wolfquest*, *Darfur is Dying*, *Harpooned*, and *September 12th* demonstrate alternative rhetorical opportunities for facilitating awareness through participatory simulations and experiences. Without useful or established precedents or a taxonomic understanding of the possibilities surrounding such initiatives, there is a high possibility of failure, and many researchers do not like the thought of time and funds invested into a project that might only be used by future programmers as an example of what not to do. One recent 'failure' is Ted Castronova's quarter-million dollar attempt to produce an online world featuring the life and works of William Shakespeare. This project is based on a modified version of *Neverwinter Nights*, and each user needs to purchase the original software to play this modification. It failed because Castronova produced a complex simulation for a general audience who rejected it because it failed to *entertain* them in the same way that commercial examples do. Rather than repurposing it for an academic audience, Castronova is busy developing *Arden 2*, which he describes as more of a "hack and slash Dungeons and Dragons-type game" in an interview with Wired Magazine's Chris Baker (2008, p. 1). Perhaps this iteration will be successful, but Castronova's shifting philosophy away from the academic focus of software design echoes the kinds of market motivations that problematize the validity of using such software for educational purposes.

Recently, Microsoft's Senior UK Regional Director, Neil Thompson, speaking at the *Games 3.0* conference in London, England, confirmed a number of reasons why the industry shies away from producing educational titles. While he did confirm that video games are useful tools for education and that increased maturity in their subject matter potentially increases their educational value, he suggested that it should be up to governments and educators to determine how to make effective use of commercial titles in this way (Martin, 2008).

Solutions and Recommendations

The prescriptive limitations of for-profit software, and the prohibitive aspects of making computer-based interactive narratives for non-commercial, educational applications seem to outweigh the projected benefits of their use. However, my work with multi-user, multi-media, object-oriented, web-based digital gamespaces over the past few years has allowed me to overcome many of the limits suggested above. My team and I have worked to convert an open-source online learning environment that was initially intended for educational purposes into an easy-to-use game-making toolkit and a web-based host for multiplayer narratives and simulations. I have directed the collaborative development and evolution of HELP, Acadia's online *Higher Education Learning Portal*, which is based on versions four and five of the enCore Xpress MOO database.[4] Although the MOO acronym reveals that this platform is dependent on 30-year-old technology, HELP represents an evolution of this 'old-school' technology. It is a flexible, cost-effective alternative to single-purpose software, and makes the creation and modification of scenarios intuitive and easy. In addition, its web-based delivery ensures compatibility across multiple hardware and browser platforms. Although the environments generated through HELP's accommodating toolkit might not meet everyone's specific ideas of what educational gamespaces should look like or be as graphically rich as the 'serious' examples I mentioned earlier, enCore has proven to be an extremely flexible and cost-effective development platform for complex, participatory experiences. In just under three years, with a research budget of approximately $15,000 CDN, and the help of three undergraduate students (one programmer and two content editors), I have been able to produce a stable, open-source virtual environment used for the exploration of theories and ideas relating to participatory narrative, social computing and collaborative learning in university education.

The EnCore Xpress database is an object- oriented, configurable and web-based virtual environment that supports multi-user interaction. Customizable multi-media frames within the browser window support both JAVA and HTML content, making it quite a flexible platform. Webpages, image files, audio files, video, flash and JAVA animations can be incorporated into the presentation, enhancing and evolving the traditional MOO experience that used to be constricted to a largely text-based presentation. No longer do MOO environments resemble text adventures or IRC chat rooms. Yet, unlike the clumsy interfaces of *Second Life* and the 3-D environments of *World of Warcraft*, enCore still preserves a good measure of textual interaction and information presentation. Text-based interactive fiction (IF) games have 25 years of developmental and commercial history, and continue to have a strong and successful independent following – enCore's multi-media environment enhances and evolves the capabilities of this genre overall, and its intended use as a learning platform for university-level literature classes easily allows for the educational application of such software. For students of literature who are being exposed to strategies for active reading and critical writing, this preservation of text-based communication *in tandem* with other media possibilities appropriately encourages multiple literacies, cultivates an understanding of the functions of textuality relative to other media, and allows them to approach textuality within and via visual, digital and procedural forms of rhetoric.

The enCore Xpress platform provides multi-user, web-based accessibility out of the box. It is a free, flexible, open source platform, and a single installation acts as a host and portal to a large number of individual gamespaces. Since enCore uses a fairly esoteric programming language, one of the goals of my project to adapt enCore was to include onboard development tools that minimize the learning curve required by programming so that students and other faculty members easily create and manage multiple projects. Another objective was to make it easy to edit, change, rearrange, delete or add anything associated with the digital narrative. To this end, we incorporated the following features in an effort to customize the enCore platform as one that could offer multi-user, easily editable gaming experiences to my literature students.

Allowing Users to Become Players and Builders

While all account-holders default to player roles, and can access any available scenario from the sign-in screen, HELP administrators may promote users to story-builder roles, which allows them access to menu options that enable the easy creation and deletion of interactive stories and scenarios. Story builders can edit multiple in-progress projects by switching between available stories, can add collaborators to any of them, and 'publish' finished stories, making them available to all registered users. Importantly, however, these developers do not have access to the HELP's programming editor and are not given any administrative privileges, thus ensuring that their localized work remains as simplified as possible and does not affect the overall operation of the platform.

Multiple Story Types

Story builders can choose to develop two main types of interactive narratives in HELP's environment. On the one hand, role-based limited-user multi-user stories allow users to role play pre-defined characters. These roles are randomly assigned when users enter an 'airlock' room prior to starting their story experience, and the number of players per game is limited. However, multiple games featuring limited numbers of concurrent users may operate simultaneously as sessions (see the *Frankenstein* example below). On the other hand, unlimited-user multiplayer stories do not restrict the number of participants and, while role playing can still be supported, users do not have to fill pre-defined character roles. Instead, they use the customizable identities that they have created within the HELP environment to navigate through a single, persistent 'world' that can be tailored to promote reflection upon particular literary scenarios (see *The Natural Daughter* example below).

Scenario Editor and Variations

Story builders do not require any programming skills to design or modify their projects within the HELP environment. Many aspects of the first interactive fiction that my team and I developed using version four of the enCore platform, including character dialogue, a money exchange, and transportation systems were hard-coded into the database and were extremely difficult to edit or fix when bugs were found. While my colleagues were enthusiastic about the experience and the platform, the programming requirement became a barrier to customization and further innovation. To remedy this, our work to modify version five of enCore was focused on programming an on-board toolkit for story creation that eliminates the need for story-builders to engage with any kind of coding or programming when developing their interactive narratives. While some commands are still necessary to generate locations, objects and non-player characters (NPCs), we designed a scenario editor which displays all of these elements in an organized and customizable table as can be seen in Figure 1.

Figure 1. The scenario viewer

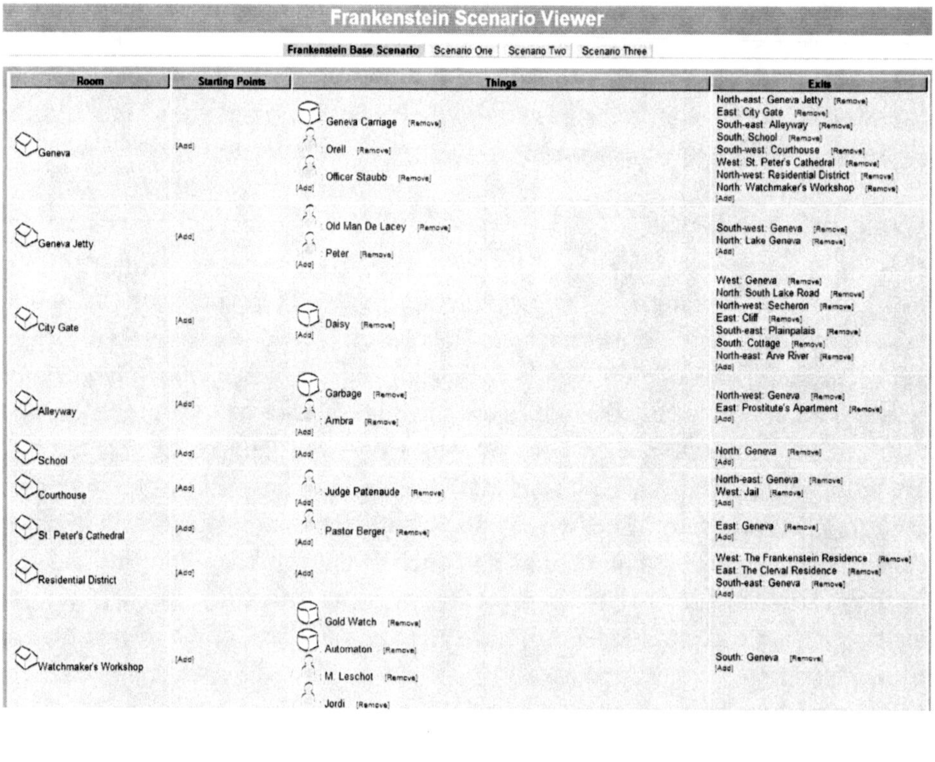

Frankenstein Scenario Viewer

Frankenstein Base Scenario | Scenario One | Scenario Two | Scenario Three

Room	Starting Points	Things	Exits
Geneva	[Add]	Geneva Carriage [Remove] Orell [Remove] Officer Staubb [Remove] [Add]	North-east: Geneva Jetty [Remove] East: City Gate [Remove] South-east: Alleyway [Remove] South: School [Remove] South-west: Courthouse [Remove] West: St. Peter's Cathedral [Remove] North-west: Residential District [Remove] North: Watchmaker's Workshop [Remove] [Add]
Geneva Jetty	[Add]	Old Man De Lacey [Remove] Peter [Remove] [Add]	South-west: Geneva [Remove] North: Lake Geneva [Remove] [Add]
City Gate	[Add]	Daisy [Remove] [Add]	West: Geneva [Remove] North: South Lake Road [Remove] North-west: Secheron [Remove] East: Cliff [Remove] South-east: Plainpalais [Remove] South: Cottage [Remove] North-east: Arve River [Remove] [Add]
Alleyway	[Add]	Garbage [Remove] Ambra [Remove] [Add]	North-west: Geneva [Remove] East: Prostitute's Apartment [Remove] [Add]
School	[Add]	[Add]	North: Geneva [Remove] [Add]
Courthouse	[Add]	Judge Patenaude [Remove] [Add]	North-east: Geneva [Remove] West: Jail [Remove] [Add]
St. Peter's Cathedral	[Add]	Pastor Berger [Remove] [Add]	East: Geneva [Remove] [Add]
Residential District	[Add]	[Add]	West: The Frankenstein Residence [Remove] East: The Clerval Residence [Remove] South-east: Geneva [Remove] [Add]
Watchmaker's Workshop	[Add]	Gold Watch [Remove] Automaton [Remove] M. Leschot [Remove] Jordi [Remove]	South: Geneva [Remove] [Add]

Via this scenario editor, a story builder can add, edit and remove entrances and exits between locations, with just a few mouse clicks. In this way, game resources are centrally organized and most of the prohibitive elements related to programming have been bypassed through the use of this graphic user interface (GUI) editor.

Encouraging Replayability Through Scenario Variations

After constructing the scenario editor, it became apparent that we could use this interface to support the creation and editing of multiple variants of a base situation. When a user plays a role-based, limited-user story multiple times, despite the variations that might be produced by choosing different roles, the experience can become repetitive. Using the scenario editor to develop and manage the multiple variants of a base setting (one of which is then randomly selected as the 'world' at the start of each new game) ensures a level of variety in the user's experience that will support multiple encounters and avoid repetition. Alternatives can involve the relocation, removal or addition of key objects and characters, and the placement or deletion of locations and exits.

Tree-Based Conversation 'Storybot'

Building believable non-player characters (NPC's) remains a challenge. NPC's are programmed, robotic (hence the abbreviation "bot") characters that players can interact with during a game. While human players can conceivably fill all of the roles necessary for a video game, NPC bots often play crucial roles in delivering expositional information or advancing the player's progress in a specific way. Since the HELP games rely heavily on description and dialogue -- hence their usefulness for literary education--, an appropriate and effective system of dialogue between players and NPC's is necessary. However, while enCore's default NPC bots try to generate responses to the text that the user enters based on keyword recognition, they usually end up producing grammatical nonsense after a few attempts at typed conversation. The functional limitations and frustrating nature of these bots became apparent after students in two of my literature classes included them in their enCore-based adaptations of William Blake's *Songs of Innocence and of Experience*. Simply put, these bots were awkward, unpredictable, and nonsensical in their dialogue, and thus mostly useless. For example, after asking the bot whether it eats beef, then following that with the comment "It's a nice day today," the bot will reply "Ah. Beef is a day. I suppose that makes sense", which makes no sense at all.

Drawing from some of the ways in which developers have attempted to manage NPC dialogue (see *Mass Effect*, *Fallout 3*, and *Elder Scrolls: Oblivion*), my team worked to generate improved storybots that the user could communicate with by selecting from a list of pre-defined responses. Despite its limitations, this tree-based response system is much easier to control and customize. However, after the grueling experience of hard coding and debugging all of the dialogue from our first attempt, we decided to direct our energies into the production of a menu-based conversation tree editor that followed the same motivations behind the scenario editor: easy management and editing capabilities without programming or coding. To this end, the storybot editor allows builders to develop branching dialogue through a menu-driven graphic user interface (GUI) as illustrated in Figure 2.

Builders can also write multiple scripts for single characters, ensuring that the NPC's react to gender, class or age differences associated with the user's character. In order to avoid conversational redundancies, a script can be written so that if players talk to a character once, any further attempts at dialogue will produce a response that acknowledges their previous encounter.

Collectively, these features have transformed enCore into HELP, a host for complex and engaging interactive narrative experiences. To allow for the widest possible use, to expedite game development and to ensure that the focus remains on experience with learning rather than technology, programming requirements have been replaced by interface options and menu-driven construction tools.

Figure 2. The script editor

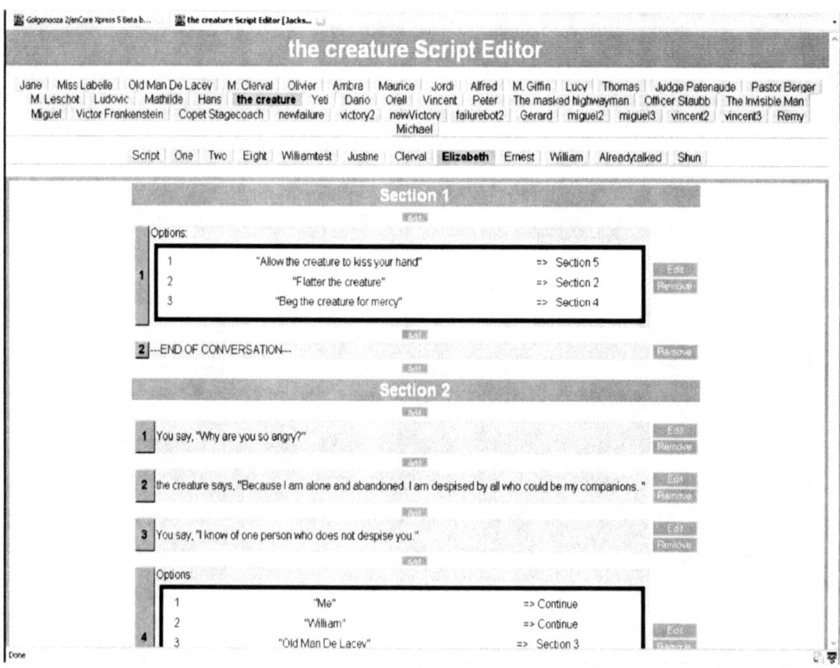

The Importance of Good Game Design

Despite minimizing the technological learning curve and easing the process of development, customization, accessibility and usage, *good game design* and a clear idea of how the technology can be used to facilitate the desired learning experience remains primary. In other words, while an adequate platform and straightforward tools are necessary, *how* these resources are used for literary education is more important than what they can do. As video games involve different types of participatory engagement, instructors and students who use computer-based, interactive narratives need to be aware of their unique aspects and the activity that they enable. Successful development and the promotion of lucid, self-reflexive strategies of play are made possible through an awareness of game design theories, and this knowledge also provides necessary background for in-class follow-up discussions about the relationship between virtual environments and literary narratives.[5] The two interactive fictions that my team and I have developed over the past three years can be used to more specifically illustrate the challenges and opportunities involved in these kinds of interactive learning experiences.

The first experience that we developed using the enCore Xpress platform was based on the situations encountered by the protagonist in Mary Robinson's novel *The Natural Daughter* (1799). In the book, the main character is wrongly accused of infidelity and from this tarnished reputation results a prolonged and largely ineffective struggle to independently sustain herself. The romantic artifice of the plot allows the protagonist to eventually triumph through her perseverance. The interactive narrative, intended to be experienced after reading the book, asks students to pursue the goal of becoming a successful late 18th-century British woman in the midst of limited opportunities. Each user is randomly assigned a social class which continuously affects their opportunities and reputation as they travel between Bath and London. Figure 3 shows the tragic events that unfold when a player's husband dies and she is left penniless in London following the posthumous repayment of his debts. The left frame features textual descriptions and conversations (as well as a space for user input), and the right frames feature graphics, a list of characters and players in the current location and a navigational compass.

Players meet and converse with various characters by selecting from a limited number of dialogue options, and can also converse with fellows (but these latter conversations amount to nothing more than gossip and do not affect the users' individual narrative opportunities). Unlike the book, and by 21st-century standards of success, there is no way to 'win' or triumphantly resolve the challenges presented by this role-playing experience – the most that can be achieved is an unsatisfactory marriage to an ignorant and largely dismissive husband. Also, risks to one's social reputation and honor (a variable that affects each user's abilities and opportunities)

Figure 3. The Natural Daughter

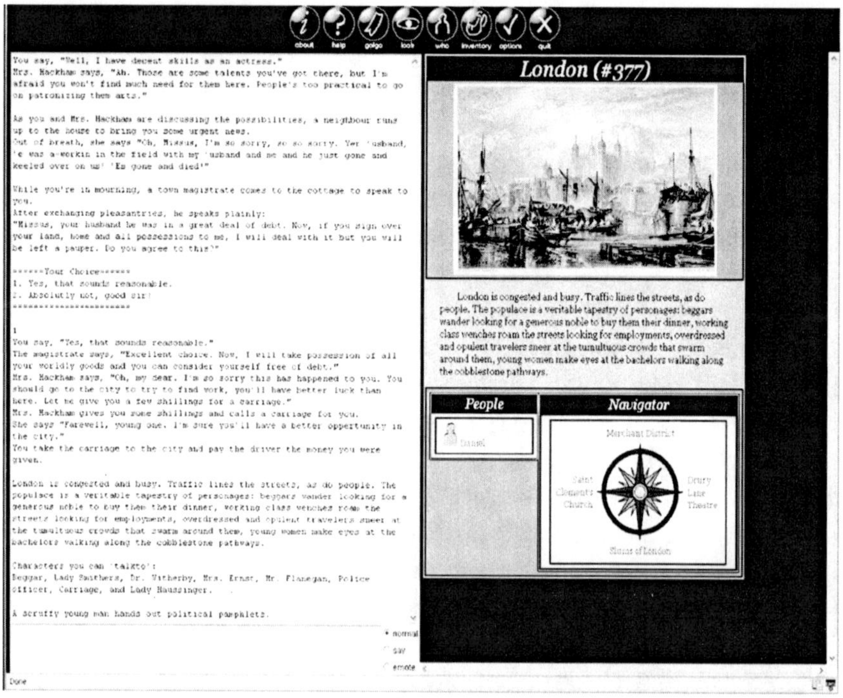

are everywhere in the game: certain professions (such as becoming a strolling actress) are dangerous, giving in to the persuasions of an upper-class gentleman can result in a debilitating sexual encounter, erratic behavior can result in a player's arrest and institutionalization in a madhouse, and hasty marriages can lead to domestic captivity. Because users are not informed of the absence of victory conditions before or during their participation in the game, their frustrations can consequently be linked to those that hopeful women might have experienced during this period.

This example provides students with an opportunity to be exposed to the historical circumstances that Mary Robinson and her main character struggled with. Students also engage in a participatory form of the novel's plot structure in an effort to precipitate discussion on the differences between observation and participation, and to relate this to reader and player roles. These exercises raise awareness of and challenge expectations regarding two aspects of mediation (narrative and technological) on human history, culture and individuality. In other words, this game is intended to initiate a comparative examination between the functions and capabilities of the novel, and those of a multi-user digital architecture – not for evaluative purposes or to determine which is better, but to point out what shared and unique functions these two forms of mediation possess. A further intention is, via role-playing, to encourage empathy, identification and understanding with characters, cultures and social situations which are temporally and spatially distant from our current position (while still understanding the distance generated via mediation). Following the experience of the game, students have an in-class opportunity to interrogate the ethics of play, role playing and puppeteering, especially in the original novel's feminist context. In other words, our subsequent classroom discussions include questions such as whether users take responsibility for their characters or whether they participate in irresponsible and frivolous ways. Such post-game dialogue is used to confront the different styles adopted by students and to explore the perceptions of freedom and inconsequence often associated with current digital games.

The Natural Daughter was designed to replicate and parallel, via interface technology, limited narrative paths, restricted interactions and an absence of satisfactory victory conditions, the frustrations that an independent, late eighteenth-century woman might have experienced in a similar situation. While there is an option for users to 'reset' themselves and start again, I do not reveal this during the first session. When such an option is revealed, I make sure to emphasize that while students can do so, women of the period could not. Whereas the book ends with a coincidental, semi-spiritual and 'positive' resolution for the protagonist (thus falsely calibrating student expectations for the trajectory followed), the interactive digital fiction offers no similar path or resolution. This becomes an opportunity to explore expectations related to games in general and to question romanticized expectations and ideals. The discord between the interactive narrative and the novel calls attention to the constructedness of both stories – yet both build the story in different ways and require different modes of participation. This dissonance raises thematic issues of agency, ability and control which are present in the novel through the software's interface and content. Finally, the digital experience catalyses an interrogation of the relationship between narrative fictions and history. Together, the role-playing experience and the novel offer two examples that provoke questions regarding the ability of virtual, imaginative creations (which unrealistically and specifically reflect real-world conditions and circumstances) to retain some historic value or cultural pertinence.

Good design takes advantage of both the limits and the opportunities inherent to the software platform. For example, in *The Natural Daughter*, two of the flawed NPC bots that were unable to support coherent conversations were placed in the asylum as insane characters who babble endlessly to each other. In this context, their nonsense makes sense. As well, in the multi-user environment that hosts *The Natural Daughter* players can chat with each other while in the midst of their role-playing experiences. As all participants in this situation are positioned as late eighteenth-century British women, their conversations might be illuminating and helpful to each other, but their collective intelligence is ultimately ineffectual in an environment that systematically prohibits success, and player-to-player dialogue adds little to the narrative. The uselessness of such interactions parallels the futile and often harmless circulation of gossip and polite conversational exchanges between women during this period and demonstrates the extent of their subjection, despite the community that such conversation affirms. This becomes an excellent opportunity to reflect on the social and political powers of language, dialogue, and linguistic mediations then and now.

Over the past three years, I have surveyed students following their experience with *The Natural Daughter* to help further the successful development and use of computer-based, interactive narratives in literary education. While some traditionally-minded students resisted this activity on the grounds that it had had little to do with the traditions and practices of literary study, one student commented that her "understanding of the period [had become] certainly more personal" as she was exposed to circumstances and consequences via her own choices. On the whole, most students agreed that this experience was an extremely useful supplement to book-based learning, and emphasized the benefits of using multiple forms of mediation that require different types of participation to explore social, historical and theoretical ideas in a more fulfilling manner.

The second major scenario was devised *in tandem* with the development of HELP's game creation toolkit. It is a limited-role, multiplayer experience based on Mary Shelley's *Frankenstein* that takes full advantage of multiple scenarios and multiple NPC scripting. If more than five users want to participate, the platform generates another session. Multiple, simultaneous sessions are easily supported. Figure 4 illustrates one location from *Frankenstein*, but also shows the history of the player's recent movements and actions in the left, text-only frame.

The intentions in this case differ considerably from those of *The Natural Daughter*. The parallels between Mary Shelley's insane academic, who makes use of older traditions to produce a monstrous challenge to contemporary theories and practices, and my own experiments with reconstituting novel-based narratives in digital forms have not been ignored. Unlike Victor Frankenstein, though, whose lack of planning and foresight causes him to abandon his creation out of fear and loathing, much like Castronova has done to his online *Arden*, my intention has been to generate communities of self-aware and engaged learners. Users are asked to role play one of five minor characters from the novel who are all threatened by the creature that Victor Frankenstein assembles (due to their various connections with the scientist). In doing so, the game extends the book's narrative beyond the three voices that Shelley uses to tell the original story, but attempts to stay as true as possible to the book's narrative progression. The role-playing experience takes place between Victor's abandonment of the creature and his confrontation with the monster on the summit of Montanvert. In due course, participants become aware

Figure 4. Frankenstein

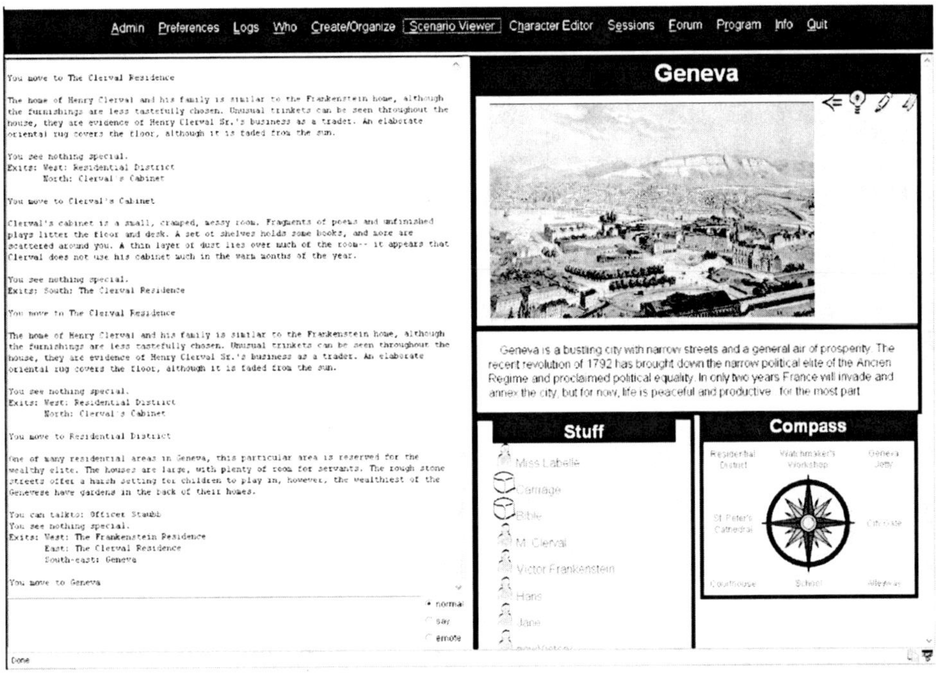

of its murderous intent toward them. Individual characters are vulnerable to fatal attacks and thus quickly learn that they must locate each other and band together in a 'party' to survive. While this is in keeping with one of Mary Shelley's explicit themes of the novel – that individuals, isolated from family and society either invent monsters or become monstrous – the game intentionally turns group mobility and cooperative agency into a necessary, but frustrating and limiting experience, subtly destabilizing the potency and polarities of Shelley's idealistic morality tale. The danger associated with individuality and independence is balanced by the difficulty associated with social interdependence and collaboration. This interactive fiction thus acts as a critical counterpoint that reveals the difficulty of Shelley's perspective, and exposes players to this challenge through performative means.

Unlike *The Natural Daughter*, where communication was inconsequential, the Frankenstein scenario necessitates that users communicate and cooperate with each other to extend their lives, understanding and chances for success. Each role has different abilities and limitations, and is presented with different opportunities. However, each character also possesses skills that are essential to the successful operation of the group. This scenario is much more ambitious in scope and operation than *The Natural Daughter* (in response to student feedback), and much more difficult as well (though not as hopeless). While, at this point, sufficient student feedback has not been gathered to offer conclusive data regarding the successful realization of its design and purpose in the classroom, it is interesting to note that the most promising sessions so far have resulted when the five players involved engage in the activity together in the same space. The spoken dialogue that takes place between them in their efforts to come up with collective strategies adds a metacritical level to their typed communications onscreen. This concurrent plurality of interaction between roles and actual people is worth pursuing in a literature classroom, as it joins two types of encounter to a text that are often segregated from each other.

FUTURE DIRECTIONS: EVOLVING CLASSROOM EXPERIENCES

In spite of all that has been said above, the particular uses of interactive digital narratives in relation to literary pedagogy need further exploration and definition. In addition, a clearer consensus of best practices and technological and design options may provide a firm foundation for others who wish to integrate video games into a comparative literary curriculum. Locating and developing other flexible construction tools that take full advantage of current 3-D, graphic and full motion capabilities of computer-based media while maintaining an ease-of-use philosophy, may help expand the uses in literature, comparative media and new media classrooms. Since the design, use and criticism of such software necessarily involve the intersections of a number of different disciplines, interdisciplinary teaching and learning opportunities can result from introducing digital games into one's pedagogical practice.

Although enCore Xpress is one of many possible platforms, its demonstrated flexibility and successful use to date confirms that further development of this older, but not-yet obsolete software could be invaluable. Despite its open-source accessibility and its straightforward, functional interfaces, a number of coding inefficiencies that result in unnecessary limitations to server operations and traffic still need to be addressed. Making tools more intuitive (perhaps involving drag-and-drop interfaces) to ensure accessibility and for broader use remains a priority for any development platform. Finally, a commitment to open-source, multi-platform development, distribution and accessibility during the creation of educational gamespaces and tools will guarantee healthy and productive exchanges and promote the exchange of ideas and practices between collective communities of cross-disciplinary researchers. To this end, preliminary work has been done to extract and clone the HELP toolkit for free distribution, installation and use on other networks.

CONCLUSION

Video gaming is an opportunity to involve students in the making and use of social computing situations that demand a complex level of critical awareness. The carefully managed development of computer-based interactive narratives can model and stimulate the same kinds of self-conscious play in the literary classroom. If used thoughtfully by instructors and students alike, these experiences will encourage users and builders to analytically and collectively resist the individualizing and isolating tendencies that persist within the dialectic, dialogic and discursive traditions of higher education, while still valuing the narrative importance and literary development of these traditions. Because such experimentation is still quite rare, the initial explorations described in this chapter are meant to catalyze and promote further innovations and applications in the university classroom. Playing through interactive narratives invites literature students to become more performatively aware of the parallel mediations that affect literary experiences. Even though I have found that enCore Xpress and its interactive fictions have served my particular purposes quite well, there are many different genres of games that have not been mentioned here and which may prove pedagogically useful and productive in ways that I have not yet anticipated. While not all types of gaming software are likely to serve post-secondary educational goals, their rich diversity is worth exploring and discussing in the classroom and between professional educators at all levels. As technology continues to evolve, so do virtual opportunities for interaction and discovery. At the time of editing this chapter, Sony Computer Entertainment and Microsoft, following in the footsteps of the Nintendo Wii's motion-based controller, have announced similar innovations in development for their consoles. Microsoft's "Project Natal" promises facial and voice recognition, along with the ability to directly translate a player's physical movements into on-screen activity without the need for a controller interface. While these developments are commercially-motivated and market-driven, they are also driven imaginative visions of more immersive and engaging virtual environments, and thus present future opportunities for post-secondary educational game development, play and criticism. Given that form is a mode of perception, then both the media content and the delivery technology to narrative experiences facilitate the depth or shallowness of our perceptions and subsequent critical engagement. Video games provide a unique and ultimately vital opportunity in the literature classroom, confirming the persistent validity of print-based narratives while evolving comparative media studies approaches to narrative and textual studies. They can promote comparative lucidity, perceptual pluralization and critical understanding in a generation of students who will benefit from the ability to interrogate the rules that they follow and the arenas in which they communicate, compete and collaborate.

REFERENCES

Baker, C. (2008, March 24). Trying to Design a Truly Entertaining Game can Defeat Even a Certified Genius. *Wired*. Retrieved October 30, 2008 from http://www.wired.com/gaming/gamingreviews/magazine/16-04/pl_games

Bakhtin, M. (1981). *The Dialogic Imagination: Four Essays* (Emerson, C., & Holquist, M., Trans.). Austin, Texas: University of Texas Press.

Barthes, R. (1978). *Image, Music, Text* (Heath, S., Trans.). New York: Hill and Wang.

Bogost, I. (2006). *Unit Operations: An Approach to Videogame Criticism*. Cambridge, MA: MIT.

Bogost, I. (2008). *Persuasive Games: The Expressive Power of Video Games*. Cambridge, MA: MIT.

Bolter, J., & Gromala, D. (2005). *Windows and Mirrors: Interaction Design, Digital Art, and the Myth of Transparency*. Cambridge, MA: MIT.

Caillios, R. (2001). *Man, Play and Games*. Champaign, Illinois: University of Illinois Press.

Carroll, L. (2003). *Alice's Adventures in Wonderland and Through the Looking Glass*. London, England: Penguin.

Derrida, J. (1980). *Writing and Difference* (Bass, A., Trans.). Chicago, Illinois: University of Chicago Press.

Galloway, A. (2006). *Gaming: Essays on Algorithmic Culture*. Minneapolis, MN: U of Minnesota Press.

Gee, J. P. (2003). *What Video Games have to teach us about Learning and Literacy*. New York: Palgrave MacMillan.

Huizinga, J. (1971). *Homo Ludens*. Boston, MA: Beacon Press.

Jenkins, H. (2006, November 27). Collective Intelligence and the Wisdom of Crowds. In *Confessions of an Aca-fan: The Official Weblog of Henry Jenkins*. Retrieved February 5, 2008 from http://henryjenkins.org/2006/11/collective_intelligence_vs_the.html

Jenkins, H. (2008, February 4). Sharing Notes about Collective Intelligence. In *Confessions of an Aca-fan: The Official Weblog of Henry Jenkins*. Retrieved February 5, 2008 from http://henryjenkins.org/2008/02/last_week_my_travels_took.html

Jones, S. (2008). *The Meaning of Video Games: Gaming and Textual Strategies*. New York: Routledge.

Juul, J. (2005). *Half-Real: Video Games between Real Rules and Fictional Worlds*. Cambridge, MA: MIT.

Krentz, A. A. (1998). 20th WCP: Play and Education in Plato's Republic. In D. Steiner (Ed.) *Twentieth World Congress of Philosophy*. Boston, MA. Retrieved October 30, 2008 from http://www.bu.edu/wcp/Papers/Educ/EducKren.htm

Martin, M. (2008, October 27). Thompson: Educational games will lose you money. Retrieved October 28, 2008 from http://www.gamesindustry.biz/articles/thompson-educational-games-will-lose-you-money

Prensky, M. (2004). *Digital Game-Based Learning*. New York: McGraw–Hill.

Salen, K., & Zimmerman, E. (2004). *Rules of Play: Game Design Fundamentals*. Cambridge, MA: MIT.

Salen, K., & Zimmerman, E. (Eds.). (2006). *The Game Design Reader: A Rules of Play Anthology*. Cambridge, MA: MIT.

Sutton-Smith, B. (2001). *The Ambiguity of Play*. Cambridge, MA: Harvard UP.

Wardrip-Fruin, N., & Harrigan, P. (Eds.). (2004). *First Person: New Media as Story, Performance and Game*. Cambridge, MA: MIT.

Wardrip-Fruin, N., & Harrigan, P. (Eds.). (2007). *Second Person: Role-Playing and Story in Games and Playable Media*. Cambridge, MA: MIT.

Wark, M. (2007). *Gamer Theory*. Cambridge, MA: Harvard UP.

ADDITIONAL READING

Atkins, B. (2003). *More than a Game: The Computer Game as Fictional Form*. Manchester, England: Manchester UP.

Atkins, B., & Krzywinska, T. (Eds.). (2007). *Videogame, Player, Text*. Manchester, UK: Manchester UP.

Burrill, D. A. (2005). Out of the Box: Performance, Drama, and Interactive Software. In Modern Drama, 48(3), 492-512.

Egenfeldt-Nielsen, S., Smith, J. H., & Tosca, S. P. (2008). *Understanding Video Games: The Essential Introduction*. New York: Routledge.

Fisler, B. (2006). Digital Extensions and Performed Players: A Theoretical Model for the Video/Computer Game. *Reconstruction: Studies in Contemporary Culture, 6*(1).

Foreman, J. (2004, Sept/Oct). Game-Based Learning: How to delight and instruct in the 21st century. *EDUCAUSE Review*, 50–66.

Fyfe, D. (2008, July 22). *Video Games are the Silver Bullet.* Retrieved October 30, 2008 from http://www.hitselfdestruct.com/2008/07/video-games-are-silver-bullet.html

Gee, J. P. (2007). *Good Video Games + Good Learning: Collected Essays on Video Games, Learning and Literacy.* New York: P. Lang.

Haynes, C., & Holmevik, J. R. (Eds.). (1998). *High Wired: On the Design, Use and Theory of Educational MOOs.* Ann Arbor, Michigan: U. of Michigan.

Haynes, C., & Holmevik, J. R. (2000). *MOOniversity: A Student's Guide to Online Learning Environments.* Boston, MA: Allyn & Bacon.

Herz, J. C. (2002). Gaming the System: What Education can learn from Multiplayer Online Worlds. In *The Internet and the University* [EDUCAUSE.]. *Forum, 2001*, 169–191.

Hitch, L., & Duncan, J. (2005). *When Halo 2, Civilization IV and XBOX 360 Come to Campus. Educause Evolving Technologies Committee. 191.* Games in Higher Ed.

Hutchison, D. (2007). *Playing to Learn: Video Games in the Classroom.* Westport, CT: Teacher Ideas Press.

Jackson, Z. A. (2002). Connecting Video Games and Storytelling to Teach Narratives in First-Year Composition. *Kairos: A Journal for Teachers of Writing and Webbed Environments, 7*(3).

Jenkins, H. (2006). *Fans, Bloggers and Gamers: Exploring Participatory Culture.* New York: NYU Press.

Lanham, R. (1997). A Computer-based *Harvard Red Book:* General Education in the Digital Age. In Dowler, L. (Ed.), *Gateways to Knowledge: The Role of Academic Libraries in Teaching, Learning, and Research.* Cambridge, MA: MIT Press.

Leitch, T. (2004). Post-Literary Adaptation. *Post Script: Essays in Film and the Humanities, 23*(3), 99–117.

Lévy, P. (1997). *Collective Intelligence: Mankind's Emerging World in Cyberspace* (Bononno, R., Trans.). New York: Plenum Trade.

Murray, J. (1997). *Hamlet on the Holodeck: The future of Narrative in Cyberspace*. Cambridge, MA: MIT.

Newman, J. (2008). *Playing with Videogames*. New York: Routledge.

O'Gorman, M. (2006). *E-Crit: Digital Media, Critical Theory and the Humanities*. Toronto, Ontario: U. of Toronto.

Ouellette, M. (2004). Critical Approaches to Video Games. *TEXT Technology*, *13*(1), 1–205.

Poole, S. (2000). *Trigger Happy: Video Games and the Entertainment Revolution*. New York: Arcade.

Raessens, J., & Goldstein, J. (Eds.). (2005). *Handbook of Computer Game Studies*. Cambridge, MA: MIT.

Ryan, M.-L. (Ed.). (2004). *Narrative across Media: The Languages of Storytelling*. Lincoln, NE: U of Nebraska P.

Ryan, M.-L. (2006). *Avatars of Story*. Minneapolis, MN: U of Minnesota P.

Selfe, C., & Hawisher, G. (2007). *Gaming Lives in the Twenty-First Century: Literate Connections*. New York: Palgrave. doi:10.1057/9780230601765

Squire, K. (2002). Cultural Framing of Computer/Video Games. *Game Studies: The International Journal of Computer Game Research, 2*(1). Retrieved on October 30, 2008 from http://www.gamestudies.org/0102/squire/

Squire, K., & Jenkins, H. (2003). Harnessing the Power of Games in Education. *Insight* 3.5. Retrieved October 30, 2008 from http://website.education.wisc.edu/kdsquire/manuscripts/insight.pdf

Tavinor, G. (2005). Videogames and Interactive Fiction. *Philosophy and Literature*, *29*(1), 24–40. doi:10.1353/phl.2005.0015

Wolf, M. J. P., & Perron, B. (Eds.). (2003). *The Video Game Theory Reader*. New York: Routledge.

Wolf, M. J. P., & Perron, B. (Eds.). (2008). *The Video Game Theory Reader 2*. New York: Routledge.

Zammit, K. (2007). Popular Culture in the Classroom: Interpreting and Creating Multimodal Texts. In McCabe, A., O'Donnell, M., & Whittaker, R. (Eds.), *Advances in Language and Education* (pp. 60–76). London, England: Continuum.

ENDNOTES

1 TAPoR, or the Text Analysis Portal for Research is the web presence related to a multi-institutional, Canadian research infrastructure initiative. This portal features a centralized 'toolbox' of independently developed text analysis tools that users can use to analyze their own documents. Collex, hosted by the NINES group (Nineteenth-century Studies Online) is a tool that allows users to explore and arrange aggregated search findings from 58 database projects relating to nineteenth-century literary studies. ZOTERO is a tool that works within the Firefox web browser to help researchers collect, manage and cite web-based resources.

2 See the EDUCAUSE Learning Initiative and the New Media Consortium's collaborative annual "Horizon Report" (http://www.nmc.org/horizon/), which identified emerging technologies that will impact the future of education practices.

3 This software was designed in 2000 by Jan Rune Holmevik as an educational tool to encourage online collaborations and interactions.

4 The web address of the first HELP platform is http://playground.acadiau.ca:7000(create a new account as an English 2386 student, then log in and progress north to access *The Natural Daughter* game). HELP's evolution is at http://playground.acadiau.ca:7001 (create a new account and either select "Frankenstein" as your login point (rather than "The Learning Commons") to play the game, or email this chapter's author (jon.saklofske@acadiau.ca) to be upgraded to a Storybuilder account so that you can construct your own scenarios). I am indebted to the assistance of undergraduate students, Acadia University's Hypermedia Humanities Centre, the Acadia Institute of Teaching and Technology and Acadia's Learning Commons for the successful development and customization of the enCore platform.

5 Indispensible resources for this purpose are Salen and Zimmerman's (2004, 2006) books, which offer a broad yet detailed survey of concepts, strategies, case studies, methods and analytical frames for understanding games from developmental and scholarly perspectives.

Chapter 7
Teaching Shakespeare in the Elementary School through Dramatic Activity, Play Production, and Technology:
A Case Study

William L. Heller
Teaching Matters, USA

ABSTRACT

In order to learn whether Shakespeare can be taught successfully in the elementary school, the author devised and implemented a unit designed to teach Macbeth to one fifth-grade class using dramatic activities, theatrical production, and technology integration. The work challenges the use of standardized testing as the final measure of student achievement. It demonstrates how Vygotsky's (1978) zone of proximal development exposes the limitations of measuring only what students can demonstrate under testing conditions, and how Gardner's (1993) Theory of Multiple Intelligences offers a variety of avenues for learning more effectively. This approach is identified with that of a reflective practitioner, and is designed to assist professionals who are looking for practical models for using Shakespeare's plays in their classrooms. The underlying motive is to help bring them to a wider audience.

DOI: 10.4018/978-1-60566-932-8.ch007

INTRODUCTION

In order to learn whether Shakespeare can be taught successfully in the elementary school, I devised and implemented a unit designed to introduce *Macbeth* to a fifth-grade class. I documented the process to provide a case study model for teachers which can be emulated as a whole, drawn from partially, or simply used as an inspiration for creating original curricula. Built into the activities were project-based tasks that I could use to assess whether I had achieved my goals, and also to see whether the ten-year-old children were able to display the higher-order thinking skills needed to meaningfully address the subject matter.

I developed my class plan knowing that the preparation and performance of a play would be at its center. I believed this strategy would allow a richer experience than only dealing with the text as a literary artifact of a bygone era. By memorizing lines and making decisions about presentation, young actors make discoveries and connections not required of the casual reader. However, in considering the age-level of the class, I felt it was necessary to preface the production with a series of interactive drama activities to familiarize the students with the play before they had to deal with language they may have had difficulty understanding. I also wanted to include a constructive task following the production, so that I could assess their understanding in an authentic way. I decided to have the students create a website guide to introduce *Macbeth* to readers who were approaching it for the first time. Underlying this project was a fundamental belief that a positive early experience with Shakespeare is more likely to foster a life-long relationship with the author than the traditional high-school introduction, which often consists of lectures and reading assignments. As Cullum (1967) suggests "The elementary school is the ideal place to introduce Shakespeare." (81). In elementary school, there is more room for fun, for tapping into the heart of what makes the plays worthwhile. At this stage, building enthusiasm and confidence with the difficult material can make a significant difference in later grades.

DEVELOPMENTAL THEORY

Performing Shakespeare in high school, or even junior high, can be challenging. In this respect, McCaslin (2000) points out that:

This is a challenge to the teacher as well as to the class, but it can be done intelligently and effectively if approached in the right way. First, the play will be far too long as it stands. If the teacher familiarizes the class with the story, has them improvise scenes from the play, and then cuts the play to a manageable length, the project will be realistic." (315)

This approach can be adapted to the elementary school by having a longer and more active familiarization process and by making even more cuts to the original text. Naturally, however, this raises the question of the ability of fifth-graders to perform in the first place, or even to understand the plays. The fact that seventh-graders can approach Shakespeare's texts in a meaningful way does not necessarily imply that they will be within the competency of a fifth-grade class.

In fact, Courtney (1989) goes so far as to describe a progression of "Dramatic Age Stages" and makes a clear distinction between the developmental level of ten- and twelve-year-old children (the typical ages of fifth- and seventh-graders respectively), and what cognitive abilities would generally be possible at each age. He defines "The Role Stage" as lasting from ages twelve to eighteen:

Their improvisation tests hypotheses practically, by trial-and-error, and reveals self doubt: "If I play my role as A, then my actions become Y; but if I play it as B, then they become Z. So who is the real me?" This hypothesis implies causality ("If I play my role as C, does it cause this effect?). It isolates and tests various actors ("If we do it this way, then..." or, "If you play a policeman as a villain, then..."), which requires the ability to think abstractly. They use logic for a conclusion, "then the play will be like this...." They imagine an ideal, use it in dramatic play, and alternate being "as if" with the actual, while combining and contrasting social masks. Facets of symbols are tested against reality. Emotional judgments can err. They explore social possibilities and moral decisions. (97-98)

Certainly, it is desirable for a class that is going to approach dramatic literature through performance to be capable of such skills as the ability to understand causality, to think abstractly, to interpret symbols, and to articulate moral decisions. But according to Courtney (1989), a ten-year-old fifth-grader would not yet be in the role stage. According to this framework, Shakespeare would be beyond the cognitive abilities of the population I have chosen at their current stage of development.

However, Courtney (1989) introduces his progression of "Dramatic Age Stages" by citing Swiss psychologist Jean Piaget's (1962) well-known framework of developmental phases as his cognitive model, which describes a series of stages that children must pass through in their cognitive development, as well as the age range where each stage is predominant:

Rational operations are, in fact, systems of aggregates, characterized by a definite and mobile structure which cannot be explained by neurology, sociology, or even psychology, save as forms of equilibrium towards which the whole development tends. In order to account for the fact that the successive structures (sensory-motor, symbolic or preconceptual, and intuitive) culminate in these general systems of action constituted by rational operations, it is essential to understand how each of these behaviours is continued in the one that follows, the direction being from a lower to a higher equilibrium. (291)

For Piaget and Inhelder (1966), mental development is dependent on physical development which "implies that child psychology must be regarded as the study of one aspect of embryogenesis, the embryogenesis of organic as well as mental growth, up to the beginning of the state of relative equilibrium which is the adult level." (xvii.) Thus, developing minds are limited by their level of physiological development.

While many rely on Piaget's work, others supplement it with the theories of Belarussian psychologist Lev Vygotsky. Davis and Lawrence (1986) discuss a 1966 paper of Gavin Bolton's, *The Nature of Children's Drama*, in which he is "using Piaget as his main theorist to argue that creative drama is built on make-believe play" (Davis and Lawrence, 1986, 26). Piaget (1962) wrote extensively on how creative play is a part of the assimilation and accommodation that the child uses to make sense of the world in each stage of development:

Once the symbol is constituted, it goes far beyond practice, and even if we confine ourselves to saying that it trains thought as a whole we then have to explain why there is any need for symbols and make-believe, and not just exercise of conceptual thought as such. Why, indeed, does the child play at being a shopkeeper, a driver, a doctor? If it is suggested that such games are pre-exercise, by analogy with the games of little goats capering or kittens running after a ball of wool, we then ask why L. played at being a church, imitating the rigidity of the steeple and the sound of the bells, and why J. lay motionless like the dead duck she had seen on a table. Far from being preparatory exercises, most of the games we have given as examples either reproduce what has struck the child, evoke what has pleased him or enable him to be more fully part of his environment. In a word they form a vast network of devices which allow the ego to assimilate the whole of reality, i.e., to integrate it in order to re-live it, to dominate it or to compensate for it. (154)

Even though Piaget's concepts were useful to Bolton in 1966, Davis and Lawrence (1986) go on to cite an unpublished 1983 interview in which Bolton discusses why Vygotsky had, to a considerable extent, replaced Piaget for him as his main theoretical influence:

For one thing, [Piaget's] developmental stages erroneously give the impression that young children are not capable of abstract thought -- teachers using drama know different, for children can think abstractly in context. (26)

This would seem to open to question the assertion in Courtney's (1989) framework, based on Piaget's, that abstract thought is not possible before age twelve. Bolton (1983 cited in Davis and Lawrence, 1986) notes that he does find Piaget's book on play useful, but explains why a shift to a new developmental theorist makes sense for drama teachers:

However, if you follow Piaget logically you would have to conclude that drama cannot be used as a tool in education because symbolic play, in his view, only reinforces what the child already knows -- either reinforces or deliberately distorts. For him, play is only dealing with the past and cannot encounter anything new: you cannot learn through play, you can only reinforce what you already know. (26-27)

And so, as useful and groundbreaking as Piaget's developmental stages have been, a newer model is required for teachers who use drama, or any other pedagogical mode that draws from the experiences of students. In *Mind in Society*, Vygotsky (1978) recognized the Piagetian developmental levels, but perceived shortcomings in traditional methods of determining these developmental levels:

In studies of children's mental development it is generally assumed that only those things that children can do on their own are indicative of mental abilities. We give children a battery of tests or a variety of tasks of varying degrees of difficulty, and we judge the extent of their mental development on the basis of how they solve them and at what level of difficulty. (85)

Unfortunately, this is no less true in today's environment of high-stakes testing than it was in his time. But standardized tests do not always give the full picture. Instead, Vygotsky (1978) observes an often-missed opportunity in measuring a student's cognitive ability:

On the other hand, if we offer leading questions or show how the problem is to be solved and the child then solves it, or if the teacher initiates the solution and the child completes it or solves it in collaboration with other children -- in short, if the child barely misses an independent solution of the problem -- the solution is not regarded as indicative of his mental development. (85)

He goes on to describe the idea of the zone of proximal development (ZPD) which "is the distance between the actual developmental level as determined by independent problem solving and the level of potential development as determined through problem solving under adult guidance or in collaboration with more capable peers" (Vygotsky, 1978, 86). Vygotsky's (1978) ZPD describes a model in which, under certain conditions, students might be able to achieve more than would be indicated in a traditional Piagetian structure such as Courtney's (1989). So it may be possible to create conditions that would allow fifth-graders to understand Shakespeare after all, if concepts such as abstract thought and the understanding of symbol are within a ten-year-old's ZPD.

An additional way to make the plays more accessible to fifth-graders might be to use a variety of strategies. In his description of Multiple Intelligences, Gardner (1993) describes areas of intelligence that exist in the human mind that are "independent of one another, and that... can be fashioned and combined in a multiplicity of adaptive ways by individuals and cultures" (9). He identifies seven such intelligences, though he allows for the possibility that there may be others, and the conversation surrounding various other possible intelligences continues today. His original seven -- Linguistic, Musical, Logical-Mathematical, Spatial, Bodily-Kinesthetic, and the two personal intelligences commonly referred to as Interpersonal and Intrapersonal -- have gained wide popularity in the field of education, and in the New York City school system. In schools across the city, the seven intelligences can be seen plastered across hallways and classrooms, and teachers are encouraged to use a variety of strategies to identify areas where students may need additional help to succeed or have talents that can be encouraged and built upon. In this unit, the various intelligences provide different venues for academic and artistic expression. As with the ZPD, the attention to Multiple Intelligences is intended to help students demonstrate skills and understandings they would not be able to show under traditional testing conditions.

Thus, with the theories of Multiple Intelligences (Gardner, 1993) and ZPD (Vygotsky, 1978) in mind, I devised a full teaching unit, which is comprised of three phases. The first one introduces the students to drama-in-education and has them begin writing about the themes of the play before they read the actual text. Phase Two opens the possibility of a live production for an audience that has not been a part of the process. In the third and last part, students apply what they have learned to a collaborative technology project. They use their classroom computers to create a web-based study guide for *Macbeth*.

In order to evaluate student work in each phase, I created rubrics, that is, descriptions of specific assessment criteria for determining what constitutes each level of achievement. Rubrics are often presented in chart form so that performance levels within a category can be easily compared. They measure the skills that students have actually demonstrated, not what they are capable of. Each set of rubrics was designed to assess students longitudinally, using similar categories to reflect the increasing level of sophistication expected from them. As the scaffolding is gradually removed, students are expected to take on more responsibility and work more independently toward the end of the unit.

As I was not the classroom teacher, I was not in a position of giving them a report card grade. I made my assessment data available to the teacher, who was present for the entire unit, so that she could use the information in her final grading. There were three rubrics with eight categories each, and a maximum score of four points for each category. This means that the maximum score for the unit was 96 (3 x 8 x 4). The final unit score, therefore, should not be viewed as a percentage or as a grade.

PHASE ONE: DRAMA IN EDUCATION

In the first phase, characters, plot, and themes of the play were explored. The original text was not used at this point though I did bring in a few samples. This was mostly process-based; no outside audiences were invited into the classroom, and no attempt was made to publish, or even refine, the writing that was produced. The purpose of this section was to provide a solid foundation for the text. Classroom activities included both creative writing assignments, and drama-in-education (DIE), which refers to the use of drama to teach other subject areas.

Here, students took on the roles of the characters in and surrounding *Macbeth* so as to gain new perspectives. They participated in role-playing and writing activities that were engaging, and at the same time, allowed them to achieve understandings that would serve them in later stages when they would be expected to read, perform, and analyze the play. As we went through different sections of the plot, the class took on roles of police detectives investigating the murder of King Duncan, they gossiped about the royals as townspeople, and they shouted improvised dialogue of what they thought Macbeth and Macduff might say to each other during their final showdown. There were no wrong answers, just an opportunity to explore and learn.

McCaslin (2000) describes the value of DIE for this purpose:

Classroom teachers find drama a valuable tool for involving children in the study of a topic. Rather than dramatizing a story or developing a play, children project themselves into a dramatic moment of the topic at hand (e.g., a mine disaster, a strike, a gold rush, an election); from there they go on to examine and learn more about the topic. They become the persons in the situation as they study it. The teacher brings in source materials and guides the study and may even play a role in the enactment. A play may result, but it is not the purpose of this use of drama. (12)

So, students were not working as theatre artists, but using the structures of drama as a learning medium. This is a distinction Courtney (1982) makes: "Drama has two places in the life of a school: as a subject and as a method. When used as a method to teach non-drama subjects, it can assist learnings in such subjects by enabling transfer to take place" (81). In this case, students were participating in activities in order to learn about Shakespeare's *Macbeth*, and not the skills for theatrical performance, though it is undeniable that such skills would be exercised and would be useful for the next phase.

The idea of an external audience is a key distinction between process-based and product-based drama work. In DIE, there is no external audience. The benefit is for the participant. While theatrical production will also benefit the actor, the focus is on what experience the audience will have. Also, in product-based work, there are long periods of preparation for a future event when the external audience will come in for the first time and experience a theatrical piece. In process-based work, the drama is spontaneous, and is intended to benefit the performer in the moment. Because of this, in product-based theatrical work, the issue of talent is relevant. One often has to decide which students possess the ability to communicate ideas and feelings most effectively to an external audience. In DIE, everyone is able to participate in the same way, and in equal measure. The activities are open-ended enough that learners of different ages and competency levels are able to approach each activity with their own level of sophistication. There may be some overlap between what is considered process-based and product-based work, but these are the qualities that will distinguish them.

In this phase, students also work together, both in small groups and as a class, making this a highly collaborative mode of instruction. They learn more from their own experiences and interaction with their peers than they are from the instructor. I give them a context and instructions, and allow them the time to make discoveries. In exploring *Macbeth* in this way, they understand why it is worth knowing about and what the themes mean for us today. Shakespeare's works resonate with us because they are rooted in the truth of human experience. This is what makes an experiential mode such a good choice to precede a theatrical production.

Because of this, performance and content objectives for this phase go hand in hand. Students participate in a range of dramatic activities (performance objectives), which will help them understand the character, plot, and themes of *Macbeth* (content objectives). If these two sets of objectives are met, the class will be well placed to approach the play in production. They will not only understand *Macbeth* well enough to begin making production decisions, but they will also have participated in a variety of activities, incidentally developing a range of skills that can be applied in a stage production.

In preparing this phase, I took advantage of activities that have already been devised to explore *Macbeth*. The Cambridge School series has published a version of *Macbeth*, which features the original text accompanied by a wealth of classroom activities to guide the reader in understanding the meaning of each scene. I drew from O'Neill and Lambert's (1982) plans liberally, as well as devised several lessons of my own.

As for assessment, it is always tricky in process-based work. With product-based work, there is something tangible to evaluate. In drama, the personal and artistic development that takes place is difficult to quantify. However, this sort of assessment is important and must be included in each phase in order to ground the unit in sound educational practice and to fit into the New York City school culture. The rubric for this section, Table 1, identifies specific areas to be assessed.

Table 1. Rubric for phase one

PHASE ONE	4	3	2	1
A. Responds to *Macbeth*	Makes warranted assertions with appropriate evidence	Makes warranted assertions about the play with little support	Makes unwarranted assertions about the play	Does not make assertions about the play
B. Understands Shakespeare	Understands Shakespeare's language and historical context	Understands Shakespeare's language or historical context	Weak understanding of the playwright and his work	Does not understand who Shakespeare is or how he writes
C. Commits to drama work	Engages fully in drama work and takes calculated risks	Engages in drama work, but takes reckless risks or none at all	Makes an effort to engage in drama work	Participates in drama work superficially, or not at all
D. Communicates through drama	Express ideas and feelings effectively via drama	Expresses ideas effectively through drama	Expresses feelings convincingly through drama	Does not express ideas or feelings effectively via drama
E. Uses drama techniques	Uses language, voice, gesture and movement effectively	Often uses language, voice, gesture and movement well	Uses language, voice, gesture or movement effectively	Does not use dramatic techniques effectively
F. Displays originality of expression	Brings original ideas and interpretations to creative work	Brings original interpretations but not ideas to creative work	Commits to creative work but without originality	Does not engage in creative work
G. Employs creative problem solving	Identifies artistic problems and finds creative solutions	Identifies artistic problems and finds workable solutions	Identifies artistic problems and finds weak solutions	Is not able to identify artistic problems
H. Displays higher order thinking skills	Displays higher order thinking skills and is aware of learning	Displays higher order thinking skills but is not aware of learning	Displays only awareness of learning	Does not display higher order thinking

In Phase One, there were three writing assignments that specifically responded to the play. Each student wrote (a) a letter from Macbeth to Lady Macbeth, (b) a police report covering the murder of Duncan, and (c) a speech from Banquo's ghost to Macbeth at the banquet. It is important to note that at this stage, they had not seen the original text yet, and were responding to my treatment of the material only. (Please note that, in order to protect the privacy of everyone involved, I am using pseudonyms.) For the third writing assignment, Ruth wrote as Banquo's ghost. Her comments were peer edited for grammar and spelling before they were added to the website, but the content was entirely from Ruth:

How could you have done this to me? I was your best friend. But my son will still be King. I am very happy. Now I understand what the witches meant when they said I will not be King but my son will. I should have known all along. I think that you killed King Duncan too, just to be King faster. But you will not kill my son. He will be King, like it or not.

I never told the class that Fleance becomes King as, in fact, he does not. But Ruth made the connection between Fleance's escape and the witches prophecy and predicted that Fleance would become King. This is an example of a warranted assertion with appropriate evidence, a 4 in "Responds to *Macbeth*," the first category of the rubric.

The police reports were a good opportunity to make assertions about the text, since the students were given a directive to report who they thought committed the murder. Most of them came up with a suspect (usually Macbeth) and explained why. Gail kept notes of all of the interviews, but simply wrote "Macbeth did it" in big letters across the bottom of the page. This is a warranted assertion about the text, but lacks the necessary support, which makes it a 3 in the "Responds to *Macbeth*" category of the rubric.

I also conducted informal assessment throughout the unit. I would take notice when Jenny, Rebecca, Alicia, George, and Linda would commit themselves fully to drama work and take calculated risks. Marsha, Randall, Johnny, and Daryl were less focused. Alex made an observation during one of the class discussions that impressed me. She noted that, in the beginning, Macbeth was a "sissy" and he did not want to kill. But then he becomes a tyrant who likes killing while Lady Macbeth is feeling guilty about killing. This is a level of analysis I was not expecting to see until the end. At this stage, I was going for an understanding of plot elements, but not necessarily to draw conclusions about characters or the play as a whole.

I only occasionally referred to the original text in the first phase. Some quoted it back in their writing assignments, particularly the "All Hail" lines in the letters from Macbeth to Lady Macbeth. The students recognized certain lines from *Mac-*

beth, such as "Something wicked this way comes" and "Double, double, toil and trouble." Whenever I would introduce some of the language, they would respond with enthusiasm. On the first day of the lesson, we discussed Shakespeare and his historical context as well.

PHASE TWO: THEATRICAL PRODUCTION

Here the class puts on a live production for an audience that has not been a part of the process. Although the students are meant to gain much from the process, this phase is product-based; the class works as a team to create a theatrical production to be viewed by others. At the completion, they are meant to have a high level of familiarity and comprehension of the play, which will then be applied in the creation of a web-based study guide to *Macbeth.*

Theatrical production follows easily from DIE, as they share many conventions that other modes of instruction, including technology integration, do not employ. Also, like drama, theatre is collaborative. The students work together to produce one shared interpretation. During the rehearsal process, they have to negotiate with each other to decide what that vision will be. The teacher's role here is to provide enough information to help them understand the artistic choices that need to be made, without doing all of the work for them. As the show's director, I also made a number of artistic decisions, but tried to give the students as much creative freedom as possible. I chose to edit the text myself as I believe that the skills involved are too advanced for fifth-graders, even taking the ZPD into account. The students were assessed according to the rubric designed for this phase, as shown in Table 2.

In editing *Macbeth* for our production, I kept a number of factors in mind. First of all, I wanted to give the students the fullest and richest experience of the original text as possible. However, decisions were also influenced by the fact that they would have to memorize each line that was kept. At the same time, the total production time had to be kept down for the young actors and audience. Finally, I tried to avoid passages that would be inappropriate or confusing for this age group.

One aspect of product-based work is that often students are not all asked to complete the same academic tasks. However, there are times when this is desirable. In the case of performing *Macbeth*, some were assigned large roles to analyze and memorize, while others had smaller ones. Roles were assigned so that they would match learners' ability to perform those tasks. This way the amount of work that each person was actually doing was much closer to being equal than it would have been if everyone had been given the same assignment.

Having said this, Garrett and Jenny were really given a lot to do in Phase Two. A lot of the work of analyzing lines was done when I was helping a particular student

Table 2. Rubric for phase two

PHASE TWO	4	3	2	1
A. Interprets *Macbeth*	Makes artistic choices that support the play	Makes artistic choices that do not contradict the play	Makes artistic choices that contradict the play	Makes unfounded artistic choices, or none at all
B. Appreciates Shakespeare	Understands Shakespeare's poetry and drama	Understands Shakespeare's poetry or drama	Somewhat understands Shakespeare's poetry and drama	Does not understand Shakespeare's poetry or drama
C. Commits to theatrical work	Engages fully in theatrical work and takes calculated risks	Engages in theatrical work, but takes reckless risks or none at all	Makes an effort to engage in theatrical work	Participates in theatrical work superficially, or not at all
D. Communicates through performance	Express ideas and feelings effectively via performance	Expresses ideas effectively through performance	Expresses feelings through performance convincingly	Does not express ideas or feelings effectively via performance
E. Uses theatrical techniques	Uses language, voice, gesture and movement effectively	Often uses language, voice, gesture and movement well	Uses language, voice, gesture or movement effectively	Does not use dramatic techniques effectively
F. Displays originality of expression	Brings original ideas and interpretations to creative work	Brings original interpretations but not ideas to creative work	Commits to creative work but without originality	Does not engage in creative work
G. Employs creative problem solving	Identifies artistic problems and finds creative solutions	Identifies artistic problems and finds workable solutions	Identifies artistic problems and finds weak solutions	Is not able to identify artistic problems
H. Displays higher order thinking skills	Displays higher order thinking skills and is aware of learning	Displays higher order thinking skills but is not aware of learning	Displays only awareness of learning	Does not display higher order thinking

speak the lines for his or her character. Thus those who had more lines also had more opportunity to work through the language. Garrett and Jenny happened to be the only two in the class who read above grade level, so it was good for them to have the added challenge of portraying the Macbeths, and they both worked hard.

One example of a student working through the language was when Melvin, playing the Doctor, was having trouble with the line "This disease is beyond my practice." I asked him what a doctor's practice was, and he understood the word. I noted that different kinds of doctors have different kinds of practices. I then asked Melvin if a doctor was saying that someone's disease was *beyond* his practice, what he might mean. He guessed that it meant that she needed a different kind of doctor. I told him he was right, and asked what kind of doctor Lady Macbeth needed. Melvin thought for a bit before asking for confirmation whether it would be a therapy doctor. If Melvin had been asked to explain this quote on a test, he would have gotten it wrong, even though he understood all of the words and the concepts involved. He just needed to be asked the right scaffolding questions to draw it out of him.

During the performance, Robert (playing Fleance) did something he had never done in rehearsal. He made a gesture towards Banquo as he was killed, as if to imply that Fleance was working with the murderers to set him up. This is an example of, as I put it in the rubric, bringing original ideas and interpretations to creative work, and taking a bold risk. Robert's interpretation of the scene is not supported by the text, or any of our discussions about it. However, we know so little about Fleance from *Macbeth* that it is hard to say for sure that Robert's choice directly contradicts the text either. This is the reason that he got the 4 in Category F, "Displays Originality of Expression."

Jack had shown much promise during our process-based work, but when he had to speak memorized lines as Banquo, he had a lot of problems making them sound organic. The witches -- Linda, Rebecca, and Ruth -- were excellent. For the cauldron scene, I told them that the ingredients were all really disgusting, but that the witches liked them. I gave them the direction to try to make the audience throw up. When our audience was in place, Rebecca began to really savor this scene. She left her blocking behind and went right to the lip of the stage to lean into the audience. I really believed she was trying to nauseate the audience. Iris did a wonderful job as Stage Manager. She was given a lot of responsibility and she rose to the occasion.

PHASE THREE: TECHNOLOGY INTEGRATION

Here students collaborated on a technology project, working together to create a website that features character biographies, original artwork, and hyperlinked annotations to an electronic copy of the text that they performed. Through a progression from the drama-in-education activities, through rehearsal, and finally to production, the students had developed a level of expertise in *Macbeth*. The annotation project allowed them to apply this knowledge, as well as reflect on what they had learned.

The Internet has a great potential in the classroom, not only to deliver education and related services, but also to serve as a publishing medium for work. Students tend to take more pride in work that will be read by an audience, and the Internet offers the possibility of a world-wide audience. In fact, the final version of the website was posted to the World Wide Web, and was accessible online for several years until the service provider shut down. This is a level of publication that was never possible to the typical classroom before the innovation of the Internet, and now can be made available to every classroom. In this unit, students are encouraged to think of the Internet as more than just a data source; it is a portal to a global community of which they can be contributing members.

This work follows the current philosophies of the field of instructional technology, because it provides an example of how to use computer technology as a teaching tool, without being computer-centered. The unit begins with learning goals, and uses the computer as one of several tools to achieve those goals. The unit also addresses a concern about computers in the classroom, well expressed by Neil Postman (1992), one of technology's most outspoken critics:

In introducing the personal computer to the classroom, we shall be breaking a four-hundred-year-old truce between the gregariousness and openness fostered by orality and the introspection and isolation fostered by the printed word. Orality stresses group learning, cooperation, and a sense of social responsibility, which is the context within which Thamus believed proper instruction and real knowledge must be communicated. Print stresses individualized learning, competition, and personal autonomy. Over four centuries, teachers, while emphasizing print, have allowed orality its place in the classroom, and have therefore achieved a kind of pedagogical peace between these two forms of learning, so that what is valuable in each can be maximized. Now comes the computer, carrying anew the banner of private learning and individual problem-solving. (17)

In this phase, students worked together as a group to create a collaborative technology project. There was also an emphasis on publication, which made learning public and reinforced the idea that proper instruction and real knowledge must be communicated. Rather than reinforcing the barriers that computer technology introduce, this study intended to demonstrate the doors that can be opened.

By the start of Phase Three, the students had reached a level of mastery of *Macbeth* such that they were ready to create a project putting their knowledge into application, reinforcing it in the process. In this case, they created a guide for those who are going to be reading the play. I then assessed their work according to the rubric for this section, as reproduced in Table 3.

The final website required a lot of writing that was a source of data for assessing students according the rubric. Of particular interest were essays written by Alicia and Jenny about the first two phases of the unit. These essays may add some additional perspective on these sections, as well as the students' reaction to them. Garrett and Charley were responsible for writing a plot summary, and even though some of the important details had been skipped over or left out completely, they did a great job. They did not only include a list of what happens, but also provided some analysis and even some dialogue in their own words. Garrett and Charley worked on this on their own, and I only saw it after it was finished. They ended their essay with

Table 3. Rubric for phase three

PHASE THREE	4	3	2	1
A. Analyzes *Macbeth*	Creates work that supports a clear decision about the play	Creates work that supports a fuzzy decision about the play	Makes decisions about the play with little or weak support	Does not make decisions about the play
B. Applies Shake-speare	Writes for an unini-tiated audience and teaches the play	Makes connections between the play and real life	Creates original work that shows an understanding of the play	Does not apply understanding of play
C. Commits to project work	Engages fully in project work and takes calculated risks	Engages in project work, but takes reckless risks or none at all	Makes an effort to engage in project work	Participates in project work superficially, or not at all
D. Communicates through language	Express ideas and feelings effectively via language	Expresses ideas effectively through language	Expresses feelings convincingly through language	Does not express ideas or feelings effectively via language
E. Communicates through image	Express ideas and feelings effectively via image	Expresses ideas effectively through image	Expresses feelings convincingly through image	Does not express ideas or feelings effectively via image
F. Displays origi-nality of expression	Brings original ideas and interpre-tations to creative work	Brings original interpretations but not ideas to creative work	Commits to creative work but without originality	Does not engage in creative work
G. Employs creative problem solving	Identifies artistic problems and finds creative solutions	Identifies artistic problems and finds workable solutions	Identifies artistic problems and finds weak solutions	Is not able to identify artistic problems
H. Displays higher order thinking skills	Displays higher order thinking skills and is aware of learning	Displays higher or-der thinking skills but isn't aware of learning	Displays only awareness of learning	Does not display higher order think-ing

"Oh and by the way, if you are in a play, good luck." This indicates that they were writing with an audience in mind, most likely another class preparing to do a similar project. They both received the maximum score in Sections B and D of the rubric.

Each student was given a different scene to illustrate for the website. The art-work was of mixed quality. I evaluated the artwork based not only on the artistic ability, but also how the image demonstrates comprehension of its subject. So, for example, while Daryl's picture did not show a lot of artistic promise, it did contain quite a bit of information about the play. Karen's picture, on the other hand, showed a lot of artistic talent, but did not tell us much. She drew her own character, Seyton, standing by a throne, and the character's big line -- "The Queen, my Lord, is dead" -- prominently displayed. Macbeth is not in the picture, and Seyton seemed to be almost smiling. However, the image is pleasing to the eye, and makes creative use of shape and color. It is important to keep both of these factors in mind when determining each student's score on the assessment rubric. Karen also painted a picture of Lady Macbeth washing her hands, with the doctor and servant watching. Karen received a 4 in Section E of the rubric, and Daryl received a 3. Both students scored a 4 in Section F. George painted a great picture of William Shakespeare which we used on the website. He also painted the picture we used for the homepage. Jack, Alicia, and Camille all included text in their illustrations. Jack drew Banquo lying dead with the caption "Who killed Banquo?" Alicia drew Rosse and Macduff and wrote a description of the scene she was illustrating. Camille painted a graveyard, and wrote epitaphs for the deceased characters at the end of the play.

The students were almost all African-American and Latino, but the characters they painted were Caucasian across the board. It seems that they were not drawing themselves as the characters they played in the stage production, but rather they were drawing the characters as they imagined them in eleventh-century Scotland. All of the paintings were done digitally on the computer. Most of them were created using ClarisWorks, a program they had used in their computer class. Adrienne was the only one who did not use ClarisWorks. She created a picture of the three witches using a program called KidPix, which is really meant more for K-3.

As we neared the end of the project, I formed a four-member student technology committee, and took two sessions to teach them Adobe Pagemill, the web-authoring software they would use to create their site. In the first session, we covered creating pages and copying and pasting text between ClarisWorks and Pagemill. In the second session, we covered creating links between documents and dividing the responsibilities within the technology committee. Iris was the overall technology manager, Melvin was the chief text editor, Karen was the art supervisor, and George took on the web authoring.

It was not a goal of the unit to make sure that all of the students learned to master Pagemill, or web authoring in general. If it were, I would have had all of the students using it in the computer lab. The technology in this case functioned as a tool which the class, as a whole, would use to publish their work. The rationale behind a student committee can be a highly effective strategy for carrying out a collaborative technology project in a classroom with a small number of computers -- in this case, four. The committee takes the burden off of the teacher of facilitating the project while managing the rest of the class. The teacher still needs to keep track of the progress of the project and make sure the committee stays on task, but does not need to be involved as directly minute by minute. This strategy also gives the students more ownership of the project, since it was actually created by them.

It can also be very empowering for the students on the committee to have this responsibility. I generally choose two boys and two girls to promote gender equity, which should not be overlooked when using technology in the classroom. In this case, I had a fitting group, with each student working in his or her strength.

UNIT ASSESSMENT

I will discuss the post-unit evaluation in two discrete sections which correspond with my dual roles as teacher and researcher. First, I will report on an assessment which will both evaluate the students based on their performance, and the unit based on its ability to improve achievement. Then, as a researcher, I will present the findings of this study by evaluating the ideas expressed in the first chapter in light of the evidence gathered during the year.

In reviewing the work done, I put all of the rubric scores for the three phases into one chart, Table 4, to get an overall sense of how the students performed longitudinally. I included on this chart their reading scores from standardized tests to see if there was any relationship between how they scored on these independent assessments and how they scored in a collaborative multi-faceted project-based unit.

The reading scores are a number indicating the grade level at which a student is reading. So George and Melvin read exactly on grade level (5.0), Garrett and Jenny read at a sixth-grade reading level (6.0), and Daryl and Adrienne read at a second-grade reading level (2.0). These scores are in increments of a half-year, meaning that Karen and Gail read between a third-grade and a fourth-grade reading level (3.5). If a student reads at slightly higher or lower than a particular grade level, the score includes a plus or a minus symbol. So Ruth reads at slightly above a fifth-grade level (5.0+) and Randall reads at slightly below a fourth-grade level (4.0-). Rebecca was given a "P" for "Primer." She does not really read at all. Freddy joined the class late, and I did not have access to his reading scores for comparison.

Based on this chart, it seems that there is a loose correlation between how a student did on the standardized test and how he or she fared in this unit, although it should be noted that there are some who performed higher or lower in their relation to the class than in the standardized tests. For the most part, however, there does seem to be a general relationship. This came as a surprise to me, since the unit taps into the range of Gardner's (1993) multiple intelligences, while the reading test relies primarily on linguistic knowledge. However, there were enough of those that outperformed better readers to make a strong case for varying teaching modes, as will be revealed by a closer examination of these individuals to see what aspects of the project gave them the opportunities to perform beyond their reading-test scores. This process will also lend support to the application of Vygotsky (1978) to this study, as it will demonstrate instances of children performing better in a collaborative, authentic project than they did under testing conditions. However, it should be

Table 4. Total evaluations based on all three rubrics

Student	Reading Level	Phase One Subtotal	Phase Two Subtotal	Phase Three Subtotal	Unit Total
Garrett	6.0	32	32	32	96
George	5.0	32	32	32	96
Alicia	3.5	32	32	29	93
Freddy	?	N/A*	32	30	62*
Jenny	6.0	32	28	28	88
Linda	4.0-	32	32	24	88
Jack	5.0+	30	32	25	87
Ruth	5.0+	26	32	27	85
Karen	3.5	27	24	32	83
Randall	4.0-	24	30	29	83
Melvin	5.0	28	25	29	82
Camille	3.0	25	25	29	79
Will	5.0+	25	27	26	78
Marsha	3.5	18	31	25	74
Iris	3.5+	22	26	23	71
Jake	5.0+	26	26	19	71
Nathan	4.0	23	N/A*	N/A*	23*
Rebecca	P	27	32	8	67
Gail	3.5	20	21	25	66
Charley	4.0	19	22	23	64
Frank	5.0+	23	22	18	63
Alex	4.0	19	21	21	61
Kathryn	3.0	18	15	27	60
Adrienne	2.0	24	13	22	59
Jane	3.0	12	18	18	48
Sarah	2.5	13	13	21	47
Margaret	2.5	11	9	25	45
Daryl	2.0	12	11	16	39
Robert	3.0-	11	18	8	37
Johnny	3.0-	12	9	15	36

* Not present for the entire unit; placed in chart based on *average* score.

noted that since different measurement scales are being used between the reading tests and the rubrics, the students can only be compared by how they performed relative to the rest of the class. Therefore, the presence of these examples alone cannot be used as quantitative evidence that there has been any improvement at all, and the discussion of the positive examples below must be considered qualitatively.

Adrienne only earned a 59, which is not a great score, but she had been tested as one of the three lowest-scoring readers in the class. She was assigned to illustrate the very first scene. Using KidPix, an application meant for younger students that none of the others used, she created an illustration of three witches around a cauldron, using a variety of colors and textures in her drawing. Two of the witches were wearing pointy hats, and next to the cauldron there was a clip art frog. These are appropriate choices for the assignment. She was also an active participant in the drama-in-education phase of the project, improvising a witch with full commitment and creativity. So, while I would not expect Adrienne to be able to write a very good essay about the witches under testing conditions, this project gave her two alternative ways to communicate her ideas about the witches.

Another example of outperforming his reading test score was George who, along with Garrett, had the highest score in the class with a 96. However, he had tested at a 5.0, exactly on grade level, which was a full grade level lower than Garrett's 6.0. Throughout the unit, George was able to demonstrate a multitude of abilities that a reading test would never be able to measure. He displayed leadership qualities, as well as a wide range of skills. From the first day, George proved that an average reading score does not necessarily indicate an average student. He showed this when he identified Scotland on the world map, when he displayed natural acting ability and mathematical skills. He also was able to memorize lines, help Daryl out on stage when he had trouble, and learn how to make hyperlinks in Pagemill very quickly.

Camille, despite testing at a third-grade reading level, scored a 79. Playing a range of characters amalgamated into a single servant, Camille's energetic performance often provided spirit and structure to the stage production at times when it needed both. For the website, Camille wrote a very short biography (claiming her character is the most important in the play) but painted a graveyard, and wrote epitaphs for the deceased characters (a forward slash is used here to indicate a line break): "RIP / LADY MACBETH / A MEAN QUEEN," "RIP / DUNCAN / A BRAVE KING," "RIP / MACBETH / THE KING OF THE PALACE," "RIP / YOUNG SIWARD / SON OF OLD MAN SIWARD." Her assignment was to illustrate the very last scene, and rather than interpreting this instruction literally by painting the characters who speak in the scene, she chose to create a painting that captured the mood and meaning of the final scene, as the battle is declared over, and the survivors mourn the dead.

Karen's reading score was a 3.5 and she scored an 83. The reason for this dramatic disparity is that Karen has a range of proficiencies that the reading test did not cover. She threw herself into the drama-in-education activities and demonstrated an ability to express ideas through improvisation. As Seyton, she gave a committed and energetic performance. Most impressive, however, was her contribution to the class website, often going over and above what was asked of her out of an enthusiasm for the project. She did three line annotations, explaining why she had chosen each line as part of her annotation, which was not part of the instructions, and which was not something any other student had chosen to do. Her art skills were advanced, and she quickly took a leadership position in filling in unfinished artwork, and eventually served as the art supervisor for the project. Her biography was brief, but like her annotations, also focused on her own reflection of why she made the choice she did: "Do you know why I picked this character? I picked this character because it's just right for me. I like to be bad. Seyton is a special character because he's all about killing and also I'm the 3rd murderer." The reading test did not account for her art skills, but in a collaborative project that includes a visual art component, she was able to take a leadership role among her peers. And reading tests do not measure ability or inclination for self-reflection, but in a multi-faceted unit with subjective rubrics, a teacher can notice those who show higher-order-thinking skills.

Alicia, who tested at a 3.5 reading level, more than one full year below grade level, scored a 93, topped only by Garrett and George. Throughout the work, she had excellent class participation, contributing to discussions and offering answers to questions that were either correct or reasonable guesses. As the Thane of Rosse, she brought clarity to the scenes she was in, speaking Shakespeare's lines with ease, and effectively communicating her speeches which often contained important exposition. The biography she wrote for the website was thoughtful, and included a couple of original conclusions that she had not discussed with me: "I think Rosse is a messenger because he also went to tell Macduff, his cousin, that his family was dead. Rosse is a very intelligent character." She even took on an additional writing assignment toward the end of the project, describing what the students did to prepare for the stage production in Phase Two for the website in Phase Three.

The most prominent example of outperforming her reading test scores was Rebecca, who scored a 67, despite the fact that she did not register on the reading scale at all. Her reading score was listed as P, for "Primer," meaning that she is an introductory reader. She was a standout in the drama-in-education phase, investing herself fully in creating a witch and participating in various improvisational activities. She was at a disadvantage at auditions, as I was initially reluctant to give such a large role to a reader at her level. But she impressed me by reciting two of the speeches from memory. This was more impressive than other students who did the same thing, not only because she would have had someone read her the lines in order to memorize them, but also because of the immense personal risk she had to take to audition at all. But she was really motivated to have a big part in the play, and so she made the necessary investment needed to get one. Casting her as the Second Witch was a big risk for me as well, but she lived up to the task. She not only knew her lines as well as any other student, but also her performance in the stage production was a standout, demonstrating an understanding of her character and a comfort, even a talent, for the spoken language. Her reading specialist, Mr. Burnett, observed the effect the project was having on Rebecca when he told me how surprised he was that a student who does not read could look him in the eye and recite a speech from *Macbeth*. She told Mr. Burnett that she wants to be an actress. Unfortunately, her lack of contribution to the website in Phase Three lowered her overall score. But there can be little question that she displayed a range of skills -- even verbal / linguistic skills -- not evident from her reading score.

Examples of outperformance of reading test scores are not the only measures of achievement worth noting. Because of the product-based nature of the second and third phases, I often asked students to take on extra responsibilities that others in the class did not have to do. They were generally chosen by their ability to contribute to the project more than educational concerns. This is the nature of product-based work. Thus, Garrett had many more lines to memorize than anyone else in the class. Jenny had to memorize more lines than anyone other than Garrett. Iris had the dual role of stage manager and technology leader, and George, Karen, and Melvin had additional responsibilities as technology committee members. It is a tricky proposition when some students are doing work that others are not doing. There is a sense that if it is an educationally-beneficial task that serves the curriculum goals, then everybody should be doing it, and if it is not, then nobody should. But the larger point is that division of labor is a part of real-world collaboration, and when work is done together as a class to create authentic products, such as stage productions and websites, everyone benefits. Also, in projects where there is an uneven distribution of responsibility in a heterogeneous class such as this one, there is more of an opportunity for performing assignments that fit individual ability levels than in lessons where everyone is given the exact same assignment regardless of ability. Ideally, every learner can be challenged at the same time, and stretch within their ZPD. I cannot say for sure whether it was more difficult for Garrett to memorize 315 lines or for Daryl to memorize 4 lines, but I can say that the tasks seem to me to be more appropriate for these two students than having both of them memorize the exact same number of lines.

There are also social considerations that should be taken into account when working on collaborative projects. Even though they are not included in the assessment rubrics, they are of interest to educators. Freddy had been transferred into Ms. MacNamara's class because he had been "having trouble getting along with the other students" in his last class. To me, this phrase suggests a kid that gets into a lot of fights, perhaps even seeks out those fights. Those described by this phrase are often behavior problems in class as well. I would describe Robert and Johnny as "having trouble getting along with other students." In my class, Freddy was always well-behaved and engaged in the lessons. In his better moments, he had a particularly wry sense of humor, an inspired creativity, and an earnest determination to do the best work he could. Perhaps the description meant he was getting picked on, and he was transferred for his own benefit. Or, perhaps, he was a behavior problem for other teachers, but was well behaved during my work with the class because he was engaged in the project. Maybe the nature of a collaborative project in which all rely on each other fosters conditions that are more conducive to them getting along with one another. I do not have any conclusive evidence to say for sure. What I do know is that Freddy took a great deal of pride from his contribution to this project, as evidenced by his participation in class, his determination to get his work correct, and the ownership that he took of each responsibility he was given. I did not see him have any trouble getting along with the others in this class.

I also observed some social development in Marsha through this project. Marsha had been left back twice, and was therefore two years older than most of the other students in the class. In the first phase, she would do good work when she chose to participate, but would choose not to participate and even disrupt the class at other times. At one point, she yelled out "BOR-RING" while another group was presenting, but I was able to bring her back in by getting her more directly involved with the activity. This leads me to believe that there was an inner conflict going on between her desire to separate herself from the others and the desire to participate in drama activities, which did seem to motivate her. She was the first one to audition, and had memorized two of the speeches. Her written audition application ended with "And when my friends ask me did I do a play on Macbeth? I'll say yes and that's not all. I went back in time to ten hundred century." Ms. MacNamara told me that Marsha did not have a lot of confidence in her school work. But she really enjoyed playing Hecate, and she found her confidence through playing what very possibly was the most powerful character in *Macbeth*, and doing it well. By Phase Three, there was no question about whether or not Marsha wanted to participate. She painted a digital picture of Hecate and wrote what ended up being the longest annotation in the project, accurately explaining the meaning of her long speech. She found herself respected by the other students for her contributions, and she took pride in them.

Daryl scored only a 2.0 on the reading exam, and his class participation, while earnest, often consisted of wild guesses and irrelevant statements. He was a very sweet-mannered and jocular child. He was not a behavior problem, and his only disruption of class would be when he was attempting to participate. From the very beginning of the project, he wanted to play Macbeth, but he was not able to memorize any of the speeches for the audition, and there was no indication that he would be able to handle such a role. Suspecting that his interest in the role had less to do with the artistic challenges and academic responsibilities of Macbeth, and more to do with the status and attention of playing the lead role, I instead chose to cast him as Donalbain, a very high-status character with only four lines. He had trouble with these lines in rehearsal, but was able to remember them during the performance. He did not write a biography, but he did annotate one of his lines. For "What is amiss," Daryl wrote "Donalbain wants to know what is wrong." And while that may not display an academic rigor appropriate for the fifth grade, for Daryl, it was a big step simply to follow directions and give an accurate description of one of the lines. His image for the website provided further evidence that he had understood what was happening in that scene. Like Adrienne, Daryl was able to communicate ideas about the play through artwork that he probably could not have using language.

RESEARCH FINDINGS

Earlier on, I raised questions about whether or not ten-year-olds could demonstrate behaviors that Courtney (1989) associates with children ranging from ages twelve to eighteen. I went back to examine whether students are able to think abstractly. I looked for evidence that they are able to understand causality. Have they expressed opinions about how their characters relate to the play as a whole? Can they make moral decisions about their characters? Do they understand the symbolism that Shakespeare uses? A lot of writing was done in Phase Three that can help answer these questions. These considerations are not listed in the rubrics, because those are for evaluating the students based on their performances, not their cognitive ability. They were being used as an assessment tool in my role as teacher. The findings presented here are my observations as a researcher.

A lot of the writing for the website demonstrated that they were able to think abstractly, which involved the use of logic to draw conclusions about that which was not in their direct experience. In the case of the play, they could demonstrate abstract thought by extrapolating from elements within the text to draw original conclusions. These conclusions should be logical, whether or not they were entirely correct. In fact, an incorrect conclusion can sometimes be stronger evidence of abstract thought than a correct assertion, because I know they were less likely to have gotten the idea from me or from another source.

Annotating the line "None of woman born shall harm Macbeth," Jane explained how the prophecy could come true:

At the end of the play, Macbeth was killed. The apparition told Macbeth that none by woman born shall harm him. Macbeth was killed by Macduff who was not born. His mother was pregnant with him when she was dying. So they cut his mother's stomach open so he was never born.

I should point out that this is the edited version of what Jane wrote as the focus does not fall on spelling and grammar. We already know that Jane tests at a third-grade reading level. As this analysis is about the depth of thought and higher order thinking skills, I will be using the edited versions of their work in this section for the purpose of clarity. What is clear from this passage is that Jane solved a problem that is presented by the text. All Shakespeare tells us is that "Macduff was from his mother's womb / Untimely ripped." The text does not state, or even imply, that Macduff's mother was dead at the time. Jane filled in the details and offered a theory to explain more clearly why Macduff was not born from a woman.

Alicia demonstrated abstract thought in her character biography of Rosse:

Rosse is a character in the play Macbeth. He is the Thane of Rosse. He was in the Norwegian war then came back to tell the King that the victory is won. He was sent out to tell Macbeth that he was now the Thane of Cawdor. One of his lines was "The king has happily received Macbeth the news of thy success." That means that Macbeth is now the thane of Glamis and Cawdor. I think Rosse is a messenger because he also went to tell Macduff, his cousin, that his family was dead. Rosse is a very intelligent character.

She noticed that Rosse came back to tell the King of victory against the Norwegians, and also brought news to Macduff of the death of his wife and children. Alicia concluded that Rosse must be a messenger. Even though this is not entirely accurate, Alicia did use observation and logic to draw this conclusion, demonstrating abstract thought.

Students also displayed evidence that they understood causality, the idea that actions have causes and consequences. Annotating the line "We have lost best half of our affair," Gail wrote "This line means that they were supposed to kill Fleance and Banquo. But they killed Banquo and Fleance escaped. So they were scared to lose half of their money that Macbeth was going to give them." Again, the conclusions do not have to be correct in order to be logical. Freddy understood that his character was wounded, so when he appeared on stage, he decided to hold his stomach to indicate his wound. Even when he appeared in a scene that took place years later, he continued to hold his stomach to indicate that he was the wounded Captain. Melvin similarly displayed an understanding of causality in his annotation of the line "This disease is beyond my practice: yet I have known those which have walked in their sleep, who have died holily in their beds:"

This line is saying that the doctor might not be able to cure Lady Macbeth. The doctor said that most people who walked in their sleep (like Lady Macbeth) die in their beds. The doctor that Lady Macbeth is seeing is a medical doctor, the doctor she needs is a therapist. If she doesn't find one fast she could die.

Of course, Lady Macbeth does die "by self and violent hands" and Melvin makes the connection here between her suicide and the mental-health problems she is experiencing.

Students expressed opinions about how their characters relate to the play as a whole. Camille wrote "The servant is the most important person in the play. She does a lot of things like: wash the dishes, clean the room and open the door for people." She did not write much, but rather than complaining that she only had a functional role, she chose to consider why her character was important. Ruth gave her character's relationship to the play a bit more thought in her character biography:

My character in Macbeth was the 3rd witch. She is very important because in the beginning she tells Macbeth that he will be king and she tells Banquo that he will never be king but his children will. If the third witch wasn't in this part of the play Macbeth wouldn't have known that he was going to be king and Banquo wouldn't have known that his sons would be kings.

Similarly, Margaret wrote a thoughtful description of her character, drawing elements from the text to enhance her description:

The third apparition is a child with a stick in her hand and a crown on her head. She has two sisters. The first apparition is a child with a metal mask over her head. The second apparition has blood all over her. The third apparition says Macbeth shall never be vanquished until Great Birnam wood high to Dunsinane hill shall come against him. That means that the Great Birnam wood is going to come to the Scottish castle. This is very important because when this happens the battle begins. Like the second witch said "When the hurly-burly's done, / When the battle's lost and won."

Like Ruth, she noticed how the actions of her character are responsible for setting the events of the play in motion.

Students not only were able to see where their characters fit into the play as a whole, but also made moral decisions regarding their characters. Robert, playing Fleance, seemed to make a decision that his character helped to set up Banquo's murder. I do not agree with his decision, but it was a strong choice. George began his character biography as follows: "Malcolm is the kind of character who obeys his father's rules. He is the person who wins a title and doesn't overjoy himself by telling everyone." This is a reference to Malcolm's being named Prince of Cumberland by his father, but George is not content just to give us this fact. He made judgments about Malcolm's character based on his behavior. Jake concluded his character biography with "Banquo's ghost now can rest in peace." Banquo's ghost appears in only one scene, and does not speak. Jake decided that the ghost could rest in peace once Macbeth was killed.

Students also demonstrated an understanding of the symbolic language that appears throughout Shakespeare. Ruth annotated the line "The Thane of Cawdor lives: why do you dress me in borrowed robes: "He says this line because Rosse and Angus tell him that he is the Thane of Cawdor but the Thane of Cawdor is still alive. Why do you dress me in borrowed robes means that why are you giving me a title that is already taken." Ruth shows an understanding here that Rosse and Angus are not literally dressing Macbeth in borrowed robes, but that Macbeth is using the idea of borrowed robes to stand for a title that does not belong to him. Similarly, Alex, annotating Lady Macbeth's line "Come, you Spirits that tend on mortal thoughts, unsex me here, and fill me, from the crown to the toe, top-full of direst cruelty," demonstrated that she understood the meaning behind the symbolic language at work in the passage:

What it means is she wants to be mean and it really means to make her feel like a man for she can kill king Duncan and than turn back to a woman. She will not really change at all, she will just be stronger for she can kill the king.

Thus, a significant number of ten-year-old students displayed a range of skills in the role stage, which Courtney (1989) associates with those who are twelve to eighteen years old. They demonstrated an understanding of abstract thought, causality, how characters relate to the play as a whole, moral decisions about their characters, and symbolic language. This demonstrates that ten-year-olds may be capable of performances associated with the role stage in the upper range of their zones of proximal development and, under certain conditions, can demonstrate evidence of these abilities. This is the chief finding here, and supports the use of Vygotsky's (1978) ZPD.

LOOKING FORWARD

This work makes a clear contribution to the field of educational theatre by providing evidence that supports Vygotsky (1978) as a developmental theorist that is more relevant to drama work than is Piaget (1962). Furthermore, it provides concrete examples of how varying teaching methods to address Gardner's (1993) multiple intelligences can provide opportunities for academic achievement that may not exist in a more traditional classroom. Taken together, these make a powerful argument for challenging a system that uses reading and math test scores as the final judgment of a child's ability. These numbers are always attractive to politicians and educational bureaucrats, because they are quantifiable and measurable in the aggregate. However, if an individual's test scores do not provide an accurate portrait of what someone can do, those aggregate numbers lose a lot of their meaning. Therefore, this study contains an inherent argument for a qualitative research methodology that can describe both in numbers and in observations, both in charts and in descriptions of ongoing reflective practice, what is really happening in the classroom, and what students are really able to achieve when the test-preparation booklets are put aside and they are able to participate in curriculum activities that were designed with their needs in mind. More work is needed, though. This study opens up avenues for future research that may help address that need. Now that there is some evidence that fifth-graders have the ability to understand Shakespeare, it would be interesting to see if there are other methods that would be effective besides the three that I have chosen. For example, one might try teaching Shakespeare to fifth-graders by having them interview experts, videotape scenes and create a video documentary. Someone else might have students update the text, create illustrations, and make original book adaptations. The methods I used are not meant to be presented as the only methods, or even the best methods. This work would be supported by a future one that uses different techniques to achieve similar goals.

Also, I assumed that an early positive experience would make a student more likely to understand and appreciate the dramatist's work later in life, but I have no evidence of this beyond the anecdotal. I would be interested to see if attitudes and competencies toward Shakespeare have any correlation with the age at which students were first introduced to his works, and the methods used to teach it to them.

If I were to do a project like this one again, I would definitely leave more time for rehearsal. I based my estimate on a production of *A Midsummer Night's Dream* I directed with another fifth-grade class in Harlem, not taking into account that those I was working with in Harlem were much more advanced than these students, not to mention more disciplined. Another thing I would want to do differently is to have the characters look the same in the different pictures of the play. As it was, each student drew all of the characters in his or her picture, so Lady Macbeth, for example, looked radically different in each picture she was in (except for the two drawn by Karen and Kathryn, who sat at computers next to each other while they drew). This did not bother me at the time, since I was more concerned with the process than with the product of the website. However, from a product-based standpoint, a viewer might be less confused if the characters had a more consistent look. This could have been accomplished by having each student design his or her character before anybody works on the scene illustrations. Then, digital copies of all of the character designs could be put in a folder on every computer, or a shared folder in the lab, so that anyone could access them when doing their scene illustrations.

There are many sources that give teachers ideas about what to do, but far fewer that document the process itself. Hopefully, this study creates a tangible record that gives more information about the various contours of a project like this. I would hope that as a result, others will decide that a Shakespearean production is appropriate and realistic. This study can also be used as a support to justify the decision to bring the playwright into a fifth-grade classroom. I truly believe that Shakespeare brings a wealth of beautiful and powerful poetry and drama just slightly beneath the thin veneer of inaccessibility. Once that surface is cracked, the rewards far outweigh the work it has taken to get there.

REFERENCES

Courtney, R. (1982). *Re-Play: Studies of Human Drama in Education. Ontario: OISE, Cullum, A. (1967). Push Back The Desks*. New York: Citation Press.

Courtney, R. (1989). *Play, Drama & Thought: The Intellectual Background To Dramatic Education* (4th ed.). Toronto: Simon & Pierre.

Davis, D., & Lawrence, C. (1986). *Selected Writings of Gavin Bolton*. Hong Kong: Longman.

Gardner, H. (1993). *Frames of Mind: The Theory of Multiple Intelligences* (2nd ed.). New York: Basic Books.

McCaslin, N. (2000). *Creative Drama in the Classroom and Beyond* (7th ed.). New York: Longman.

O'Neill, C., & Lambert, A. (1982). *Drama Structures: A Practical Handbook for Teachers*. London: Stanley Thornes.

Piaget, J. (1962). *Play, Dreams and Imitation in Childhood.* New York: Norton.

Piaget, J., & Inhelder, B. (1966). *The Psychology of the Child.* Paris: Presses Universitaires de France.

Postman, N. (1992). *Technopoly: The Surrender of Culture to Technology*. New York: Random House.

Vygotsky, L. (1978). *Mind in Society: The Development of Higher Psychological Processes* (Cole, M., Eds.). Cambridge: Harvard University Press.

ADDITIONAL READING

Bolton, G. (1979). *Toward a Theory of Drama in Education*. London: Longman.

Bolton, G. (1992). *New Perspectives on Classroom Drama*. Hemel Hempstead: Simon & Schuster Education.

Cuban, L. (1997). Preface. In Sandholtz, J., Ringstaff, C., & Dwyer, D. C. (Eds.), *Teaching with Technology: Creating Student-Centered Classrooms*. New York: Teachers College Press.

Dewey, J. (1910). *How We Think*. Boston: D. C. Heath & Co.doi:10.1037/10903-000

Dewey, J. (1938). *Experience and Education*. New York: Macmillan.

Dewey, J. (1944). *Democracy and Education: An Introduction to the Philosophy of Education*. New York: The Free Press.

Ely, M. (1991). *Doing Qualitative Research: Circles Within Circles*. London: Falmer.

Gibson, R. (1998). *Teaching Shakespeare*. Cambridge: Cambridge University Press.

Heathcote, D., & Bolton, G. (1995). *Drama for Learning: Dorothy Heathcote's Mantle of the Expert Approach to Education*. Portsmouth: Heinemann.

Knapp, L. R., & Glenn, A. D. (1996). *Restructuring Schools with Technology*. Needham Heights: Allyn & Bacon.

Kohl, H. R. (1988). *Making Theatre: Developing plays with Young People*. New York: Teachers and Writers Collaborative.

Moll, L. C. (Ed.). (1990). *Vygotsky and Education: Instructional Implications and Applications of Sociohistorical Psychology*. Cambridge: Cambridge University Press.

Morgan, N., & Saxton, J. (1987). *Teaching Drama: A Mind of Many Wonders*. London: Stanley Thornes.

National Center on Education and the Economy and the University of Pittsburgh. (1997). *New Standards Performance Standards: English Language Arts, Mathematics, Science, Applied Learning*. Washington, DC: Harcourt Brace.

Neelands, J. (1984). *Making Sense of Drama: A Guide to Classroom Practice*. London: Heinemann.

Neelands, J. (1990). *Structuring Drama Work*. Cambridge: Cambridge University Press.

O'Neill, C. (1995). *Drama Worlds: A Framework for Process Drama*. Portsmouth: Heinemann.

Papert, S. (1980). *Mindstorms: Children, Computers, and Powerful Ideas*. New York: Basic Books.

Papert, S. (1993). *The Children's Machine: Rethinking School in the Age of the Computer*. New York: Basic Books.

Perkins, D. (1992). *Smart Schools: Better Thinking and Learning for Every Child*. New York: The Free Press.

Schön, D. A. (1983). *The Reflective Practitioner: How Professionals Think in Action*. USA: Basic Books.

Schön, D. A. (1987). *Educating the Reflective Practitioner*. San Francisco: Jossey-Bass.

Stake, R. E. (1995). *The Art of Case Study Research*. London: Sage.

Taylor, P. (Ed.). (1996). *Researching Drama and Arts Education: Paradigms and Possibilities*. London: Falmer.

Taylor, P. (2000). *The Drama Classroom: Action, Reflection, Transformation*. New York: Routledge/Falmer.

Vygotsky, L. (1986). *Thought and Language* (Kozulin, A., Ed.). Cambridge: MIT Press.

Wagner, B. J. (1976). *Dorothy Heathcote: Drama as a Learning Medium*. Washington, D.C.: National Education Association.

Wagner, B. J. (1998). *Educational Drama and Language Arts: What Research Shows*. Portsmouth: Heinemann.

Afterword

READING THROUGH THE MACHINE

Finally, let's dream for a moment – a literary scholar's dream. Most of us who regularly turn to a computer to support our work might venture to have such a dream. In it, I am sitting comfortably reading, the computer next to me readily accessible. My thoughts about the text as I read can be recorded by the computer as they occur to me (perhaps I speak aloud while the computer's voice recognition system transcribes my words). Perhaps I begin to wonder about a prominent image in a novel I am reading: I can search for this image across the rest of the text or the whole corpus of the novelist's other writings. Or I may recall a thought I had while reading a particular poem last year and now wish to revisit it, perhaps add to it in the light of my present understanding. All the literature I have read (and perhaps much that I propose to read) is available through the computer; all the thoughts I have had during my reading are similarly available. As I read on the screen (sitting with my notebook computer, that is, in a comfortable armchair, with its wireless network connection), the system that I am accessing is an online portal personalized to access my selection of texts and the records of my reading, together with a powerful set of Internet tools for organizing and searching these texts (cf. the portal technology described by Siemens, 2009). Through the portal I can also semi-automatically create personal web pages, the outcome of my searches and the connections I build between my responses and the texts I read. These are also stored online, available only to me, and for as long as I wish to keep them. The Internet also provides access to the reference works I might need: a dictionary, an encyclopedia, a chronology; each can be activated merely by highlighting a word or phrase on screen and requesting the relevant resource. This system is available to me whether I am an occasional, ordinary reader, a student, or a professional scholar of literature – it will adjust to my needs and offer me the resources appropriate to my interests. It will accommodate both the absorbed, experiential mode of the ordinary reader reading for pleasure, and the analytical, focused mode of the student. Moreover, a part or whole of this virtual structure could be designated as available for public access or access by a limited set of users, thus making it a central tool for discussions in an educational context.

This is just a preliminary sketch of the system I am dreaming about. Many of the elements needed to create it already exist, scattered across different applications, including several described in this book, but not yet brought together on the Internet in the way I have envisaged. As Susan Hockey (2000) remarked, introducing her survey of research with digital texts, these are "tools and techniques which ought to be available via the Internet, but at present are not [...] The expectation is that these tools will be available in future versions of the Internet" (p. v). In this context, my primary focus will be on text analysis: the systematic analysis by computer of language, style, narrative forms, and other features. I will suggest that it is here, rather than in hypertext or virtual reality, that the power of the computer can provide an appropriate basis for literary reading. This will require developing and testing text analysis methods rather more systematically than hitherto. In addition, we will interface text analysis methods with another dimension rarely considered: the responses of actual readers.

Thus the computer will offer a facility for registering and mapping the responses of readers to the literary texts they read. Since the computer screen seems destined to become a medium on which readers of the future will experience literature, the scenario I sketch here – albeit a somewhat speculative one – will enable the computational power of the computer to be brought into play in support of reading and understanding literary texts. In particular, the power of the computer will support the significance of the individual's acts of reading. As Lev Manovich (2001) points out, the computer allows for individual variability as never before: "new media technology acts as the most perfect realization of the utopia of an ideal society composed of unique individuals. New media objects assure users that their choices – and therefore, their underlying thoughts and desires – are unique, rather than preprogrammed and shared with others" (p. 42). In this respect, the computer will provide the ideal medium for exploring the individuality of our responses to the texts we read and then, if desired, sharing them with others.

Why would anyone choose to read a literary work on computer screen? Because the computer can help us to co-create and explore the imaginative world of the text. Our computer tools so far are not adept at this, but in this commentary I mention a little of what has been done, and what we might try to do.

The research I will draw upon in support of this model, then, comes both from the text analysis tradition, and from empirical studies of literary response (Miall, 2006). Both fields have largely been disregarded by mainstream literary scholarship. In combination, however, they offer, first, an opportunity to rethink our expectations of the computer in literary studies, and subsequently, with appropriate research, to help model and support what ordinary readers experience when reading. As I suggest, we can develop a system for the individual reader, whether engaged in a book for pleasure or a student of literature, drawing both on our knowledge of texts and on the systematic recording and analysis of the responses of groups of readers. Individuals will benefit in the long run from being able to engage at any given moment with their own image as readers, that is, with the encoded history of their responses, with the forms and processes embodied in each text they have read, and with the concerns they express through reading (i.e., the issues they are engaged with in their own lives). This will depend on building systems that do not yet exist, but many of the central pieces are already evident, certainly sufficient for a sketch of what the first stage of the building might include. My proposal might seem a Quixotic endeavour, but it is, to cite Jerome McGann (1998), an exercise in "imagining what we don't know" (p. 617).

So far the computer as a literary medium has been developed in three ways. First, as an expressive medium, it has been used to present hypertexts and, more recently, to open the prospect of immersive virtual reality narratives – a problematic development, as Ryan (2001) has suggested. Second, as a delivery medium, the computer is being used as an alternative to the book: editions of existing literary texts are being digitized, or "repurposed," in order to be read on screen or, at least, distributed digitally for printing out. Neither of these applications provides any knowledge about the texts they transmit, nor are they attentive to the reader on the other side of the screen beyond the basic executive functions of interaction, that is, clicking links in hypertext (virtual reality is more complex, but lacks the self-reflective role of literature). Here, then, we must turn to the third way, that of text analysis, which not only presents texts but can enrich our experience of them with all the computational power that is available through this machine. The computer can become a tool for thinking, for enlarging the conversations we have with ourselves while reading, and for focusing and systematizing our experiences. As McGann (1998) observes, "Computerized environments implicitly argue for dialectical models" (p. 617). The machine will, in this respect, become our symbiotic partner as a reader, simultaneously "reading" both the literary text and our responses to it in order to pattern our identity.

This may also restore to readers the authority they have supposedly lost in post-modern (i.e., Foucauldian) theory, as sites acted upon rather than acting, appropriated by the discursive formations that in literature as in other discourses are said to define what is known. This, however, we can consider a research question that the reading machine may enable us to explore. The machine leaves open the question of how we are to understand the literary system: whether it can be considered text-based, driven by the distinctiveness of literature as a medium (as we have argued in previous studies: e.g., Miall and Kuiken, 1999), or is the effect of certain conventions in classifying and processing texts that came into place primarily in the eighteenth century, as the social constructivism of recent schools of literary theory now argue. The machine will offer us opportunities to assess these alternative views, since it will enable us to collect and analyze data about texts and about readers, as well as their interactions. It will allow us to consider whether the formal structures of a literary text influence reading regardless of the disposition or experience of the reader, or whether it is only the reader's knowledge of the conventions of literary reading that promotes formal features to become agents of influence.

This last issue, of course, echoes a debate of twenty years ago in which critics such as Stanley Fish (1980) and Barbara Herrnstein Smith (1988) attacked stylistics for its formalist premises. I mention this debate, since my proposed reading machine might be considered vulnerable to the same attack. Before I do so, I should clarify three other issues which might otherwise distract from the positions I present later.

First, I am not attempting to describe a machine that reads. Although research on natural language processing has been taking place for several decades, the building of a computer that can read any text it is offered with understanding (let alone aesthetic pleasure) is still a long way off. My aim is not a computer similar to the one imagined by Richard Powers (1995) in his fiction *Galatea 2.2* which is taught to interpret literary texts (and becomes too self-aware for her own good). Reading, especially literary reading, is one of the most complex activities we perform, and seems dependent not only on cognitive functions, but on feeling, and kinaesthetic and other bodily responses. We have recently begun to recognize the embodied nature of thinking, as scholars as diverse as Hayles (1999) and Damasio (1999) have shown. Thus, for a computer to read as we do would require something equivalent to the porting of human subjectivity into the computer. While in 1988 Hans Moravec announced this as a possibility within a few decades, Hayles's (1999) discussion provides strong grounds for considering it improbable, a roboticist's fantasy. By the shorthand phrase "reading machine" I mean a support system for reading, a knowledge-base, a program with some similarity to an expert system, able to model information, to reason about it using Bayesian logic or a similar stochastic process, and to reflect its findings in an intelligible way to the reader.

Second, the attempt to model literary reading might be considered misguided. Isn't reading too fugitive and idiosyncratic to be amenable to systematic analysis? This certainly seems to be the view implied by current scholarship, which continues to elaborate theories and readings of texts with no regard for the empirical support that might be obtained from actual readers. While reader response theory has formed a significant part of this work, it has been the tradition here as in the rest of literary theory to ignore the actual reader. Jonathan Culler (1975), for instance, declared his indifference to such investigations, remarking that the important question was "what an ideal reader must know implicitly in order to read and interpret works in ways which we consider acceptable, in accordance with the institution of literature" (p. 123; see also Culler, 1981, p. 129). This was a question for theoretical reflection, not data collection. At the same time, complex theoretical arguments continue to be advanced about the interpretive moves that an ideal reader must make. Yet the question of idiosyncrasy is answered in numerous empirical studies of reading: almost all show that in various ways reading is systematic, that different readings, although they may differ interpretively, do so on grounds that are partly recoverable; and on examination, such readings are found to be determined in part by rules that we can trace either to texts or to the psychological processes of reading (including the cultural influences that mediate the process). It is this systematicity that will form an essential core of the reading machine and that will account for its fruitfulness.

Third, my reference to producing data on the formal structures of literature may remind some of my readers of an earlier debate about stylistics, focused in particular on the analysis of Baudelaire's "Les Chats" by Roman Jakobson and Claude Levi-Strauss (1972). This, for Stanley Fish (1980) was an example of the "monumental aridity" (p. 94) of Jakobson's stylistic analyses in general, in which every formal feature that could be analysed was included. As Fish (1980) puts it, in this approach there is nothing in place to govern the field of description, thus "there is no way of deciding either where to begin or where to stop, because there is no way of deciding what counts" (p. 94). While Fish (1980, pp. 322-326) appeals to the experience of the reader as the domain in which formal features are recognized, he is one more theorist for whom actual readers remain of no interest (that is, beyond his bizarre and much-cited "experiment" in asking his students to read a list of names left on a blackboard as a poem). Thus, he fails to suggest the appropriate response to Jakobson's work: that in collecting formal features the task should, first, be driven by hypotheses about reading; and second, the results should be tested against the responses of actual readers. In other words, in the light of a hypothesis about what is at issue in reading, we devise some measure of the reading process. Then we use an array of formal features we believe to be implicated in reading as predictors of the reading measure – measures range from collecting brain scans during reading, to the analysis of talk-aloud protocols.

Fish's (1980) objection to Jakobson is a double-edged sword. It could apply equally well to Fish's (1980, pp. 21-67) own postulated data about the reading process, his "affective stylistics" which was based on a model of supposed expectations and disappointments as readers construe, or misconstrue, each line of a text. We could, indeed, consider a good deal of literary theory and interpretation in the same light, as unchecked fields of description with no principles in place to define the limits of what might count. While Fish (1980) or Culler (1981) would answer that the conventions of literary reading control what counts, I suggest that this is also an empirical question. What counts should, where possible, be investigated by examining what actual readers are doing. If Fish's (1980) affective model is correct, then it should be possible to design a study to validate it with the experiences of actual readers. The elaboration of such theories, proposing specific types of interaction between text features and readers, is the essential first step in outlining what an analysis of reading should be taking into account. But invariably this is as far as literary scholarship ever gets (including hypertext theory): it makes "implicit premises" on texts and on readers, as Cees van Rees (1985, p. 445) expressed it, in his critique of Gerard Genette's (1980) narrative theory. So many categories of narrative mood, tense, time, etc., are elaborated by the theorist: but, the question should then be, are readers actually influenced by them? Almost certainly they are, at particular times and in specifiable ways, but Genette (1980) is typical in his indifference to this question (although late in his book he acknowledges the importance of Proust's remark, that as readers we are reading ourselves).

Here, then, is the first step towards the computer system we wish to build. On the text side, we take a poem such as Coleridge's (1924) "The Rime of the Ancient Mariner" (186-209) and we not only encode the poem for presentation on screen (so that readers know which part they are reading, which line numbers), but also we analyze the narrative and stylistic aspects of the poem: the turning points of the narrative, the most ambiguous parts, the lines with the most striking poetic features (metaphors, alliteration, etc.) that also seem to typify the tone of the poem overall (but keeping this information off-screen until readers request it). We will initially glean much of the information we need in this respect from systematic empirical studies with readers of the poem. When a reader pauses at a passage that seems particularly interesting or surprising (a passage that the readers in our prior empirical studies will probably also have found striking), the system can be queried: what is known about this passage in terms of the narrative, or its stylistic qualities? With additional facilities, that I will describe later, the system can also sketch its relation to other work by the poet or other poets (a menu of such choices will be offered on screen). In this way, readers can explore their understanding of the poem, whether to reflect on it, to extend it, or perhaps help to correct it (if, say, a reader has misunderstood a phrase).

"The Mariner" has been interpreted in widely different ways. While critics have diverged from each other in their view of the poem, so have the readers we have studied. While critical differences can be imputed primarily to the theoretical position held by the professional reader (intent on expounding a historicist reading, say, or an ecological one), our volunteer readers more typically depended on their own experience and understanding of life. The reading machine will also accommodate this. Here is one brief example: the responses of two readers to a passage late in the poem. As his ship travels home, the Mariner describes himself as looking out and seeing nothing but the ocean, yet he is:

Like one, that on a lonesome road
Doth walk in fear and dread,
And having once turned round walks on,
And turns no more his head;
Because he knows, a frightful fiend
Doth close behind him tread. (Coleridge 1924: 203)

This passage is undoubtedly disturbing and represents a challenge for interpretation. Both of the readers I cite below made quite extensive commentaries after choosing this passage, but I pick out what seems to be a central concern in each. One of them said:

It feels like, this, there's this certain point in your life that you can't turn back. You know that if you try and turn back or stop what you're doing, it's over, nothing good will come out of it. You have to continue on. It's like riding a bike downhill, you know you can't stop it because if you stop, you know you'll crash... It could be a metaphor for life, there's no turning back once you get started.

In contrast to this sense of the imperative forward movement of life, another reader spoke of guilt over missed opportunities:

This passage also describes someone who lacks a high self-confidence, I guess. It's like the person seems to see his abilities. And so he's trying to avoid things. I know I've done that at times, in situations when I don't feel like I mingle to do things the way I want to. I sometimes turn away. But afterwards, the frightful fiend that follows me, it's not really anything that's external, it's more internal. It's my, well, guilt is a strong word, sort of regret that I didn't have the courage to deal with it better. It's something that haunts me sometimes.

Whether the concern of either of these readers is more than a passing response to the poem is not clear, although each seems to touch on some long-standing issue in his or her lives. In both cases this was the last of five passages considered by the reader, and in response to previous passages both protocols show indirect anticipations of the concerns reported here, but we cannot tell how important these might be. The reader may not be clear what importance the concern has either, but given a facility for recording such comments, the place of the concern in the reader's life might become evident in the longer term. Other readings may evoke the same issue, allowing it to be reconsidered or developed – or resolved. Just as the features of the poem can be indexed by the computer, so the comments of the reader can be coded, sorted, and ordered for later retrieval, for the reader's reconsideration, whether in another context or in rereading the same text.

A reader might also wish to turn back to the poem itself and probe its language a little further. For instance, given the mysterious nature of the "fiend" in this verse, we can ask if the word occurs elsewhere in Coleridge's writing, in case some similarity in use casts a light on its occurrence here in "The Mariner." The "fiend" appears only once in this poem, and it is the more problematic for being a figurative fiend, not a literal one (the Mariner describes himself as "Like one, that on a lonesome road"). The question can be explored by means of a text analysis program. Here we envisage a facility for surveying all of Coleridge's poetry and picking out passages where the word "fiend" (or "fiends") occurs. While such concordance programs have existed for some time as free-standing computer applications, only very recently has the same activity become possible through the Internet, although only basic look-up facilities are available so far, e.g., *Open Source Shakespeare* (http://www.opensourceshakespeare.org), and these are tied to a specific text, except for Sinclair's *HyperPo* (http://hyperpo.org/). In the Coleridge example, we wish to know, of course, where other occurrences of "fiend" are located, so the text of the poetry is encoded with the titles of the poems, at a minimum, and preferably line numbers as well to help us find our place in longer poems.

A concordance of Coleridge's poetry for "fiend" and "fiends" yields 19 instances. Several of the fiends turn out to be rather conventional: they are mostly from hell (Milton seems responsible for some of these), or they are figurative representations of evil. But two of the examples seem more relevant to the mysterious fiend of "The Mariner": in "Religious Musings" (Coleridge 1924, pp. 108-125) and, especially, "Pantisocracy" (Coleridge 1924, pp. 68-69). These suggest that the Mariner's fiend may, like those in "Pantisocracy," be internal, an agent beneath consciousness known only from dream states or other unconscious promptings. This would help elucidate the obscure lines that introduce the simile, where the Mariner says he "looked far forth, yet little saw / Of what had else been seen." "Pantisocracy," in other words, helps to gloss the Mariner's comment: it suggests that what he would have seen if he had looked in the right place (within instead of "far forth") would have been like a pursuing fiend. The fiend, then, may be a part of the self.

As a reader of "The Mariner," making use of the reading machine, I can thus quickly put in place a verbal environment drawn from the rest of Coleridge's poetry that will help enrich my understanding of the verse before me. This depends both on facilities which are commonplace in concordance programs and several other facilities that could readily be developed to support the reader. At the same time, my own responses to the verse I am reading are being recorded, if I wish, on the computer. Since we can envisage using the reading machine over many years, a large body of comments will accumulate over time. These too, however, will be searchable through the same concordance and collocation facilities that gave instant access to Coleridge's poetry. Thus, if I wish to review what I have thought about a particular concern I enter a word, or a combination of words for a collocation search, and bring up all the recorded instances. At any time during my reading of "The Mariner" (once I have performed the inquiry into the "fiend," for example), or after assessing a particular concern, I can output the screen pages that record the results of my inquiry as a web page, and have this permanently linked to the contents of my record. In other words, while engaged with the text, I can produce and interlink a hypertextual representation of my image as a reader. When I wish, I can switch to this representation (sidelining the text I am currently looking at, perhaps) and examine, by clicking from one linked view to the next, what has moved me as a reader, how I explored it, when a given insight occurred and in what context, and, in summary, who I am as a reader (information that will be kept secure, private to my Internet portal). Then, if appropriate, designate part of my response record available for viewing by others (if working within an educational context, or a reading group).

I could, of course, simply keep a written diary of my reading, which I index from time to time. What reasons are there to believe that a computer-based system, offering encoded texts and comments, will provide a significantly more powerful context for reading to make it worth building? Here is where the design of a knowledge-base containing literary texts and readers' comments about them is critical: it will take its shape, at least initially, from what we know about the structures of literary texts and their determining effect on readers. This presupposes that literary response is far from idiosyncratic, that it is impelled in systematic ways by the structural and linguistic features of texts. Put another way, even though individual interpretations may diverge, certain kinds of attention are promoted by the underlying field of forces that each reading encounters. The interactive processes that are set in play can then be analyzed and modeled, and a support system put in place through the computer that includes information about both the text and the individual's responses.

What is currently little appreciated is that a number of examples of empirical research now show that readers' responses to literature are far from idiosyncratic, although they may vary one from another on interpretive grounds (e.g., Martindale & Dailey, 1995). The source of the commonalities we find in response appears to be located to a significant degree in the literary text itself, in its phonetic, figurative, narrative, and other features, which compel a certain kind of attention from readers. This makes possible a range of text analysis techniques which we can apply to map texts and to provide a support system for readers, since we know that readers are likely to be addressing the same features of texts as they read, even if the questions differ that they bring to the system. While further studies of readers' responses are required to test and validate such computer-based techniques, this approach alone will not be enough. The main limitation of text analysis methods on their own is that they cannot address the fundamental feature of reading literary texts: their modifying power over the reader. Text analysis methods typically produce static maps of features. It is the recording and patterning of readers' responses that overcome this limitation.

The system I have described comprises the first stage in building the reading machine. Next we envisage a set of programs for recording and analyzing a group of readings, in which the probabilities and rules of interpretation are inferred from the text elements noticed by readers and from their verbal or written responses to such elements. This would contribute to the building of the subsequent program, where this information is made available to the current or a later reader. This would provide all the facilities we have already sketched, drawn from text analysis and from representations of the reader's own responses. But now this can be enhanced by information from others. Once a reader had entered some data about the response, the system would match the new data to its existing data, and make predictions about the likely path of the reading and about its overall direction. If the user requested it, the program would thus be able to provide advice specific to the point the reader had reached. Each time more data was entered, the program would update its probabilities. A system built on these principles would thus allow for a range of different (and possibly incompatible) readings of the same text: more interestingly, it would also give access to some of the underlying causes for differences in readings and provide a logical basis for analyzing such differences.

The reading machine will thus not only accommodate such divergences of interpretation, it will facilitate them. It will enable readers to engage in a dialogue with the computer about their understanding of a text, and through the computer to relate their developing understandings to what other readers have thought, and what other evidence supports such readings. "Computer technology," as William

Winder (1996) puts it, "like the codex itself, is the basis of a new incarnation of dialogue, and the source of renewed collaboration. The *reincarnation of dialogue* is the ultimate object of humanities research and the source of humanists' fascination." For the same reasons, the reading machine will reinvigorate reading, and may one day become the preferred medium for our experience of literary texts.

David S. Miall
University of Alberta, Canada

REFERENCES

Coleridge, S. T. (1924). *The poems* (E. H. Coleridge, Ed.). Oxford: Oxford University Press.

Culler, J. (1975). *Structuralist poetics: Structuralism, linguistics, and the study of literature.* London: Routledge & Kegan Paul.

Culler, J. (1981). *The pursuit of signs: Semiotics, literature, deconstruction.* London: Routledge & Kegan Paul.

Damasio, A. R. (1999). *The feeling of what happens: Body and emotion in the making of consciousness.* New York: Harcourt Brace.

Fish, S. (1980). *Is there a text in this class?* Cambridge, MA: Harvard University Press.

Genette, G. (1980). *Narrative discourse.* (J. E. Lewin, Trans.). Ithaca: Cornell University Press.

Hayles, N. K. (1999). *How we became posthuman: Virtual bodies in cybernetics, literature, and informatics.* Chicago: University of Chicago Press.

Hockey, S. (2000). *Electronic texts in the humanities: Principles and practice.* Oxford: Oxford University Press.

Jakobson, R., & Lévi-Strauss, C. (1972). Charles Baudelaire's 'Les Chats.' In R. T. De George & F. M. De George (Eds.), *The structuralists: From Marx to Lévi-Strauss* (pp. 123-146). New York: Anchor.

Manovich, L. (2001). *The language of new media.* Cambridge, MA: MIT Press.

Martindale, C., & Dailey, A. (1995). I. A. Richards revisited: Do people agree in their interpretations of literature? *Poetics, 23,* 299-314.

McGann, J. (1998). Textual scholarship, textual theory, and the uses of electronic tools: A brief report on current undertakings. *Victorian Studies, 41*, 609-619.

Miall, D. S. (2006). *Literary reading: Empirical and theoretical studies.* New York: Peter Lang.

Miall, D. S., & Kuiken, D. (1999). What is literariness? Three components of literary reading. *Discourse Processes, 28*, 121-138.

Powers, R. (1995). *Galatea 2.2.* New York: Farrar, Straus, Giroux.

Ryan, M.-L (2001). *Narrative as virtual reality: Immersion and interactivity in literature and electronic media.* Baltimore: Johns Hopkins University Press.

Siemens, R. (2005). Text analysis and the dynamic edition? A working paper, briefly articulating some concerns with an algorithmic approach to the electronic scholarly edition. *Text Technology, 14*, 91-98. Retrieved from http://texttechnology.mcmaster.ca/pdf/vol14_1_09.pdf

Smith, B. H. (1988). *Contingencies of value: Alternative perspectives for critical theory.* Cambridge, MA: Harvard University Press.

Van Rees, C. J. (1985). Implicit premises on text and reader in Genette's study of narrative mood. *Poetics, 14*, 445-464.

Winder, W. (1996). Texpert systems. *Computing in the Humanities Working Papers* B.35 (1996). Retrieved from http://www.chass.utoronto.ca/epc/chwp/winder2/

Compilation of References

Albert, H. (2000). *Kritischer Rationalismus. Vier Kapitel zur Kritik illusionären Denkens.* Tübingen: Mohr Siebeck.

Alvarez-Altman, G., & Burelbach, F. M. (Eds.). (1987). *Names in literature: Essays from Literary Onomastics Studies.* Lanham, MD: University Press of America.

Anderson, L. B. (1986). Evidentials, Paths of Change and Mental Maps: Typologically Regular Symmetries. In Chafe, W. L., & Nichols, J. (Eds.), *Evidentiality: The Linguistic Coding of Epistemology.* Norwood, NJ: Ablex.

Ayer, A. J. (1954). *Philosophical Essays.* London: Macmillan.

Baayen, R. H., van Halteren, H., Neijt, A., & Tweedie, F. (2002). An experiment in authorship attribution. In [St. Malo: Universite de Rennes.]. *Proceedings of JADT, 2002*, 29–37.

Bacon, F. [1605] (1985). The Advancement of Learning. Harmondworth: Penguin.

Baker, C. (2008, March 24). Trying to Design a Truly Entertaining Game can Defeat Even a Certified Genius. *Wired.* Retrieved October 30, 2008 from http://www.wired.com/gaming/gamingreviews/magazine/16-04/pl_games

Bakhtin, M. (1981). *The Dialogic Imagination: Four Essays* (Emerson, C., & Holquist, M., Trans.). Austin, Texas: University of Texas Press.

Ballaster, R. (2007). What is reading? Ros Ballaster asks us to think about what we do when we read. *The English Review, 17*(3), 6–9.

Barthes, R. (1973). *Le plaisir du texte.* Paris: Editions du Seuil.

Barthes, R. (1978). *Image, Music, Text* (Heath, S., Trans.). New York: Hill and Wang.

Barton, E. (1993). Evidentials, argumentation, and epistemological stance. *College English, 55*, 745–769. doi:10.2307/378428

Bauer, R., & Maier, J. (2003). Schwebendes Schreiben. Vom Schreiben an/in kontextualisierenden Medien wie nic-las.com. In Fehr, J., & Grond, W. (Eds.), *Schreiben am Netz. Literatur im digitalen Zeitalter* (pp. 164–171). Innsbruck: Haymon.

Baurmann, J. (2002). *Schreiben Überarbeiten Beurteilen. Ein Arbeitsbuch zur Schreibdidaktik.* Seelze-Velber: Kallmeyer.

Beach, R., & Anson, C. M. (1992). Stance and Intertextuality in Written Discourse. *Linguistics and Education, 4*, 335–357. doi:10.1016/0898-5898(92)90007-J

Beck, E., Guldimann, T., & Zutavern, M. (1994). Eigenständiges Lernen verstehen und fördern. In Reusser, K. (Ed.), *Verstehen* (pp. 207–225). Bern: Huber.

Bergermann, U. (1997). *Verkörpert Hypertext Theorien vom Schreiben?* Retrieved December 18, 2007, from http://www.uni-paderborn.de/~bergerma/texte/zmm.html

Berofsky, B. (1971). *Determinism*. Princeton: PUP.

Biber, D. (1990). Methodological Issues Regarding Corpus-based Analyses of Linguistic Variation. *Literary and Linguistic Computing, 5*(4), 257–269. doi:10.1093/llc/5.4.257

Biber, D. (2006). Stance in spoken and written university registers. *Journal of English for Academic Purposes, 5*, 97–116. doi:10.1016/j.jeap.2006.05.001

Biber, D., & Finegan, E. (1988). Adverbial Stance Types in English. *Discourse Processes, 11*, 1–34. doi:10.1080/01638538809544689

Biber, D., & Finegan, E. (1989). Styles of stance in English: lexical and grammatical marking of evidentiality and affect. *Text, 9*, 93–124. doi:10.1515/text.1.1989.9.1.93

Binongo, J. N. G. (2003). Who wrote the 15th book of Oz? An application of multivariate analysis to authorship attribution. *Chance, 16*(2), 9–17.

Bleich, D. (1978). *Subjective Criticism*. Baltimore, London: Johns Hopkins University Press.

Bogost, I. (2006). *Unit Operations: An Approach to Videogame Criticism.* Cambridge, MA: MIT.

Bogost, I. (2008). *Persuasive Games: The Expressive Power of Video Games.* Cambridge, MA: MIT.

Bolter, J., & Gromala, D. (2005). *Windows and Mirrors: Interaction Design, Digital Art, and the Myth of Transparency.* Cambridge, MA: MIT.

Bontcheva, K., Dimitrov, M., Maynard, D., Tablan, V., & Cunningham, H. (2002). Shallow methods for named entity coreference resolution. In *Proceedings of Traitement Automatique des Langues Naturelles.* Nancy: TALN.

Borin, L., & Forsberg, M. (2008). Something old, something new: A computational morphological description of Old Swedish. In *LREC 2008 Workshop on Language Technology for Cultural Heritage Data (LaTeCH 2008)* (pp. 9-16). Marrakech: ELRA.

Borin, L., Kokkinakis, D., & Olsson, L.-J. (2007). Naming the past: Named entity and animacy recognition in 19th century Swedish literature. In *Proceedings of the ACL Workshop: Language Technology for Cultural Heritage Data (LaTeCH)* (pp. 1-8). Prague: ACL.

Boud, D., & Feletti, G. (Eds.). (1997). The Challenge of Problem-Based Learning (2nd ed.). London, Stirling (USA): Kogan Page.

Bradley, J. (2005). What you foresee is what you get: Thinking about usage paradigms for computer assisted text analysis. *TEXT Technology, 2*, 1–19.

Bransford, J. D., Brown, A. L., & Cocking, R. R. (2000). How Experts Differ from Novices. In Bransford, J. D., Brown, A. L., & Cocking, R. R. (Eds.), *How People Learn: Brain, Mind, Experience, and School* (pp. 31–50). Washington, DC: National Academy Press.

Brienza, S. D. (1987). *Samuel Beckett's New Worlds. Style in Metafiction.* Norman, Oklahoma: Univ. of Oklahoma Press.

Bullock, A., & Trombley, S. (Eds.). (2000). *The New Fontana Dictionary of Modern Thought.* London: HarperCollins.

Burrows, J. F. (1987). *Computation into Criticism: A Study of Jane Austen's Novels and an Experiment in Method.* Oxford: Clarendon Press.

Burrows, J. F. (1996). Tiptoeing into the Infinite: Testing for Evidence of National Differences in the Language of English Narrative. In S. Hockey & N. Ide (Eds.), Research in Humanities Computing '92 (pp.1-33). No. 4 in the series Research in Humanities Computing. Oxford: Clarendon Press.

Caillios, R. (2001). *Man, Play and Games.* Champaign, Illinois: University of Illinois Press.

Carnap, R. (1928). *Der Logische Aufbau der Welt.* Berlin-Schlagtensee: Weltkreis-Verlag.

Carnap, R. (1956) Meaning and Necessity: A study in Senmantics and Modal Logic. Chicogo: University of Chicago Press.

Carroll, L. (2003). *Alice's Adventures in Wonderland and Through the Looking Glass.* London, England: Penguin.

Caspi, J. L. (1998). *The Cambridge Quintet: A work of scientific speculation.* London: Abacus.

Chafe, W. L. (1986). Evidentiality in English Conversation and Academic Writing. In Chafe, W. L., & Nichols, J. (Eds.), *Evidentiality: The Linguistic Coding of Epistemology.* Norwood, NJ: Ablex.

Chapman, S. (2008). *Language and Empiricism: After the Vienna Circle.* New York: Palgrave. doi:10.1057/9780230583030

Chateau, C. (2007). Drift and shift: How "continental" moves in geological English. Dijon: mimeo.

Conrad, S., & Biber, D. (2001). Adverbial Marking of Stance in Speech and Writing. In Hunston, S., & Thompson, G. (Eds.), *Evaluation in Text. Authorial Stance and the Construction of Discourse.* Oxford: Oxford University Press.

Courtney, R. (1982). *Re-Play: Studies of Human Drama in Education. Ontario: OISE, Cullum, A. (1967). Push Back The Desks.* New York: Citation Press.

Courtney, R. (1989). *Play, Drama & Thought: The Intellectual Background To Dramatic Education* (4th ed.). Toronto: Simon & Pierre.

Cudden, J. A. (1980). *A Dictionary of Literary Terms.* Harmondsworth: Penguin.

Davis, D., & Lawrence, C. (1986). *Selected Writings of Gavin Bolton.* Hong Kong: Longman.

Davis, T. F. (2002). *Formalist Criticism and Reader-Response Theory.* Gordonsville, VA: Palgrave Macmillan.

de Morgan, A. (1851/1882). Letter to Rev Heald 18/08/1851. In de Morgan, S. E. (Ed.), *Memoirs of Augustus de Morgan by his wife Sophia Elizabeth de Morgan with selections from his letters.* New York: Adamant Media.

Deci, L. E., & Ryan, R. M. (1993). Die Selbstbestimmungstheorie der Motivation und ihre Bedeutung für die Pädagogik. *Zeitschrift fur Padagogik, 1*(39), 223–238.

Derrida, J. (1980). *Writing and Difference* (Bass, A., Trans.). Chicago, Illinois: University of Chicago Press.

Dilthey, W. (1970). Der Aufbau der geschichtlichen Welt in den Geistewissenschaften. Frankfurt/M.: Suhrkamp.

Eco, U. (1964). *Apocalittici e integrati.* Milano: Bompiani.

Eco, U. (1979). *The Role of the Reader: Explorations in the Semiotics of Texts.* Bloomington: Indiana University Press.

Ellis, N. C. (2002). Frequency effects in language processing. *Studies in Second Language Acquisition, 24*(2), 143–188.

Enkvist, N. E. (1973). *Linguistic Stylistics.* The Hague: Mouton.

Evans, R., & Orasan, C. (2000). Improving anaphora resolution by identifying animate entities in texts. In *Proceedings of the DAARC 2000.* (pp. 154-162). Lancaster, UK.

Fan, W., Wallace, L., Rich, S., & Zhang, Z. (2006). Tapping the power of text mining. *Communications of the ACM, 49*(9), 77–82. doi:10.1145/1151030.1151032

Firth, J. R. (1957). *Papers in Linguistics 1934-1951.* Oxford: OUP.

Fish, S. (1980). *Is There a Text in This Class? The Authority of Interpretive Communities.* Cambridge, MA: Harvard University Press.

Flanders, J., Bauman, S., Caton, P., & Cournane, M. (1998). Names proper and improper: Applying the TEI to the classification of proper nouns. *Computers and the Humanities, 31*(4), 285–300. doi:10.1023/A:1001066508011

Fleischman, M., & Hovy, E. (2002). Fine grained classification of named entities.In *Proceedings of the 19th International Conference on Computational linguistics* (pp. 1-7). Taipei: ACL.

Flusser, V. (2004). *Writings. Electronic Mediations.* Minneapolis, MN: University of Minnesota Press.

Foster, I., Kesselman, C., & Tuecke, S. (2001). The anatomy of the Grid: Enabling scalable virtual organizations. *The International Journal of Supercomputer Applications, 15*(3), 200–222. doi:10.1177/109434200101500302

Foucault, M. (1969). *L Archéologie du savoir.* Paris: Gallimard.

Frege, G. (1884). *The Foundations of Arithmetic: A Logico-Mathematical Enquiry into the Concept of Number (J.L. Austin, Trans., 1974).* Oxford: Blackwell.

Galloway, A. (2006). *Gaming: Essays on Algorithmic Culture.* Minneapolis, MN: U of Minnesota Press.

Gardner, H. (1993). *Frames of Mind: The Theory of Multiple Intelligences* (2nd ed.). New York: Basic Books.

Gee, J. P. (2003). *What Video Games have to teach us about Learning and Literacy.* New York: Palgrave MacMillan.

Giesecke, M. (2002). Von den Mythen der Buchkultur zu den Visionen der Informationsgesellschaft: Trendforschung zur aktuellen Medienökologie. Frankfurt/M: Suhrkamp.

Habermas, J. (1973). Wahrheitstheorien. In H. Fahrenbach (Ed.), Wirklichkeit und Reflexion. W. Schulz zum 60. Geburtstag (pp. 211-265). Pfullingen: Neske.

Halliday, M. A. K. (1994). *An Introduction to Functional Grammar* (2nd ed.). London: Edward Arnold.

Hamilton, C. A., & Schneider, R. (2002). From Iser to Turner and Beyond: Reception Theory Meets Cognitive Criticism. *Style (DeKalb, IL), 36*(4), 640–658.

Harker, W. J. (1992). Reader Response and Cognition: Is There a Mind in This Class? *Journal of Aesthetic Education, 26*(3), 27–39. doi:10.2307/3333011

Hirsch, E. D. (1967). *Validity in Interpretation.* New Haven, London: Yale University Press.

Hoey, M. H. (2005). *Lexical Priming: A New Theory of Words and Language.* London: Routledge.

Hoey, M. H., Mahlberg, M., Stubbs, M., & Teubert, W. (Eds.). (2007). *Text, Discourse and Corpora: Theory and Analysis.* London: Continuum.

Holmes, D. I. (1994). Authorship attribution. *Computers and the Humanities, 28*(2), 87–106. doi:10.1007/BF01830689

Holmes, J. (1988). Doubt and Certainty in ESL Textbooks. *Applied Linguistics, 9*, 20–44. doi:10.1093/applin/9.1.21

Hoover, D. (2006). Stylometry, chronology, and the styles of Henry James. In [Paris: Sorbonne.]. *Proceedings of Digital Humanities, 2006*, 78–80.

Hoover, D. L. (2003). Multivariate Analysis and the Study of Style Variation. *Literary and Linguistic Computing, 18*(4), 341–360. doi:10.1093/llc/18.4.341

Hoover, D. L. (2004). Altered Texts, Altered Worlds, Altered Styles. *Language and Literature, 13*(2), 99–118. doi:10.1177/0963947004041970

Hoover, D. L. (2007). Corpus Stylistics, Stylometry, and the Styles of Henry James. *Style (DeKalb, IL), 41*(2), 174–203.

Huizinga, J. (1971). *Homo Ludens.* Boston, MA: Beacon Press.

Hunston, S. (1994). Evaluation and organization in a sample of written academic discourse. In Coulthard, M. (Ed.), *Advances in Written Text Analysis* (pp. 191–218). London: Routledge.

Hyland, K. (1996). Talking to the Academy: Forms of Hedging in Scientific Research Articles. *Written Communication, 13*, 251–281. doi:10.1177/0741088396013002004

Ide, N., & Romary, L. (2002). Standards for language resources. In *Proceedings of the Third Language Resources and Evaluation Conference (LREC)* (pp. 839-844). Las Palmas: ELRA.

Iser, W. (1974). *The Implied Reader.* Baltimore: Johns Hopkins University Press.

Jackson, P., & Moulinier, I. (2007). *Natural language processing for online applications: Text retrieval, extraction and categorization.* Amsterdam: John Benjamins.

Jauss, H. R. (1982). *Toward an Aesthetic of Reception.* Hemel Hempstead: Harvester Wheatsheaf.

Jenkins, H. (2006, November 27). Collective Intelligence and the Wisdom of Crowds. In *Confessions of an Aca-fan: The Official Weblog of Henry Jenkins*. Retrieved February 5, 2008 from http://henryjenkins.org/2006/11/collective_intelligence_vs_the.html

Jenkins, H. (2008, February 4). Sharing Notes about Collective Intelligence. In *Confessions of an Aca-fan: The Official Weblog of Henry Jenkins*. Retrieved February 5, 2008 from http://henryjenkins.org/2008/02/last_week_my_travels_took.html

Jessop, M. (2004). The visualization of spatial data in the humanities. *Literary and Linguistic Computing, 19*(3), 335–350. doi:10.1093/llc/19.3.335

Johannessen, J. B., Hagen, K., Haaland, Å., Björk Jónsdóttir, A., Nøklestad, A., & Kokkinakis, D. (2005). Named entity recognition for the mainland Scandinavian languages. *Literary and Linguistic Computing, 20*(1), 91–102. doi:10.1093/llc/fqh045

Johnson, D. W., & Roger, T. Johnson (1992). Encouraging Thinking Through Constructive Controversy. In D. W. Davidson & T. Worsham (Eds.), Enhancing Thinking Through Cooperative Learning (pp. 120-137). Teachers College Press: New York City.

Jones, S. (2008). *The Meaning of Video Games: Gaming and Textual Strategies.* New York: Routledge.

Juola, P. (1997). What can we do with small corpora? Document categorization via cross-entropy. In *Proceedings of the Workshop on Similarity and Categorization (SimCat 97).* Edinburgh: University of Edinburgh.

Juola, P. (2002). Humanities mathematics: when computing doesn't work. In (Ed.), *Proceedings of COSH/COCH 2002.* Toronto: University of Toronto.

Juola, P. (2004). Ad-hoc authorship attribution competition. In *Proc. 2004 Joint International Conference of the Association for Literary and Linguistic Computing and the Association for Computers and the Humanities (ALLC/ACH 2004).* Gothenberg: Univerity of Gothenberg.

Juola, P. (2006). Authorship attribution. *Foundations and trends in information retrieval, 1*(3), 1-112.

Juola, P. (2008). Killer applications in digital humanities. *Literary and Linguistic Computing, 23*(3), 73–85.

Juola, P., & Baayen, H. (2005). A controlled-corpus experiment in authorship attribution by cross-entropy. *Literary and Linguistic Computing, 20*(1), 59–67. doi:10.1093/llc/fqi024

Juola, P., & Ramsay, S. (in press). *Mathematics for humanists.* Oxford: Oxford University Press.

Juola, P., Sofko, J., & Brennan, P. (2006). A prototype for authorship attribution studies. *Literary and Linguistic Computing, 21*(2), 169–178. doi:10.1093/llc/fql019

Juul, J. (2005). *Half-Real: Video Games between Real Rules and Fictional Worlds.* Cambridge, MA: MIT.

Kärkkäinen, E. (2003). *Epistemic stance in English conversation: a description of its interactional functions, with a focus on I think.* John Benjamins.

Keller, S. (2008). 'I Have A Dream!' – mit dialogischem Lernen in Englisch eine gute Rede schreiben. In U. Ruf, S. Keller & F. Winter (Eds.), Besser lernen im Dialog. Dialogisches Lernen in der Unterrichtspraxis (pp. 70-82). Seelze-Velber: Klett/Kallmeyer.

Kittler, F. A. (1985). [München: Fink.]. *Aufschreibesysteme, 1800,* 1900.

Kittler, F. A. (1992). *Discourse Networks 1800/1900.* Palo Alto, CA: Stanford University Press.

Knowlson, J., & Pilling, J. (1979). *Frescoes of the Skull.* London: John Calder.

Kokkinakis, D. (2004). Reducing the effect of name explosion. In *Proceedings of the LREC Workshop: Beyond Named Entity Recognition – Semantic Labeling for NLP.* Lisbon: ELRA.

Kokkinakis, D., & Thurin, A. (2007). Anonymisation of Swedish clinical data. In *Proceedings of the 11th Conference on Artificial Intelligence in Medicine (AIME 07).* Amsterdam.

Koppel, M., Argamon, S., & Shimoni, A. R. (2002). Automatically categorizing written texts by author gender. *Literary and Linguistic Computing, 17*(4), 401–412. doi:10.1093/llc/17.4.401

Krentz, A. A. (1998). 20th WCP: Play and Education in Plato's Republic. In D. Steiner (Ed.) *Twentieth World Congress of Philosophy.* Boston, MA. Retrieved October 30, 2008 from http://www.bu.edu/wcp/Papers/Educ/EducKren.htm

Krishnamurthy, R. (2004). *English Collocation Studies: The OSTI Report.* London: Continuum.

Kristeva, J. (1969). Le mot, le dialogue et le roman. In J. Kristeva, Sémiotiké: recherches pour une sémanalyse (p. 82-112). Paris: Seuil.

Kruh, L. (1982). A basic probe of the Beale cipher as a bamboozlement: Part I. *Cryptologia, 6*(4), 378–382. doi:10.1080/0161-118291857190

Kruh, L. (1988). The Beale cipher as a bamboozlement: Part II. *Cryptoogila, 12*(4), 241–246. doi:10.1080/0161-118891863007

Lempert, M. (2008). The poetics of stance: Text-metricality, epistemicity, interaction. *Language in Society, 37,* 569–592. doi:10.1017/S0047404508080779

Levorato, A. (2009). Be steady then, my countrymen, be firm, united and determined. Expressions of stance in the 1798-1800 Irish paper war. *Journal of Historical Pragmatics, 10*(1), 132–157. doi:10.1075/jhp.10.1.11lev

Lewis, D. D. (1998). Naïve Bayes at forty: The independence assumption in information retrieval. In *Proc ECML-98* (pp. 4-15).

Louw, W. E. (1989). Sub-routines in the integration of language and literature. In Carter, R. (Ed.), *Literature and the Learner: Methodological Approaches*. London: MEP/British Council.

Louw, W. E. (1991). Classroom concordancing of delexical forms and the case for integrating language and literature. In Johns, T., & King, P. (Eds.), *Classroom Concordancing, ELR Journal 4*.

Louw, W. E. (1993). Irony in the text or insincerity in the writer? The diagnostic potential of semantic prosodies. In Baker, M. (Eds.), *Text and Technology: In Honour of John Sinclair*. Amsterdam: John Benjamins.

Louw, W. E. (2000). Contextual Prosodic Theory: Bringing Semantic Prosodies to Life. In Heffer, C., & Sauntson, H. (Eds.), *Words in Context. In Honour of John Sinclair*. Birmingham: ELR.

Louw, W. E. (2003). Dressing up waiver: a stochastic-collocational reading of the Truth and Reconciliation Commission (TRC). Harare: mimeo. Also available in the *Occasional Papers dei Quaderni del CeSLIC*. Retrieved from http://www.lingue.unibo.it/ceslic/e_occ_papers.htm

Louw, W. E. (2004, May 20). Unravelling the ideological from the authentic. *Guardian Weekly*. Retrieved August 2006 from http://www.guardian.co.uk/education/2004/may/20/tefl4

Louw, W. E. (2007a). Truth, literary worlds and devices as collocation. Closing Keynote presentation at TaLC6 on 7th July 2004. In E. Hidalgo, L. Quereda, & J. Santana (Eds.), *Proceedings of the Sixth Conference on Teaching and Language Corpora*. Amsterdam: Rodopi.

Louw, W. E. (2007b). Collocation as the determinant of verbal art. In Miller, D., & Turci, M. (Eds.), *Verbal Art Re-Visited* (pp. 149–180). London: Equinox.

Louw, W. E. (2007c). Corporibus Phlogiston: A Gentle Refutation of Michael Hoey's Theory of Lexical Priming. Harare: mimeo.

Louw, W. E. (2007d). *Are literary texts and their worlds 'thrown together' as collocation?* Keynote presentation to ACORN Symposium, in Honour of John Sinclair, on 4th May 2007. Retrieved from http://www.aston.ac.uk/symposium.htm

Louw, W. E. (2007e). Literary worlds as collocation. In Watson, G., & Zyngier, S. (Eds.), *Literature and Stylistics for Language Learners: Theory and Practice*. Basingstoke: Palgrave.

Louw, W. E. (2008a). Consolidating empirical method in data-assisted stylistics: towards a corpus-attested glossary of literary terms. In Viana, D., & Zyngier, S. (Eds.), *Directions in Empirical Literary Studies. In Honour of Willie van Peer*. Amsterdam: John Benjamins.

Louw, W. E. (2008b). Two chapters in D. Hoover, et al (Eds.), Approaches to Corpus Stylistics. London: Routledge.

Louw, W. E. (2008c). Establishing a historiography for corpus-events from their frequency: a celebration of Bertrand Russell's (1948) five postulates. Harare: mimeo.

Louw, W. E. (2008d). What is a homogenized corpus? Harare: mimeo

Louw, W.E. (2010). Automating the extraction of literary worlds. *Textus*, special edition on stylistics. Genoa: Tilgher.

Maingueneau, D. (1991). *L'Analyse du discours. Introduction aux lectures de l'archive*. Paris: Hachette.

Malinowski, B. (1935). *Coral Gardens and their Magic*. London: Allen and Unwin.

Martin, J. R. (2001). Beyond Exchange: Appraisal Systems in English. In Hunston, S., & Thompson, G. (Eds.), *Evaluation in Text. Authorial Stance and the Construction of Discourse* (pp. 142–175). Oxford: OUP.

Martin, M. (2008, October 27). Thompson: Educational games will lose you money. Retrieved October 28, 2008 from http://www.gamesindustry.biz/articles/thompson-educational-games-will-lose-you-money

Mauthner, T. (2000). *The Penguin Dictionary of Philosophy*. London: Penguin.

McCallum, A. (2005). Information extraction: Distilling structured data from unstructured text. *Queue, 3*(9), 48–57. doi:10.1145/1105664.1105679

McCaslin, N. (2000). *Creative Drama in the Classroom and Beyond* (7th ed.). New York: Longman.

McKenna, C. W. F., & Antonia, A. (2001). The Statistical Analysis of Style: Reflections on Form, Meaning, and Ideology in the 'Nausicaa' Episode of *Ulysses*. *Literary and Linguistic Computing, 16*(4), 353–373. doi:10.1093/llc/16.4.353

Mendenhall, T. C. (1887). The characteristic curves of composition. *Science, 9*(241), 237–249. doi:10.1126/science.ns-9.214S.237

Mikheev, A. (2000). Document centered approach to text normalization. In *Proceedings of the 23rd ACM SIGIR Conference on Research and Development in Information Retrieval* (pp. 136-143). Athens.

Mosteller, F., & Wallace, D. L. (2007). *Inference and Disputed Authorship: The Federalist Papers (with a new introduction by John Nerbonne).* Stanford: CSLI.

O'Neill, C., & Lambert, A. (1982). *Drama Structures: A Practical Handbook for Teachers.* London: Stanley Thornes.

Ochs, E. (Ed.). (1989). The Pragmatics of Affect. Special issue of Text, 9(1).

Olsson, F. (2008). *Bootstrapping named entity annotation by means of active machine learning: A method for creating corpora.* Data linguistica 21. Department of Swedish Language, University of Gothenburg. Retrieved from http://spraakdata.gu.se/publikationer/datalinguistica/DL21.pdf

Opas, L. L. (1990) *Aspects of Style in Samuel Beckett's Prose Works.* Unpublished DPhil. Thesis. University of Oxford.

Opas, L. L. (1996). A Multi-Dimensional Analysis of Style in Samuel Beckett's Prose Works. In S. Hockey & N. Ide (Eds.), Research in Humanities Computing '92 (pp.81-114). No. 4 in the series Research in Humanities Computing. Oxford: Clarendon Press.

Opas, L. L., & Tweedie, F. J. (1999). The Magic Carpet Ride: Reader Involvement in Romantic Fiction. *Literary and Linguistic Computing, 14*(1), 89–101. doi:10.1093/llc/14.1.89

Oser, F. K., Achternhagen, F., & Renold, U. (2006). *Competence Oriented Teacher Training. Old Research Demands and New Pathways.* Rotterdam, Taipei: Sense.

Palmer, F. R. (1968). *Selected Papers by J.R. Firth 1952-1959.* London: Longman.

Paradis, C. (1997). *Degree modifiers of Adjectives in Spoken British English.* Lund: Lund University Press.

Paradis, C. (2000). It's well weird. Degree modifiers of adjectives revisited: the nineties. In Kirk, J. (Ed.), *Corpora Galore: Analyses and Techniques in Describing English* (pp. 147–160). Amsterdam, Atlanta: Rodopi.

Pears, D. (1971). *Wittgenstein.* London: Fontana Collins.

Peirce, C. (1932). Collected Papers of Charles Sanders Peirce: *Vol. 2. Elements of Logic.* Cambridge: Cambridge University Press.

Pennebaker, J. W., & King, L. A. (1999). Linguistic styles: Linguistic use as an individual difference. *Journal of Personality and Social Psychology, 77,* 1293–1312. doi:10.1037/0022-3514.77.6.1296

Pennebaker, J., Mehl, M., & Niederhoffer, K. (2003). Psychological aspects of natural language use: Our words, our selves. *Annual Review of Psychology, 54,* 547–577. doi:10.1146/annurev.psych.54.101601.145041

Pettersson, G. (2005). *Svenska språket under sjuhundra år: En historia om svenskan och dess utforskande.* Lund: Studentlitteratur.

Piaget, J. (1962). *Play, Dreams and Imitation in Childhood.* New York: Norton.

Piaget, J., & Inhelder, B. (1966). *The Psychology of the Child.* Paris: Presses Universitaires de France.

Pilz, T., Ernst-Gerlach, A., Kempken, S., Rayson, P., & Archer, D. (2008). The identification of spelling variants in English and German historical texts: Manual or automatic? *Literary and Linguistic Computing, 23,* 65–72. doi:10.1093/llc/fqm044

Plett, H. (1979). *Textwissenschaft und Textanalyse. Semiotik, Linguistik, Rhetorik.* Heidelberg: UTB für Wissenschaft.

Popper, K. R. (1959). *The Logic of Scientific Discovery.* London: RKP.

Postman, N. (1992). *Technopoly: The Surrender of Culture to Technology.* New York: Random House.

Prensky, M. (2004). *Digital Game-Based Learning.* New York: McGraw–Hill.

Preston, J. (2008). *The Structure of Scientific Revolutions.* London: Continuum.

Ravin, Y., & Kazi, Z. (1999). Is Hillary Rodham Clinton the President? Disambiguating names across documents. In *Workshop on Coreference and Its Applications.* Maryland.

Rayson, P., Archer, D., Baron, A., Culpeper, J., & Smith, N. (2007). Tagging the Bard: Evaluating the accuracy of a modern POS tagger on Early Modern English corpora. In *Proceedings of Corpus Linguistics 2007, University of Birmingham, UK.* Retrieved September 14, 2008 from http://www.corpus.bham.ac.uk/corplingproceedings07/index.htm

Riddle Harding, J. (2007). Evaluative stance and counterfactuals in language and literature. *Language and Literature, 16*(3), 263–280. doi:10.1177/0963947007079109

Riffaterre, M. (1978). *Semiotics of Poetry.* Bloomington: Indiana University Press.

Rudman, J. (1998). The state of authorship attribution studies: Some problems and solutions. *Computers and the Humanities, 31,* 351–365. doi:10.1023/A:1001018624850

Rudman, J. (2005). The non-traditional case for the authorship of the twelve disputed Federalist Papers: a monument built on sand. In *Proceedings of ACH/ALLC 2005.* Victoria, BC: University of Victoria.

Russell, B. (1912). *The Problems of Philosophy.* London: RKP.

Russell, B. (1946). *The History of Western Philosophy.* London: Routledge.

Russell, B. (1948). *Human Knowledge: Its Scope and Limitations.* London: Routledge.

Russell, B. (1960). *Bertrand Russell Speaks his Mind.* London: Arthur Baker.

Salen, K., & Zimmerman, E. (2004). *Rules of Play: Game Design Fundamentals.* Cambridge, MA: MIT.

Salen, K., & Zimmerman, E. (Eds.). (2006). *The Game Design Reader: A Rules of Play Anthology.* Cambridge, MA: MIT.

Salmon, G. (2002). *E-tivities – The Key to Active Online Learning.* London: Kogan Page.

Sauter, A., Sauter, W., & Bender, H. (2004). Blended Learning: effiziente Integration von E-Learning und Präsenztraining (2nd extended ed.). Neuwied: Hermann Luchterhand.

Schulmeister, R. (2004). Didaktisches Design aus hochschuldidaktischer Sicht – ein Plädoyer für offene Lernsituationen. In Rinn, U., & Meister, D. M. (Eds.), *Didaktik und neue Medien* (pp. 19–39). Münster: Waxmann.

Scott, M. (2004). *WordSmith Tools version 4.* Oxford: Oxford University Press.

Sekine, S. (2004). Definition, dictionaries and tagger for extended named entity hierarchy. In *Proceedings of the Language Resources and Evaluation Conference (LREC).* Lisbon: ELRA.

Selden, R., Widdowson, P., & Brooker, P. (1997). A Reader's Guide to Contemporary Literary Theory. (4th ed.). Hemel Hempstead: Prentice Hall.

Simon-Vandenbergen, A. (2008). Almost certainly and most definitely: Degree modifiers and epistemic stance. *Journal of Pragmatics, 40,* 1521–1542. doi:10.1016/j.pragma.2008.04.015

Simon-Vandenbergen, A., & Aijmer, K. (2007). The discourse functionality of adjectival and adverbial epistemic expressions: evidence from present-day English. In Butler, C. S., David, J., & Hidalgo Downing, R. (Eds.), *Functional Perspectives on Grammar and Discourse: In Honour of Angela Downing* (pp. 419–445). Amsterdam, Philadelphia: John Benjamins.

Sinclair, J. M. (1987). Fictional Worlds. In Coulthard, R. M. (Ed.), *Talking about Text* (pp. 43–60). Birmingham: ELR.

Sinclair, J. M. (1991). *Corpus, Concordance, Collocation.* Oxford: OUP.

Sinclair, J. M. (1995). *Collocation on CD-ROM.* Glasgow: HarperCollins.

Sinclair, J. M. (2004a). *Trust the Text.* London: Routledge.

Sinclair, J. M. (2004b). *Reading Concordances.* London: Longman.

Sinclair, J. M., & Maurenen, A. (2006). *Linear Unit Grammar: Integrating speech and writing.* Amsterdam: John Benjamins.

Sinclair, J.M. (2006). *Phrasebite.* Pescia: TWC.

Singh, S. (2000). *The code book: The science of secrecy from ancient Egypt to quantum cryptography.* London: Anchor.

Smith, M. W. A. (1983). Recent experience and new developments of methods for the determination of authorship. *Bulletin of the ALLC, 11*, 73–82.

Stockmann, R. (2005). Die Erfindung des Rades – universitäres E-Learning aus Sicht der Nutzenden. In C. Thimm (Ed.), Netz-Bildung – Lehren und Lernen mit neuen Medien in Wissenschaft und Wirtschaft (pp. 51-73). Frankfurt/M.: Peter Lang.

Sutton-Smith, B. (2001). *The Ambiguity of Play.* Cambridge, MA: Harvard UP.

Svedjedal, J. (2004). Almqvist och namnen. En studie i litterär onomastik. *Samlaren, 125*, 52–77.

Tabata, T. (1995). Narrative Style and the Frequencies of Very Common Words: A Corpus-Based Approach to Dickens's first person and third person narratives. *English Corpus Studies, 2*, 91–109.

Tabata, T. (2004). Differentiation of Idiolects in Fictional Discourse: A Stylo-Statistical Approach to Dickens's Artistry. In Hiltunen, R., & Watanabe, S. (Eds.), *Approaches to Style and Discourse in English* (pp. 79–106). Osaka: Osaka UP.

Teleman, U. (2005). Language cultivation and language planning II: Swedish. In Bandle, O. (Eds.), *The Nordic languages: An international handbook of the history of the North Germanic languages* (*Vol. 2*, pp. 1970–1983). Berlin: Walter de Gruyter.

Text Encoding Initiative. (n.d.). Retrieved September 13, 2008, http://www.tei-c.org

Thompson, G., & Hunston, S. (2001). Evaluation: An Introduction. In Hunston, S., & Thompson, G. (Eds.), *Evaluation in Text. Authorial Stance and the Construction of Discourse* (pp. 1–27). Oxford: OUP.

Tjong Kim Sang, E., & De Meulder, F. (2003). Introduction to the CoNLL-2003 Shared Task: Language-independent named entity recognition. In [Edmonton, Canada: ACL.]. *Proceedings of CoNLL, 2003*, 142–147.

Tognini-Bonelli, E. (2001). *Corpus Linguistics at Work.* Amsterdam: John Benjamins.

Urmson, J. O. (1956). *Philosophical Analysis: Its development between the two World Wars.* Oxford: Clarendon Press.

van Dalen-Oskam, K. (2005). Comparative literary onomastics. Retrieved September 6, 2008, from http://www.huygensinstituut.knaw.nl/index.php?option=com_content&task=view&id=197&Itemid=118

van Dalen-Oskam, K., & van Zundert, J. (2004). Modelling features of characters: Some digital ways of looking at names in literary texts. *Literary and Linguistic Computing, 19*(3), 289–301. doi:10.1093/llc/19.3.289

van der Sluijs, K., & Houben, G.-J. (2008). Metadata-based access to cultural heritage collections: The RHCe use case. In *Proceedings of the 2nd International Workshop on Personalized Access to Cultural Heritage (PATCH'2008).* (pp. 15-25). Hanover.

van Halteren, H., Baayen, R. H., Tweedie, F., Haverkort, M., & Neijt, A. (2005). New machine learning methods demonstrate the existence of a human stylome. *Journal of Quantitative Linguistics, 12*(1), 65–77. doi:10.1080/09296170500055350

Vygotsky, L. (1978). *Mind in Society: The Development of Higher Psychological Processes* (Cole, M., Eds.). Cambridge: Harvard University Press.

Wardrip-Fruin, N., & Harrigan, P. (Eds.). (2004). *First Person: New Media as Story, Performance and Game.* Cambridge, MA: MIT.

Wardrip-Fruin, N., & Harrigan, P. (Eds.). (2007). *Second Person: Role-Playing and Story in Games and Playable Media.* Cambridge, MA: MIT.

Wark, McKenzie. (2007). *Gamer Theory.* Cambridge, MA: Harvard UP.

Watson, G., & Zyngier, S. (Eds.). (2007). *Literature and Stylistics for Language Learners.* Basingstoke, New York: Palgrave.

Weinert, F. (2001). Concept of Competence: A Conceptual Clarification. In Rychen, D. S., & Salganik, L. H. (Eds.), *Defining and Selecting Key Competencies. Theoretical and Conceptual Foundations* (pp. 45–65). Göttingen: Hogrefe & Huber.

Wellman, F. L. (1936). *The art of cross-examination.* New York: MacMillan.

Willke, H. (2000). *Systemtheorie I: Grundlagen.* Stuttgart, Jena: Gustav Fischer UTB.

Willke, H. (2001). *Systemtheorie III: Steuerungstheorie. Grundzüge einer Theorie der Steuerung komplexer Sozialsysteme.* Stuttgart: Lucius&Lucius.

Windelband, W. (1894). *Geschichte und Naturwissenschaft. Rektoratsrede. Rede zum Antritt des Rektorats der Kaiser-Wilhelms-Universität Straßburg.* Strassburg.

Wittgenstein, L. (2005). *Philosophical Investigations.* Oxford: Blackwell.

Wittgenstein, L. 1922. Tractatus Logico-Philosophicus. (D.F. Pears & D.F. McGuiness, Trans., 1960). London: Routledge and Kegan Paul.

XCES. (2008). *XCES: Corpus encoding standard for XML*. Retrieved September 13, 2008, from http://www.xces.org

Yule, G. U. (1938). On sentence-length as a statistical characteristic of style in prose, with application to two cases of disputed authorship. *Biometrica, 30*, 363–390.

About the Contributors

Willie van Peer holds a Ph.D. from Lancaster University, and is Professor of Literary Studies and Intercultural Hermeneutics at the University of Munich, former President of IGEL (International Association for the Empirical Study of Literature and Media) and of PALA (Poetics and Linguistics Association). He has been Visiting Scholar in the Departments of Comparative Literature at Stanford and at Princeton University, and in the Department of (Cognitive) Psychology at the University of Memphis. He is also a Fellow of Clare Hall of Cambridge University. He is the author of several books and many articles on poetics and the epistemological foundations of literary studies, including Stylistics and Psychology: Investigations of Foregrounding (London, 1986). He edited The Taming of the Text: Explorations in Language, Literature and Culture (Routledge, 1988), together with Seymour Chatman, New Perspectives on Narrative Perspective (SUNY Press, 2001), and together with Max Louwerse, Thematics. Interdisciplinary Studies (Benjamins, 2002).

Sonia Zyngier is Associate Professor of English Language and Literature at the Postgraduate Programme of Applied Linguistics at the Federal University of Rio de Janeiro, Brazil, where she was also Director of Cultural Affairs and Continuing Education for 5 years. She also acted as Secretary of PALA (Poetics and Linguistics Association) and is the current Secretary of IGEL (International Society for the Empirical Study of Literature and Media). She has an M.A. in English Literature from the University of Liverpool and a Ph.D. in Applied Linguistics from the University of Birmingham. Much of her work has been on stylistics and the teaching of literature to EFL students. Specific research interests include discourse analysis and pedagogical stylistics. She has published widely on literary awareness, stylistics, and corpus analysis of literary discourse. She has developed a program of research in the area of the Empirical Science of Literature and its implications for literary education. In 2006 she edited, together with Greg Watson, Literature and Stylistics for Language Learners, published by Palgrave, and published Muses and Measures: Empirical Research Methods for the Humanities in 2007 together with Willie van Peer and Jèmeljan Hakemulder.

Vander Viana is a PhD candidate at Queen's University Belfast. He holds an MA in Language Studies from the Catholic University of Rio de Janeiro and a BA in English Language and Literature from the State University of Rio de Janeiro. He has been the student representative at the International Society for the Empirical Study of Literature (IGEL) since 2008. He is a member of the editorial board of seven international journals in Colombia, South Korea, and the United States. His main research interests and publications focus on Corpus Linguistics, English Language, Applied Linguistics, Distance Learning and Teacher Development. In addition to several published chapters, he has also been in charge of editing a number of books. *Acting and Connecting: Cultural Approaches to Language and Literature*, edited in collaboration with Sonia Zyngier and Anna Chesnokova is among his latest publications.

* * *

Michael Toolan (MA Edinburgh, D.Phil. Oxford) is Professor of English Language at the University of Birmingham, where he teaches courses in Stylistics, Language and the Law, and Narrative Analysis. He also convenes the MA programme in Literary Linguistics, and is editor of the Journal of Literary Semantics (de Gruyter). He is currently Head of the Department of English. He has published extensively on stylistic and narratological topics; his most recent book is Narrative progression in the short story: a corpus stylistic approach (Benjamins 2009).

Patrick Juola received his Ph.D. in computer science (including a certificate in cognitive science) from the University of Colorado at Boulder, then worked as a post-doc in the department of experimental psychology at Oxford University (UK). He is currently associate professor of computer science at Duquesne University (Pittsburgh, USA). He is the author of several books, including a 2006 monograph for Foundations and Trends in Information Retrieval on Authorship Attribution and a textbook on basic computer science for Prentice-Hall. His research interests include text analysis, digital humanities, e-science, and computer security.

Lisa Lena Opas-Hänninen is Adjunct Professor and University lecturer in English Philology at the University of Oulu in Finland, where she teaches courses in corpus linguistics, stylistics and humanities computing. She received her DPhil.

degree from the University of Oxford in 1990 for a linguistic study on the style of Samuel Beckett's prose. Her research interests include computational stylistics, building tools for the collection and analysis of multimodal corpora, language variation and imagology. She leads the LInguistic and Cultural Heritage Electronic Network –project (LICHEN), which aims to facilitate the collection and preservation of minority languages in the North. She has been an active member of the Association for Literary and Linguistic Computing, serving as its Secretary for over 10 years.

Lars Borin holds a PhD in computational linguistics from Uppsala University (1992). He is currently professor of natural language processing at the University of Gothenburg, where he heads Språkbanken (the Swedish Language Bank) and the Centre for Language Technology. Among his current research interests are: Language technology infrastructure development, computational lexicography and lexical semantics, language technology-based e-science for humanities research (in particular linguistics, literature and history), language technology for less-resourced languages, and computer-assisted language learning. (Email: <lars.borin@svenska.gu.se>)

Dimitrios Kokkinakis, received his PhD in Computational Linguistics from the University of Gothenburg in December 2001. He is currently associate professor at the Department of Swedish Language, University of Gothenburg, Sweden. His research interests include Computational lexical semantics (particularly word-sense disambiguation and automatic lexical acquisition), Medical and Clinical informatics, Corpus linguistics (particularly standardization of resources and shallow syntactic/semantic analysis) and Text mining (particularly information extraction, machine learning and visualization of linguistic and multidimensional data). (Email: dimitrios.kokkinakis@svenska.gu.se)

Bill Louw is head of the Department of English at the University of Zimbabwe. He studied stylistics at Reading University under David Crystal. His researches at COBUILD in the 1980s led to his establishing Corpus Stylistics as a discipline in 1987. John Sinclair produced the first computer concordanced dictionary at COBUILD. Their collaboration brought about the recognition of semantic prosody as a digital collocational phenomenon that is largely opaque to human intuition. He continues to add rigour to the theory of corpus linguistics through the falsification of intuitively derived theories and the automation of the pre-computational theories of the analytical philosophers, in particular, Frege, Russell, (early) Wittgenstein and Carnap. Applications of his work have recently appeared in translation studies, humour studies, negotiating skills and political 'spin'. His earlier work on LITRAID (1996), a national literacy programme for Zimbabwe, was apparently censored because it pioneered Firthian, Malinowskian and Sinclairan approaches to meaning as collocation.

Stefan Hofer (* 1972, Zurich, Switzerland) studied German Literature, Linguistics, Latin American Studies and Communications Studies at the University of Zurich and the University Complutense of Madrid. He received his PH. D. in German Literature from the University of Zurich in 2006. His main research topics include Literature and Ecology, Literature and Systems Theory, Migrant Literature and e-learning in the Humanities. He teached German Literature at the Universities of Zurich, Rome II and Leipzig and worked as a journalist. Since 2001 he has been participating in the conceptual design and the didactic and practical implementation of the e-learning environment tEXtMACHINA at the University of Zurich. Currentely, he works as a scientific assistant for e-learning at the University of Zurich, as lecturer in German Literature at the Zurich University of Teacher Education (PHZH) and as a high school teacher for German and Spanish Language and Culture in Baden, Switzerland.

René Bauer (*1972, Kreuzlingen, Switzerland) develops since 1998 the autopoietic collaborative system nic-las (www.nic-las.com). Since 2001 he has been participating in the conceptual design and the technical and practical implementation of the e-learning environment tEXtMACHINA (www.textmachina.uzh.ch) at the University of Zurich. Since 2004 he is a lecturer in Gamedesign at the University of Applied Science Zürich (ZHDK, gamedesign.zhdk.ch). He also works in the field of GameArt (www.and-or.ch).

Imre Hofmann was born 1972 in Stuttgart, Germany. He studied German Literature, Linguistics, Philosophy and Cultural Anthropology at the University of Zurich. Since 2001 he has been part of the developer team of the e-learning environment tEXtMACHINA at the University of Zurich. tEXtMACHINA was funded in order to design an e-learning tool that suits the particular needs of the Humanities. In addition to his e-learning employment he works as a webdesign teacher for the educational programm of the Fachverein Arbeit und Umwelt (a Swiss organisation for the further education of jobless persons: www.fau.ch) and as a self-employed practical philosopher (www.elenchos.ch).

Jon Saklofske is an Assistant Professor at Acadia University in Nova Scotia, Canada. His specialization in the writing of the British Romantic period and continuing interest in the ways that William Blake's composite art illuminates the relationship between words and images on the printed page has inspired current research into larger correlations between media forms and cultural perceptions. In addition, he is actively pursuing the use of "serious games" in university-level research and learning. Recent and forthcoming publications include an exploration of William Blake's participation in late-eighteenth-century gallery culture and spectacles, an interrogation of player agency in Grand Theft Auto: San Andreas, and an investigation of the use of data visualization tools in Humanities teaching and research practices.

William L. Heller. Since 1997, Dr. Heller has taught the graduate-level course Dramatic Activities in the English Classroom as an adjunct Assistant Professor for the Program in English Education at New York University. He has also taught two distinct graduate-level Shakespeare courses for NYU's Program in Educational Theatre, and has been an instructor for the Folger Shakespeare Library's Teaching Shakespeare Institute. His personal website can be found at http://shakespeare-teacher.com.

David S. Miall is professor of English at the University of Alberta. Previous publications include, as editor, Humanities and the Computer: New Directions (Oxford UP, 1990), Romanticism: The CD-ROM (Blackwell, 1997), and Literary Reading: Empirical and Theoretical Studies (Lang, 2006). While he specializes in literature of the British Romantic period, his research interests also include the empirical study of literary reading – a field in which he has collaborated with Don Kuiken (Department of Psychology) since 1990 – and the role of computers in literature. His work on reading has been supported by a series of research awards from the Social Sciences and Humanities Research Council of Canada since 1992. He teaches courses in Romantic literature, Gothic fiction, literary computing, and empirical and historical studies of literary reading.

Index

S

T

U

V

W

Z